"We Gather Together"
Food and Festival in American Life

"We Gather Together"
Food and Festival in American Life

Edited by
Theodore C. Humphrey
and
Lin T. Humphrey

Utah State University Press
Logan, Utah
1991

Cover Design and Illustration: Lori Herdegen
Utah State University Press
Logan,Utah 84322-7800

We gather together : food and festival in American life / edited by
Theodore C. Humphrey and Lin T. Humphrey.
     p. cm.
     Originally published: Ann Arbor : UMI Research Press, 1988.
     Includes bibliographical references and index.
     ISBN 0-87421-155-7
     1. Festivals—United States. 2. Food habits— United States.
3. Cookery. American. 4. United States—Social life and customs.
I. Humphrey, Theodore C. (Theodore Carl), 1938- . II. Humphrey,
Lin T. (Lin Tufts). 1940-
GT4803.W4   1991
394.1'2'0973—dc20

91-29267
CIP

To the memory of friends and mentors
Susan Camille Samuelson (1956-1991)
Mary Celestia Randolph (1905-1981)
Vance Randolph (1892-1980)
Richard Mercer Dorson (1916-1981)
and D. K. Wilgus (1918-1989)

Contents

Preface

The phrase "We Gather Together" is taken from a rather militant seventeenth-century Netherlands folk hymn that many of us recall singing at Thanksgiving, that prototypic American folk food festival. Separated from the hymn, the phrase is pleasant and playful. We play with the similarity in sound; we are pleasantly reminded of various warm and friendly gatherings, usually involving food as a main ingredient. Because this book is about gatherings and about food and about how people come together to create meaningful bonds, the phrase seemed an appropriate title. We do gather together—to share our food, to share our lives, and to create community.

On behalf of all the authors of the studies in this book, we want to extend our deepest appreciation to the people who allowed us—and you—into their lives to steam clams and lobsters, celebrate soup, share potlucks, and dine with them in dozens of different communities. They—and we—mark calendar holidays and personal celebrations by preparing and sharing food, gathering ingredients, acquaintances, and close friends into temporary but important unions. Through the food, the sharing, and the celebration they—and we—have established relationships that transcend both the food and the occasion. In gathering together, they define what it means to be human.

In our cultural memories, we recall our ancestors gathered around the fire in front of the dark cave, around the campfire on the prairies as they crossed this great country, and around the heavy-laden table as they feasted together. In times of trouble and in joy we seek each other's company. We comfort and console with food; we acknowledge our commitment and relationship with each other through shared food and drink. However we say it, however we do it, human beings gather together, and thus we enhance our power through the very act of gathering.

Thus it is appropriate that we gather our thoughts at this moment and thank those who have helped us with this book. Special thanks to Simon Bronner, mentor and friend, for his careful reading of all of the essays and his many helpful suggestions. While he is in no way responsible for any shortcomings of the volume, his keen eye and extensive knowledge of American material culture and folklore have contributed significantly to whatever merits this book may possess. As editors, we thank especially all of the contributors to this book who have written and rewritten without complaint; the staff at UMI Research Press, whose enthusiasm and commitment to the project have kept our spirits from flagging; and good friends and family members who have put up with our involvement with this project, especially our daughter Merritt and son Carter; and those folklorists who encouraged us—Mary C. Parler, Vance Randolph, Richard Dorson, and D. K. Wilgus—and who led us into the fields of folklore.

Introduction:
Food and Festivity in American Life

Theodore C. Humphrey, Sue Samuelson, Lin T. Humphrey

In this book, we celebrate celebration. Not the huge (and impersonal) festivals such as Mardi Gras or the Super Bowl but the family and community get togethers that characterize the life of thousands of communities and millions of individuals in this country. And we celebrate the role of foods and the behaviors associated with those foods in such festive events as clambakes, barbecues, birthday parties, Seders, Halloween, and Old Folks Days among others. We think it is the nature of human beings to seek community and to define those communities in symbolic fashion through the foods that are prepared and consumed in those festive contexts.

In *The Feast of Fools: A Theological Essay on Festivity and Fantasy,* Harvey Cox argues that "both our enjoyment of festivity and our capacity for fantasy have deteriorated in modern times. We still celebrate but our feasts and parties lack real verve or feeling."[1] Mr. Cox is entitled to his view, but we think the evidence examined in this book suggests an abundance of "real verve or feeling" and nowhere more pervasively than in the small group festive gatherings and celebrations that characterize the "ordinary" life of Americans. In these festive gatherings and celebrations, we eat: we ritualize and consume the clams and corn of New England clambakes; the barbecued meats of Oklahoma, Utah, and Arizona; the calf fries, the okra, the chitlings, the "crawdads" and booya, the birthday cakes, and a thousand other dishes in thousands of festive contexts. We eat well when we celebrate.

In doing so, we do more than sustain the physical body. The foods consumed express a variety of messages about the individual and the culture; some have to do with the sheer availability of the foods, their seasonality, their economic nature; others make powerful statements about status, tradition, and the nature of the particular context in which the foods are being consumed. As Roland Barthes suggests, food is "a system of communication, a body of images, a protocol of usages, situations, and behavior."[2] Foods become metaphor and metonym, expressing not only the fundamental assumptions or world view of individuals and groups but also the emotional associations that begin, as Peter Farb reminds us, with the "earliest eating experiences associated with the mother."[3]

The analyses presented in this volume suggest that the sociological and semiotic aspects of foods are especially significant in festive contexts, events in which the intention is not principally to satisfy physical hunger and the need for nutrition (although these are powerful and legitimate motives, even in a mentalist interpretation), but rather to celebrate. It becomes clear in these analyses that a festive context need not be characterized by a certain number of performers, or by exotic or unusual dishes, or even by a recognized "tradition" of a certain duration, although, of course, a particular group[4] may define these characteristics as being critical within its festive event. Such recognition occurs because the participants in a festive event understand that traditional foods, events, and contexts encode more meaning than the single food or event. Thus, the foods that appear in a particular festive environment are not mere collections of nutrients upon a table. Because communities of individuals select, transform, and "perform" foodstuffs in ways (often in complex and disorderly ways) appropriate to the full set of traditional expectations that govern a particular festive context, they define and perform significant aspects of that community, its values, its sense of itself. Whether in a family reunion, a birthday party, a periodic dinner, or a coffee klatch; a community barbecue, clambake, or fish fry; or a small romantic candlelight dinner for two, we who participate in such events transform foods into markers of meaning. Perhaps the exchange of food within festive events becomes so potent a marker of community values because food is so fundamental to our sense of nurturing.

Among earlier writers who have addressed the question of community identification based on ethnic origins, C. Paige Gutierrez considered how the crawfish became the essential symbolic totem for Cajuns. She argued that the qualities of "the [intrepid] crawfish are paralleled in the Cajuns' own image of themselves as a people who have managed to fight and survive in the face of deportation, economic hardship, social oppression, and a sometimes hostile environment."[5] She noted how the lowly crawfish, once the food of poor folk, has become a very upscale status symbol of ethnic and regional identity. In this book, we argue that the idea of food as a symbolic marker of identity may be extended beyond the boundaries of ethnicity and regionalism. Family, neighborhood, temporary associations, ephemeral interest groups, traditional work environments, and other "made" communities all create festive events in which food becomes symbolic of identity. A food item may be a traditional staple in a given area (probably for reasons of availability and necessity) and thus become identified with the group that cultivates it, both within the group and from the outside. But other traditions and associations, such as those of a family, can be strongly preserved by food items and behaviors. You may well find yourself here. In the Humphrey family, for instance, fried okra (sliced raw okra, rolled in corn meal, and slowly fried in cooking oil—it used to be lard, of course) is served at family reunions whenever possible because, aside from its wonderful taste, it clearly symbolizes home, growing up on the farm in Oklahoma, working in the garden with the family, and Mom cooking and nurturing. It marks the Humphrey family in that context as belonging symbolically to a southern time and a rural place, defining ourselves again— if only for a moment—as Oklahoma farmers who fought gumbo soil, grasshoppers, drought, flood, and adverse economic conditions. The food depends upon its total context in our memories and with our associations to develop such meaning and identification and such warmly positive and tasty connotations.

Anthropologist and food scholar Ravindra Khare has pointedly argued that "the materialist view of food remains incomplete without . . . appropriate attention to the symbolic, moral, and communicational dimensions" of foodways.[6] These are precisely the dimensions that most reward scholarly investigation of the festive events of groups, and especially (though not exclusively) of the foods that are focal points of the events, the rituals associated with them, and their location in the overall context of festivity. Here we may see a performance of a particular vision of the community, of its values, assumptions, world views, and prescriptive behaviors, for it is within festive contexts that the transformation from staple to symbol becomes most apparent. The complex of behaviors associated with selecting, preparing, serving, and consuming foods creates a symbolic vocabulary of the basic assumptions of the community, with meaning and significance that may or may not rise to the conscious level. Over time with "continuity and consistency"[7] in performance (and even possibly with the very first performance) the separate elements fuse into a symbolic language. The festive event allows the everyday items or behaviors to be elevated, made special and invested with multivalent resonances, creating and affirming the very idea (or even ideal) of the community that performs them.

Such meaning may be possible because festivity seems to be inextricably linked with ritual at the point of community, that is, at the point where the individual participates in traditional structured ways in the social network. We suggest, further, that all rituals function to mediate our progress through life toward death, informing us of the inevitability of it, and preparing us emotionally and intellectually for it; festive events likewise have such a deep function and, in addition, create a sense of joy in us even as they reconcile us to our fate in a myriad of ways. Thus, when we participate in celebratory exchange and consumption of food, the behaviors become ritualized over time and function to mediate our passage. The exchange of food in such events is crucial because food is life. While we run the risk of oversimplifying the fascinating and complex processes at work in creating the enormous diversity seen around the world and in history for celebrating with food (or in the enforced and ritualized absence of food) in festive contexts,[8] the central function seems clear. Foods are indeed both good to eat and "good to think."

The essays in this volume spring from a substantial history of scholarship and work in foodways by folklorists, sociologists, anthropologists, and other food scholars, who, when they investigate the origins of their discipline's interest in food, often consult Don Yoder's 1972 essay on "Folk Cookery." Found in a classic text, *Folklore and Folklife: An Introduction,* edited by Richard M. Dorson, Yoder's article was the first clear "call to arms" for an intensive study of foodways by Americans interested in folk culture. Yoder had long been interested in studying food as a type of material culture, as evidenced by a series of articles on Pennsylvania German specialities such as *sauerkraut* and *schnitz*.[9] His orientation was primarily historical and comparative in nature, stressing the importance of "family cookery based on regional tradition" as opposed to "the commercial, institutional, and scientific-nutritional versions of cookery" (325). The concern for regional variations was partnered by an interest in comparing American practices to those of the Europeans.

Yoder's work, with its emphasis on historical and descriptive approaches, sums up the basic questions informing food research at the time. Although he mainly used the term "folk cookery," Yoder recognized the usefulness of the term "foodways" (a reduction of an older term, "food folkways") and the importance of the "total cookery complex, including attitudes, taboos, and meal systems—the whole range of cookery and food habits in a society" (325).

His essay was written at a time of great activity in the area of foodways research. In 1970, Don Yoder attended the first International Symposium on Ethnological Food Research held in Lund, Sweden[10] and organized by Nils-Arvid Bringéus. In that same year, Bringéus's book *Mat och Miljö* (*Food and Milieu,* 1970)[11] appeared, a milestone in establishing new approaches to the study of food and culture. Yoder was familiar with Bringéus's ideas through Alexander Fenton's prompt translation of a chapter of the book, published as "Man, Food and Milieu" in the journal *Folk Life* (1970).[12]

Much of what Bringéus proposed was a definite departure from the

European folklife scholars' ethnological and historical approaches to the study of food, especially in terms of his interest in class issues and the relationship between culture, food, and environment, presaging later work in the field of cultural ecology. He insisted that food patterns operate within a network that is "affected by our immediate environment as well as what is past and distant" (45).

Bringéus also paid close attention to what he called "food and fellowship." Following his discussion of eating habits as "lines of demarcation between the classes of a community," Bringéus acknowledged how "they also serve as links between people" (50). His statements included perceptive assessments of the role of food in what would later be called "small group festive gatherings."[13] "The organization of a feast was based on neighborhood. It covered seasonal as well as personal festivals, Christmas and parish catechism parties as well as church and funeral feasts, *and it did not exclude more everyday activities*" (Bringéus, 51; emphasis added).

Also participating at the Lund conference was another American, Jay Allan Anderson. Portions of his summary of American foodways research were published in *Ethnologia Scandinavica* and in *Keystone Folklore Quarterly*. In the latter journal, Anderson presented something of a split personality. Initially, he clung to a regional and historical emphasis much like Yoder's but outlined future prospects as using the "conceptual model" of foodways:

> The concept refers to the whole interrelated *system* of food conceptualization and evaluation, procurement, distribution, preservation, preparation, consumption, and nutrition shared by all the members of a particular society. It is essentially a cultural *complex, a bundle of ideas* carried around by men as part of their conceptual equipment, and the patterned behavior and material phenomena these ideas shape.[14]

Here Anderson was making one of the earliest statements by a folklorist that food is not only an item or thing, but also a way people express themselves, a means by which they can communicate with one another. He took a much broader perspective on the study of food in its social and cultural context than had previously been the case.

Illustrating Anderson's statements, the same issue of *Keystone Folklore Quarterly* contained articles on specific groups and their use of food. Roger Welsch wrote about Omaha Indians, Charles Joyner about Black slaves, and David Hufford about health food enthusiasts. Welsch in particular stressed the role of food in expressing the notion of community identity as he looked at the status of changing foods. Milkweed soup was once simple fare but then became a dish prepared only on special occasions. Frybread, a nontraditional Omaha food, is now treated as traditional because it is unique to Great Plains Indians in general. "It quickly becomes evident to the observer of Omaha culture that the importance of food like frybread transcends historicity, economics, and taste. It is viewed as an embodiment of Indian-ness"[15] (169). Here again is an example, in an early foodways article, of an awareness of the role of foods in festivity. Welsch notes, "Community occasions of all sorts, from simple committee meetings to funerals, and games and protest meetings, are always followed by a 'feast'— called that no matter how humble it might be" (166). The feast too is a part of the expression of Omaha culture. Food as a whole becomes a "bastion" of identity in the face of assault from the outside world. "To an Omaha, you are indeed what you eat" (170).

Surprisingly, there was little immediate response to this flurry of activity in the early 1970s intent on reshaping the configuration of foodways research. With her discussions of British meal structure and food as art form, anthropologist Mary Douglas may have been the impetus for renewed interest in the late 1970s on the part of American folklorists. One example of this "second phase" of foodways studies was the debut of *The Digest, A Newsletter for the Interdisciplinary Study of Food,* published initially by the University of Pennsylvania's Department of Folklore and Folklife under the auspices of the Foodways Section of the American Folklore Society. Guest editor Eliot A. Singer exulted that the *Digest*'s presence demonstrated that "The ethnographic study of food seems finally to have come of age.... Eating, no longer considered mundane, has become central to a definition of humanity" (2). In his assessment of four main orientations to the study of foodways, Singer proclaims the folklife studies or material culture approach as the one "responsible for insisting that food is not trivial and is deserving of serious scholarly attention." As was the case with the increasing stature of children's folklore studies, foodways had to pass through a sort of "triviality barrier"[16] to prove its scholarly mettle. Partly this was also accomplished by researchers who found "food habits interesting primarily where they are implicated in the etiology of malnutrition" (2). This approach was considered a form of applied science and thus tapped by academics as a "socially responsible outlet" to justify food studies, as was a similar orientation developed by the cultural ecologists. Singer felt the fourth area of foodways research, that of semiotics, turned away from the study of food itself to emphasize its use as vehicle for studying something else. Food was approached as a means to an end, and the "ends" were such subjects as identity, community, and status. Eating was seen as a conventionally organized expressive act. Researchers had therefore to try to decipher and interpret the meaning of eating (3). But while such efforts were important, Singer stressed that both the applied and the historical viewpoints were significant as well. "Internal dialectic, external pressure, and the necessities of survival may combine to lead to a changing fit between cultural, productive, and biological systems thus creating new ways of eating and of feeding" (4).

Reinforcing Singer's plea for historical perspective was Charles Camp's review of federal foodways research in the 1930s and 1940s, particularly the America Eats program of the Works Progress Administration. Such documentation laid the groundwork for his own presentation of theories for foodways study in his 1978 dissertation and later articles.[17] Camp was among the first folklorists to acknowledge that many food researchers were talking past each other. Folklorists had little idea of what the nutritionists were up to, and vice versa. The same could be said for work in the popular arena.

> A proportionately high amount of information on foods and food habits is published each year in the United States, but this mixture of popular and scholarly material does not have a central point of passage.... The state of foodways research today is very much the same as it was before World War Two, as specialized research takes place without the benefit of cross-pollination of ideas and methods. (Camp 251)

Part of the problem stemmed from the use of the food item as the basic unit of analysis. Most people assumed the place to begin was with food itself, thus preventing the integration of data based on broader social and cultural contexts.

Camp's solution to the problem was to emphasize food *events*. "While it is true that the foods which are actually consumed during the meal constitute the basic physical material of the meal, it is not necessarily true that any accurate or telling description of food habits must begin with what is eaten" (Camp 298). He made it clear that he was not simply widening the descriptive focus of food consumption, but that an event orientation would provide valuable information on the "relationships in which these foods participate and the socially-derived meanings they take on as the event develops from an impulse through performance to conclusion" (301). Camp basically stressed the need to explore the act of eating together and the implications and interpretations evolving from it, acknowledging that "even when the foods are physically identical at a family dinner and a church supper their consumption may represent very different values" (305). A chicken dinner is not always just a chicken dinner.

Many of the events Camp was interested in fall into the category of small group festive gathering (SGFGs) as defined by Lin T. Humphrey (1979). In looking at picnics, potlucks, box socials, reunions, progressive dinners, and cocktail parties, Humphrey joined Camp in proclaiming the need to study "how people use food as a catalyst for social interaction"

(190). Why is it that so many of our social actions, at least in America, take place in the company of food? Rarely do people get together to socialize without incorporating food. Even a workout at the gym may include sharing a diet soda or stopping at the juice bar.[18] Approaching her topic more from a background in festival scholarship than a grounding in foodways research, Humphrey developed a typology for various kinds of SGFGs, offered historical and contemporary examples, and posited several explanations as springboards for further research. Perhaps it is contrary to our Puritan heritage to meet or talk or visit unless there is some more tangible reason for getting together, such as harvesting, preparing or sharing food and drink. Perhaps this need to eat together is part of our underlying assumption that America is the land of plenty, a plenty which can and must be shared with others. Perhaps there is something in our temperament, a nervousness that is eased in these small social events by eating together (L. Humphrey, 190). Above all, SGFGs "impart a sense of community, of belonging, of intimacy, that is often lost in modern urban society" (198). Thus Humphrey brought together the topics of community and festivity and combined them with foodways research to generate a new, more fully integrated approach to all three.

At about the same time as Humphrey's article appeared, several new foodways volumes also were published. One of these was a special issue of *Western Folklore*[19] containing 13 essays exploring the nature of eating. It would later appear as a separate book entitled *Foodways and Eating Habits, Directions for Research* (edited by Michael Owen Jones, Bruce Giuliano, and Roberta Krell). The *Journal of American Culture* also published a special issue on American foodways.[20] The guest editors of that issue, Kay Mussell and Linda Keller Brown, soon followed with another anthology, *Ethnic and Regional Foodways in the United States.* Taken together, these collections of analytic essays on American food behaviors represent a third phase in foodways research.

If one word could be chosen to describe the emphasis of the *Foodways and Eating Habits* volume it would be eclectic. The editors puzzled over many of the seeming inconsistencies in people's eating patterns. They were not eating what previous research indicated they should eat: Montana natives were not expected to nosh on a chile relleno. Food choice did not depend simply on accessibility of foodstuffs in the environment or upon historical, technological or economic variables. Neither did selections strictly relate to "what the culture permits and what the society insists is appropriate" (vii). Americans seemed to be eating "all over the map," eating anything anywhere. Such diversity suggested an approach that took into account Americans' multiple "registers" of identity in terms of selecting what they eat, from tacos to Tang. In addition, researchers needed to consider the many types of interpersonal networks that individuals tap into. Where and with whom we eat are increasingly important. "[W]hat is crucial to much of foodways research is the matter of consuming food. Often the sensory quality is prominent for us when preparing, serving, and eating food, and usually these activities take place in, and thus affect and are affected by, social settings" (xi).

The "Prologue" to *Foodways and Eating Habits* acknowledged the matters of global concern relating to questions of nutrition, agriculture, education and marketing. Such issues "require that the question of food choice be answered as completely as possible in regard to as many populations and situations as feasible; this requirement in turn demands information about specific behavior in particular circumstances" (xi). Thus the local and specific become the basis for understanding the broader patterns, the potential universals. All people eat out of biological necessity, but eating may also be an intellectual and a social experience. Eating communicates information and establishes associations, as well as providing nourishment, both physiologically and emotionally.

The essays in *Foodways and Eating Habits* covered a broad range: the "rules" for eating Oreo cookies and other foods, the role of gender in American households as it applies to food appropriated by male cooks (e.g., pancakes on Sunday, backyard barbecues), and food-sharing issues in cooperative households (such as in college communities). Among the disciplines represented by the contributors are folklore, history, experimental psychology, and consumer research.

The array of specialities is equally apparent in the later volume by Brown and Mussel, *Ethnic and Regional Foodways in the United States*.[21] Here folklorists, anthropologists, nutritionists, urban planners, and scholars from the fields of American Studies, popular culture, and public health survey a fascinating range of groups and communities, including Italian-Americans, Russian Molokans, Cajuns, American Hindus, Seminole Indians, and residents of New Jersey's Pinelands. Once again the study of a small unit is championed to help develop broader perspectives. "Each essay highlights a particular strategy within a larger, integrated framework" (3). Because of the concentration on ethnic and regional groups, an organizing principle for the volume was to determine how groups define themselves, how they establish boundaries both internally and externally, especially through foodways. Borrowing from Mary Douglas, these researchers considered foodways as a kind of code, as interactions "encoding a highly ritualized, although taken-for-granted, set of behaviors" (7). More recently, Anne R. Kaplan, Marjorie A. Hoover, and Willard B. Moore in *The Minnesota*

Ethnic Food Book (1986), working with fourteen ethnic groups in Minnesota, demonstrate how these groups use foods to maintain their ethnic identity and community.

Brown and Mussell also proposed "directions for future foodways research." These included studying the nature and meaning of intragroup variation (i.e., examining group identity as a continuum of allegiance and interest); expanding the notion of affinity groups (such as age, occupation, socio-economic, in addition to ethnicity and region); using structuralism to view eating as a system; and increasing support for interdisciplinary interpretation (which the editors call "nexus studies").

Ethnic and Regional Foodways came out of a somewhat different perspective from that of *Foodways and Eating Habits*. Only one author, Leslie Prosterman, appears in both volumes. The essays in the two books utilize many of the same perspectives: folklore, anthropology, communication studies. Yet Keller Brown and Mussell focus more exclusively on notions of group and community. Jones, Giuliano and Krell seem more intent on revealing the ramifications of the food event. Taken together, however, both works set the stage for the volume currently in hand, one that explores the relationship between community and food at the level of the event, specifically the small group festive gathering.

Once again, Lin T. Humphrey's 1979 article "Small Group Festive Gatherings" marks the beginning of concerted research in the area of the small-scale festive event. Festivals in general, despite the allure their complexity offers the skilled researcher, have remained relatively untouched throughout much of American folklore scholarship. Until recently it has been mainly Old World survivals, such as harvest festivals or customs related to the major religious holidays such as Christmas and Easter, that have received the most attention. But starting in the mid-1970s, with work on community festivals by John Moe and John Gutowski quickly followed by the work of many young scholars such as Jack Santino on Halloween, Leslie Prosterman on county fairs, Carter Craigie on picnics, and Sue Samuelson on Christmas, not to mention the contributions of Roger Abrahams and Robert Smith,[22] there has been a definite trend towards exploring the productions of *homo festivus,* man the celebrator.

It is difficult to think of a festival that does not have some type of food component. Just as we use food to alleviate some of the tension of everyday socializing, such as talking about our problems over a cup of coffee, perhaps we need it even more in such a highly charged situation as a celebration. Festivals are very intense occasions when social and cultural order is affirmed or challenged (albeit within a sanctioned structure). But when one looks at a particular kind of festive event, the smaller, more community-based occasions, or those involving family, friends, church members, and so forth, the festival's free-for-all nature is somewhat curtailed. We still see the event as something special, but its scale keeps it more tightly bound. Thus, more than ever, we use food to keep the interactions and communications flowing smoothly. Food serves as a balm or salve, something which helps to soothe the rough edges. As anyone who has ever stood nervously on the fringe of a cocktail party exploring the hostess's wall paintings can acknowledge, such activity feels far more comfortable with a glass of some beverage in hand. One wonders what would happen at a high school reunion if the dinner dance or picnic that the get-together ostensibly revolves around did not exist. Congregators at a family reunion would probably find other ways to break the ice besides raving over Aunt Jane's banana bread or the size of the watermelon in the cooler, but these topics provide ready-made "mixers."

It is on this very personal level that studies of food still have far to go and to which this volume is a contribution. If we truly want to understand how food "works," how it operates in different "networks," how it "communicates," then one of the best ways is to look at situations where its power is most heightened, in those events which also utilize the frames of play, frivolity, relaxation, or celebration.

The following essays move generally from the very small, family-centered festive context outward to larger community gatherings, and they may be read that way. But one might think of them in a number of equally interesting (perhaps more so) ways. One could, for instance, read them to validate or broaden one's own way of celebrating, of creating community. One may also find within several of these essays useful insights into creating community where no community existed before, a relevant skill in these often rootless days. Then too, if we examine these pieces according to the motive for the gathering—work, commemoration, homecoming, promotion, fund-raising—we can see more clearly how the symbolic values of the foods and food-associated behaviors are formed from the elemental functions of a community regardless of its basis.

However arranged, the essays describe events that are nearly universal in their appeal. They cover a representative variety of communities in North America: Claremont, California; Toronto; Bala Cynwyd, Pennsylvania; Hough's Neck, Quincy, Massachusetts; Allen's Neck, Massachusetts; a farm near Surry, Virginia; Boone County, Missouri; Koosharem and Fountain Green, Utah; Morrison, Oklahoma; St. Paul, Minnesota; Lexington, Kentucky; Hartford, Connecticut; Tucson, Arizona. Who among us would not attend a community barbecue, a family clambake, a birthday party, a soup night? Fundamental to the sense of well-being of most of us are the twin elements of food and fellowship which both create and are stimulated by the sense of community without which our lives are significantly diminished. Here in this nexus of foods (often with a strongly regional identity) and festivity, we see the essentials of human community, the idea (and ideal) which serves as a bulwark against the strong currents of partisan strife.

Notes

1. Harvard University Press, 1969: 8.

2. "Toward a Psychosociology of Contemporary Food Consumption," in *European Diet from Pre-Industrial to Modern Times,* ed. Elborg and Robert Forster (New York: Harper and Row, 1975): 50.

3. Peter Farb and George Armelagos, *Consuming Passions: The Anthropology of Eating* (New York: Washington Square Press, 1983): 76.

4. By group we mean any number of individuals from one to a theoretically infinite number, although practically speaking we are talking about dyadic groups and small group festive gatherings of family, friends, and other types of social organizations that can maintain some sort of face-to-face interaction. See, for example, Alan Dundes, *The Study of Folklore* (Englewood Cliffs: Prentice-Hall, 1965); Barre Toelken, *The Dynamics of Folklore* (Boston: Houghton Mifflin Company, 1979); Jan Brunvand, *The Study of American Folklore: An Introduction,* 3rd. ed. (New York: Norton, 1987).

5. "Cajuns and Crawfish in South Louisiana," *Ethnic and Regional Foodways in the United States: The Performance of Group Identity,* Linda Keller Brown and Kay Mussell, eds. (Knoxville: University of Tennessee Press, 1983): 174.

6. Announcement of the 1987 NEH Summer Seminar, "Anthropological Perspectives on the Study of Foods and Foodways."

7. Robert A. Georges and Barre Toelken have provided much useful discussion of this concept.

8. In an unpublished paper "Divine Food for Better Bodies," (NEH Summer Seminar on Anthropological Perspectives of Food, University of Virginia, 1987), Manuel Moreno discusses the Hindu emphasis on "feeding," the giving away of food, as being culturally more important than "eating," particularly as seen in a ritual of a Tamil trading caste (Nattukkottai Cettiyar) involving the god Murukan in his winter festival. The ritual involves bathing the image of the god in certain foods, a process that consecrates the food and the bodies of devotees who then eat "divine food-leavings or washings (*prasad*)."

9. Don Yoder, "Sauerkraut in Pennsylvania Folk-Culture," *Pennsylvania Folklife* 12.2 (Summer 1961): 56–69; "Schnitz in the Pennsylvania Folk-Culture," *Pennsylvania Folklife* 12.3 (Fall 1961): 44–53.

10. "The First International Symposium on Ethnological Food Research," *Keystone Folklore Quarterly* 16 (1971): 185–88.

11. Nils-Arvid Bringéus, *Mat och Miljö: En bok om svenska kostvanor* (Lund: Gleerups, 1970).

12. Alexander Fenton's prompt translation of a chapter of the book was published as "Man, Food and Milieu" in the journal *Folk Life* 8 (1970): 45–56.

13. Linda T. Humphrey, "Small Group Festive Gatherings," *Journal of the Folklore Institute* 16 (1979): 190–201.

14. Jay Allan Anderson, "The Study of Contemporary Foodways in American Folklife Research," *Keystone Folklore Quarterly* 16 (1971): 155–63.

15. Roger Welsch, "'We Are What We Eat': Omaha Food as Symbol," *Keystone Folklore Quarterly* 16 (1971): 165–70.

16. Brian Sutton-Smith, "The Psychology of Childlore: The Triviality Barrier," *Western Folklore* 29 (1970): 1–8.

17. John Charles Camp, "America Eats: Towards a Social Definition of American Foodways" (Ph.D. diss., University of Pennsylvania, 1978). Published versions of his research include Charles Camp, "Foodways in Everyday Life," *American Quarterly* 34 (1982): 278–89; "Food in American Culture: A Bibliographic Essay," *Journal of American Culture* 2 (1979): 559–70; and "Foodways" in *The Handbook of American Popular Culture,* vol. 2, ed. William Inge (Westport, Conn.: Greenwood Press, 1980): 141–61.

18. As pointed out by Lindsy van Gelder, "Inventing Food-Free Rituals," *Ms. Magazine* 11.6 (December 1982): 25–26.

19. 40:1 (January 1981).

20. *Journal of American Culture* 2 (1979): 392–570. (Note: This is not a special issue in the strict sense because it does contain articles unrelated to foodways. However, the bulk of this issue, a section entitled "Focus on American Food and Foodways" and edited by Kay Mussell and Linda Keller Brown, is devoted to the subject.)

21. Linda Keller Brown and Kay Mussell, eds., *Ethnic and Regional Foodways in the United States: The Performance of Group Identity* (Knoxville: University of Tennessee Press, 1984).

22. John Moe, "Folk Festivals and Community Consciousness; Categories of the Festival Genre," *Folklore Forum* 10:2 (1977): 33–40; John Anthony Gutowski, "American Folklore and the Modern American Community Festival: A Case Study of Turtle Days in Churubusco, Indiana" (Ph.D. diss., Indiana University, 1977); and John A. Gutowski, "The Protofestival: Local Guide to American Behavior," *Journal of the Folklore Institute* 15 (1978): 113–32; Jack Santino, "Halloween in America: Contemporary Customs and Performances," *Western Folklore* 42 (1983): 1–20; Leslie Mina Prosterman, "The Aspect of the Fair: Aesthetics and Festival in Illinois County Fairs" (Ph.D. diss., University of Pennsylvania, 1982); Carter Walker Craigie, "A Moveable Feast: The Picnic as a Folklife Custom in Chester County, Pennsylvania, 1870–1925" (Ph.D. diss., University of Pennsylvania, 1976); Susan Camille Samuelson, "Festive Malaise and Festive Participation: A Case Study of Christmas Celebrations in America" (Ph.D. diss., University of Pennsylvania, 1983).

Part I

**Family and Friends,
Ritual and Renewal**

Introduction to Part I

Family and the widening gyre of family concerns are the themes of the food-centered events described in this section. The essays here suggest some of the ways that personal and individual yet traditional events can create community in our stress-filled contemporary lives. Personal and group ritual is an important part of such traditions and thus of many recurring food-centered festive events. Ritual is one response to our expectations of significance that are created by an event's cyclic performance. Ritual sustains tradition because we human beings create meaning and significance through ritualizing our activities and calling forth deeper responses to our celebrations of life's events. Part One describes and analyzes four such events, two of them traditional family-centered celebrations—a family birthday party and a Seder—and two of them created responses to a perceived need for community—a Montessori school's Halloween Brunch and one woman's weekly "Soup Night." Readers will recognize in these events their own forms for marking thresholds, for celebrating religious and secular holidays, and their own creative power. Furthermore, the symbolic nature of food, a constant theme of this book, is explored.

Theodore Humphrey examines a family celebration of a daughter's birthday and in so doing examines the significance of the birthday cake, a powerful and symbolic celebratory food in much of western culture. Sharon Sherman analyzes the full range of individual and group meanings associated with a contemporary Jewish family's celebration of Seder and explores the nature of a religious tradition within the context of a family's history and experience of a culture symbolized in the foods of the Seder plate. Nancy Klavans explores how a menu for a "Halloween Brunch" evolved so that it features an idealized "country breakfast," the function of which is clearly to create for an ephemeral educational group a unifying and community celebration within an otherwise disparate community. Finally, Lin Humphrey describes how she creates and conducts a small group festive gathering nearly every Thursday night in Claremont, California. Demonstrating the power of simple foods—soup, bread, and wine—as the catalyst for shaping and maintaining a community of friends within the megalopolis of Greater Los Angeles, she examines the issues of hospitality and responsibility and analyzes the significance of establishing such a food-centered forum for human connectivity, an extended family in which the actions of preparing and consuming soup create a community of warmth and caring for "friends who are present and those who are not."

A Family Celebrates a Birthday: Of Life and Cakes

Theodore C. Humphrey

When our family recently observed our daughter's 24th birthday, we were not thinking about its nature as a small group festive gathering[1] or about the symbolic nature of the expressive behaviors and forms of that celebration. We were simply celebrating her birthday the way many people celebrate birthdays in our culture—with food and drink in a festive manner.[2] It was one of the smaller, more intimate celebrations of birthdays that have occurred in our house or among our circle of friends recently. But after the celebration I began to think about it and to consider it more deeply, especially within the framework of how birthdays are presently celebrated in European and North American culture generally. Its analysis will serve to illustrate how foods are turned into highly symbolic forms in a context of festivity and ritual that characterizes a widely observed family and personal festive event.

Four people were present, all immediate family. My mother, her grandmother, who ordinarily resides in Oklahoma, had spent the winter in Claremont and thus was able to attend this birthday dinner for Merritt. Her brother, however, was absent, being away at school. None of her intimate friends were present because, in part, the celebration fell on a Tuesday this year, a work day for them. But most of them, although not physically present, made their presence and best wishes known with phone calls. My wife Lin, in her role as mother and "chief kitchen person," Merritt in her role as birthday girl, and I as father, son, host, and husband completed the list—four people in all. The dishes served included a green pea and peanut salad, 40-garlic clove chicken, baked potatoes, green tossed salad, French sourdough bread with garlic butter, and a chocolate cake with chocolate icing and raspberry filling that I had ordered from a local bakery with a reputation for producing wonderful confections. On it was a candle, writing

("Happy 24th birthday Merritt") and flowers and curls made with white butter icing. Of these foods, only the cake is culturally imbued with heavy symbolic identification, as we shall see (although peas, peanuts, garlic, potatoes, and bread each has had symbolic and folkloric significance). The meaning of these other foods, however, derived in this instance from their having been chosen by Merritt in consultation with her mother, having been then prepared by her mother, and having been served in this celebratory context. These foodstuffs were then consumed by Merritt in the company of most of her close family (grandmother, mother, father) at a meal frequently interrupted by phone calls from, among others, her brother (who sang "Happy Birthday" to her over the phone from Pittsburgh) and various friends who wished her happy birthday. Later, as we were finishing the meal, a friend came over to take her out to be in the company of others of her age group to celebrate the birthday further.

The important thing here as for any festive event is to see these foods not as individual entities on a menu but rather as part of the celebratory, festive context, the purpose of which was to mark an important threshold in a manner heightened by ritual and festive elements. Individually each of these foods has appeared on our table more than once in the past year. The green pea and peanut salad, for instance, is a fairly recent addition to Lin's repertoire as a cook, as is the garlic chicken. Both are cookbook recipes, not "traditional." The baked potato and the tossed mixed green salad as well as the garlic buttered French sourdough bread have been appearing for a good 25 years in our household. And a chocolate cake of one sort or another was always a traditional birthday cake for me as a child, and even today it is not that unusual an item on our table, although a growing concern for overweight and other dietary matters may diminish its frequency.

For all participants the event was clearly understood as a festive event, an event different from ordinary board in our house, even though characterized by food items that are in some sense ordinary. It was different not in the individual item or behavior so much as in the total scene, the total concatenation of behaviors and performances, the order and sequencing of the individual items and behaviors, and the emic understanding of the intention, the significance, and the meaning of the total event, a threshold event, a birthday. It was marked by a heightening of setting, of ritual, especially of the birthday cake with candle lit, singing (in a family that does not generally sing), blowing out of candle, birthday wishes and greetings; the day was identified in everyone's mind as "special." Ritual and expressive verbal and gestural behaviors all contributed to making it festive—and significant.

The meaning of a particular food behavior (the entire complex of food item, selecting, preparing, serving, consuming, and reflecting upon it) is totally ascribed within the culture but not necessarily in a conscious fashion. The power of tradition comes in part from the weight of the unselfconscious assumptions about "the way" to do or say anything, about "the meaning" of a behavior. These assumptions are, of course, largely but not entirely the result of the group's historical experiences coupled with the individual's possession and adaptation of them. We participate in tradition, as folklorist Kay Cothran has noted,[3] in a variety of ways—by continuing elements of it, by modifying elements of it, or by denying elements of it. A close reading of the foods and the behaviors at that birthday meal demonstrate in detail the validity of Simon Bronner's observation that the "disparities as well as [the] continuities in individual behavior and thought must be significant to the analysis of foodways."[4] In just this way, the presence of chocolate cake at Merritt's birthday celebration constitutes an identifiable tradition in our family. This particular cake was not "homemade" as so many of them have been for birthdays in our home, nor had, I should add, any of the earlier cakes ever had a raspberry filling between the layers. And most of the earlier cakes had candles that more directly represented the number of birthdays being celebrated. Rather than having been baked by myself or her mother, it had been purchased from a bakery and "customized" by the baker, who wrote "Happy 24th Birthday Merritt" on it at my request. We adorned it with a single large household candle, all we could find at the time. Yet, because of the nature of the total context of this celebration, all present clearly understood that the candle represented the full extent of 24 years, and that our following the ritual associated with it appropriately commemorated her birthday.

Similarly, the other foods present at that birthday celebration, foods rendered special by their being prepared and served within the larger context of a birthday celebration, became meaningful because of the occasion. Lin asked the birthday girl what she would like to have for her birthday dinner. The relative sophistication of the menu suggested to all of us her maturity, status, and individuality within the continuities and consistencies of the culturally significant and sanctioned venue for celebration and threshold marking. All in all, the foods served, the details of their selection, preparation, and consumption, and the total performance all worked together to provide a powerful expression of the family's vision of itself, a matrix of meaning as rich and significant as one may find in any set of traditional behaviors.

To see more clearly the validity of these correspondences, let us examine in more detail the ritual of the cake since it is clearly the central and most significant element. To understand it, we must first consider the culinary form that we identify as a birthday cake as well as the complex of behaviors that characterizes a typical birthday celebration. Typically, but not always, it is a sweet, baked confection of flour, baking powder, salt, sugar (usually a lot of it), shortening, flavor (such as chocolate, lemon extract, vanilla, etc.), eggs, and milk, baked in a variety of shapes including but not limited to round, square, oblong, loaf, and specialty shapes, and usually enhanced or set apart from other, more ordinary baked goods by being covered with a sugar-based icing and decorated with sugared forms deemed appropriate for the person either in terms of a vocabulary of forms generally used (e.g., leaves, flowers, tendrils) or in a personal iconography, and finished off with candles, typically one for each year of age. Although the typical form is a cake, "birthday cakes" may also take the forms known as pies, loaves of bread, shaped ice cream, or, theoretically, any food item whatsoever that is denominated "birthday cake" and is adorned with at least one candle or candle substitute. The form is so deeply imbedded in the culture that a nearly infinite series of variations may occur. The tradition is so solid, in other words, so widespread and so often observed that so long as the context carries other signs that signify "birthday," the actual form the cake may take is very free. It is conceivable that I could serve a cabbage with a candle stuck in it to a vegetarian friend of mine, wish her happy birthday, and she would recognize the event—and accept the form. Furthermore, it is possible to parody the form by varying specific components of it including, but not limited to, the item itself as we have seen, perhaps designating a cabbage as the cake as I have suggested, or decorating the cake with motifs or colors in opposition to the expected norms. The colors might be black, the iconography placed on it might contain images of death, or the sentiments expressed in writing on it could be insulting or in some other way at odds with the normal expectations. If humor is essentially an aggressive act, then preparing a birthday cake for someone at one of the "critical" age thresholds, e.g., 30, 40, and perhaps 50, with colors, images, and written sentiments that call into question the birthday person's virility, sexiness, power, health, or other attributes typically associated with life and vigor (found often in humorous or "contemporary" birthday cards) may be understood to be a kind of shared "gallows" humor, attacking directly the problem of aging. Or it might be a covert attack upon the vanity or other personality attribute of the honoree. (However, it may well be that as a person advances into years felt more truly to be "old age," such parodies would not occur. This is a topic to be explored further.) Such rich possibilities for parody suggest that the form is well understood, widely observed, and a fully functional element within the culture's repertoire of expressive behaviors.

Moving from the cake itself to the candles, we enter into an area profoundly rich in symbol and meaning. First of all, traditionally each candle corresponds directly to a year of life. Up to about 40 or so, it is common practice for the correspondence to be direct and one-for-one. After 40, however, it is a common but by no means universal practice to substitute candles on an equivalency bases, e.g., one large candle for each ten years, or candles in the shape of the numbers themselves. For my 48th birthday, Lin got candles in the shape of a "4" and an "8." (I saved them for my 84th, which will occur soon, I suspect.) Other variations are permitted within this element of the form. While the typical candle will stay out when blown out, one may get candles which relight, and in terms of the central cake ritual (discussed below) that substitution makes a powerful symbolic statement of its own. We have celebrated other birthdays in which a household candle was substituted for the cake candles that we had forgotten to get. But a candle need not even be a candle. The important thing seems to be to have a flame in conjunction with the cake so that the ritual of "blowing out the candles" may take place. One could even use kitchen matches or paper matches stuck in the icing of the cake. It is the flame itself, this flickering, wavering, rapidly oxidizing symbol of the years that have passed, that is of principal importance.

We do not have to look far to discover a cause. Our atavistic relationship with fire is found in the imagery of our poetry, our paintings, in the tribal lore. Walter Pater urged us to "burn with a hard, gem-like flame." Othello muses on Desdemona's fate thus: "And if I quench thee, thou flaming minister, /I can again thy former light restore, /Should I repent me; but once put out thy light, / Thou cunning'st pattern of excelling nature, /I know not where is that Promethean heat /That can thy light relume" (V.II.7–13). Charles Dickens has Miss Havisham's wedding cake, the central symbol of thwarted expectations, consumed by fire in *Great Expectations.* And, of course, in the Christian complex, Christ is the "light of the world." The idea that our lives and their passages are seen generally in the flickering of the flame is surely in the minds of nearly everyone who reflects on the meaning of the central ritual of the cake.

It is worth looking at the ritual that generally accompanies the cake in some detail, to provide, as it were, a close reading of every commonplace and detail. Typically the birthday cake (or whatever food has been chosen to *be* the cake in this instance) is adorned with the requisite number of candles (or the substituted symbol for the symbol) usually out of sight of the birthday honoree. The entire custom of the "surprise" birthday party partakes even more fully in the idea of secrecy. But in both instances, surprise party or expected gathering, the cake is typically prepared in alleged or assumed secrecy, from baking to decorating to lighting, and then is brought into the presence of the honoree with the house lights dimmed, all eyes upon the "flaming minister" and the honoree as it is placed before him or her.[5] The "Happy Birthday" song usually accompanies the procession. The honoree is instructed and exhorted by those present to "Make a wish" and is often instructed in the proper procedures to be followed next: "Make a wish." "Close your eyes." "Don't tell anyone what the wish is." "Blow out all the candles." And so on. The honoree takes a deep breath and attempts to put out all the candles with one expulsion, perhaps assisted if very young or old or infirm by significant others such as parents, children, or close friends. This is, despite the general festive mood, a serious moment, high drama, and the center of the birthday ceremony. And it is justly so.

Consider what has happened. The entire history of conception, birth, life, and death has been played out in this small compact drama, filled with objects and behaviors and meanings that are part of the cultural equipage of many (though of course not all) people in the North American and European cultural complex. Because the cake is often prepared in "secret" and because the candles by general agreement signify the years of life from conception, before which the honoree did not exist, onward and because the candles are often lit by several people working together in a kind of communal activity, the honoree's existence not only as an individual but as a social creature, as a part of a community, is clearly symbolized by this ritual. This creation and identification continue with the rest of the ceremony. For example, usually the triumphal procession in which the cake is borne into the presence of the honoree is accompanied with song,[6] with light, with that perfectly focused attention that was hers at the moment of birth; the event is a communal celebration of life that mediates the progress toward death. Traditionally, the honoree pauses before the blazing cake, and makes a wish, which, regardless of the actual form and content of it, is clearly by the very definition of the act itself an affirmation of life, an expressed prayer for continued life and vigor. Blowing out the candles, which occurs next, each one representing one year of life, is at once an affirmation of life and power because of the vigorous intake of life-sustaining air and the exertion of control over it through its vigorous expulsion. Extinguishing the candles, these markers of one's past years, wipes them out, halts their destruction through an exaggeration of the process of respiration, surely one of the great central facts of our form of life, without which we are dead. (Besides, only by blowing them all out are we assured of having our wish come true.) Thus, in this drama, life and death are brought into symbolic conjunction, the cake becoming both metaphor and metonym. The breath of the honoree becomes symbolic of the divine afflatus, the life-giving and sustaining force of the universe, and by breathing it over this culturally encoded symbolic food, the cake, the birthday honoree endows it with magic power. It becomes *mana*, carrying with it divine force and power, blessed by the divine spirit which has been inhaled and exhaled in the first of several great sharing rituals that mark this rite.

With the candles blown out and removed, the honoree typically cuts and serves the cake to the guests assembled, urging each to "have some cake." I contend that the cake is certainly made special if not holy or blessed by the honoree through the ritual of blowing out the candles, by breathing on it and then sharing it directly with the guests. Thus, we have a direct and potent symbolic connection enacted here, the purpose and main business of which is the celebration of life and the triumph over death performed in the fellowship of others, the human community; the candles, their flame now extinguished, become the closest representatives of death allowed in the celebration and are cast aside. The morphological and symbolic similarities to the Eucharist are direct, powerful, and no accident. "Eat of this my body, drink of this my blood."

Consider too that those things which are essential to life—conception, birth, respiration, eating, drinking, and nurture—all come together in this central ritual, one that many, many people celebrate every year of their lives with their family and friends. Although central, the cake does not generally occur in isolation. Although important to our understanding of the meaning and significance of the birthday celebration, the cake takes on a large part of its meaning by being embedded in a complex ritualized context, each part contributing its meaning to the meaning of the whole and its variety of formal characteristics, sources, and functions. As Robertson-Smith says, there is "no separation between the spheres of religion and ordinary life"[7] if both are properly understood.

Thus people who celebrate birthdays in the ways just described create and manipulate powerful symbolic systems from their traditions, especially within the customs that center on foods in this festive context. They establish and maintain *communitas,* the idea and the reality of community, not as a permanent and unchanging entity, but as a source of individual and group identity and power. In the celebration of birthdays, the group creates a powerful and affective core of meaning that in turn creates the community through the ritual and binds it together. In this simple and widely observed traditional form, we can begin to glimpse some of the complex ways in which food lies at the center not just of our corporeal existence but of our social and spiritual selves, individually and collectively.

Notes

I am grateful to the National Endowment for the Humanities for participation in the Summer Seminar on Anthropological Perspectives on the Study of Food directed by Dr. Ravindra H. Khare, Professor of Anthropology, University of Virginia, in which I amplified an earlier version of a portion of this paper which was read at the annual meeting of the California Folklore Society, April 26, 1987, U.C.L.A., in the session entitled *Defining Folklore from Inside and Out.*

1. Linda T. Humphrey, "Small Group Festive Gatherings," *Journal of the Folklore Institute* 16 (1979): 190–201.

2. Karin Lee Fishbeck Calvert argues, in "To Be a Child: An Analysis of the Artifacts of Childhood" (Ph.D. diss., University of Delaware, 1984), 196–201, that the "practice of giving children's birthday parties to commemorate the importance of the individual child" occurred no earlier than the nineteenth century in America. She offers as evidence a number of entries from nineteenth-century diaries. For a somewhat different view as to the history of celebrating birthdays, see Linda Rannells Lewis, *Birthdays: Their Delights, Disappointments, Past and Present, Worldly, Astrological and Infamous* (Boston: Little, Brown and Company, 1976).

3. Kay L. Cothran, "Participation in Tradition," in *Readings in American Folklore,* ed. Jan Brunvand (New York: W. W. Norton, 1979): 444–48.

4. *Foodways and Eating Habits,* Michael Owen Jones, Bruce Giuliano, and Roberta Krell, eds. (Los Angeles: The California Folklore Society, 1983): 121.

5. Notice that the ritual may often be performed in restaurants complete with waiters singing songs adapted from a variety of sources while serving an ice cream sundae or a cupcake with a flaming candle stuck in it and observing other aspects of the ritual, showing how completely the ritual is understood and accepted in contemporay society.

6. Perhaps the most popular song in American culture presently, "Happy Birthday" was published by Patty Smith Hill in 1893 as "Good Morning to All" with music by Mildred J. Hill in *Songs, Stories for Children.*

7. Quoted by Mary Douglas, *Purity and Danger* (London, Boston and Henley: Ark Paperbacks, 1966): 21.

2

The Passover Seder:
Ritual Dynamics, Foodways, and Family Folklore

Sharon R. Sherman

Food, family, and ethnic identity are at the core of the Passover ritual. Despite a lengthy and strong tradition governing the formal observance of Passover, the meaning given to each of these elements changes with each enactment, building on earlier interpretations (both "official" and family-generated ones). Such family folklore thus appears to be not merely "a creative expression of a common past"[1] but rather the reflection of a constantly evolving process. To understand this process better and to appreciate more fully the nature of my family's celebration of Passover, I studied the behaviors of members of my own extended Gershenowitz family during two Passover Seders held in Toronto by Stan and Brenda Kates.[2] Many of the events described in this chapter relate to that festive occasion, but my study of changes in one family's Seder has continued to evolve, along with my own participation in that family's Seders, in subsequent years. By their levels of participation in the family Seder, participants define their relationships within the family. The meanings of those relationships arise then from the rich mix of the generations within the family, the varying intensities of their involvement in Judaism, the differing sorts of family membership, as well as their experiences with previous Seders.

One might assume that a "common past" does exist for the Gershenowitz family as for other Jews, and, indeed, most Jews see the Passover event as a symbol for the Jewish people or Jewish "family" as a whole.[3] One of the rituals connected with the yearly cycle of seasons, Passover creates a sense of *communitas* with Jews throughout time—from the Exodus upon which it is based to the present. Added to this diachronic dimension, Jews sense the synchronic simultaneous celebration of the event with all Jews at one specific time of the year throughout the world. On a more intimate level, Jews mark the celebration as one which has symbolic meanings acquired within individual families.

Since "Seder" means "order," the Haggadah, or prayer book for this holiday, has a definite structure which must be followed, giving the Seder ritual, therefore, an ingrained continuity. As the leader of a Seder once remarked to me, the Seder is oriented "to bring the tradition along, year after year after year." Certain passages of the Haggadah text, for example, are commonly read by most families, yet other sections allow for familial improvisation. Thus, the Seder integrates both continuity and change. Beatrice Weinreich, in "The Americanization of Passover," has described generalized cultural transformations in the Passover Seder resulting from external change (such as mechanization, urbanization, and cross-cultural acculturation) and internal change ("adaptations to internal historical events," such as the Holocaust and "a general trend toward secularization").[4] The changes she describes have affected the ritual for most North American Jews of East European ancestry, but Weinreich does not analyze change within a specific family, the multi-layered dynamics of prescribed and personal food symbolism, or the family inter-relationships which underlie the Seder ritual and serve to shape the event.

Although religious studies scholars have researched the origins of Passover to pre-Exodus rituals, these early symbols, reinterpreted in the light of the Exodus event, are generally ignored by many contemporary Jews. Indeed, when I mentioned their historical significance during a family Seder, I was met with uneasy short comments and a quick shifting of topic. These rituals were "too primitive" to consider as foundations for an event which had acquired immediate relevance to each year's current world situation.

Nevertheless, we do know that two nature festivals predate the Exodus.[5] In ancient times, Jews who lived as nomadic shepherds in the desert sacrificed a sheep or goat from their flocks during the spring month when the lambs and kids were born. The animal's blood was smeared on the tent posts to ward off misfortune and ensure good luck for the coming year. This festival, observed within family groups, was called "Pesach," derived from "paschal offering."

The agricultural Jews who lived in Palestine also celebrated the cutting of the grain in the spring with a Festival of Matsos or Unleavened Bread. They first removed all the fermented dough and old bread made with the leaven or "chomets" of the preceding year's crop. After this cleaning out was completed, the first new sheaf of grain, the "omer," was cut and sacrificed to God by a priest, while the entire community attended. According to other scholars, agricultural groups also baked their freshly harvested grain into unleavened cakes eaten in a special ceremony to thank God for the harvest.

These early nature rituals eventually merged and came to symbolize the exodus of the Jewish people from Egypt—an event which had occurred in the first spring month (Nisan) of the year—reinterpreting the Pesach sacrifice. When the Angel of Death slew the first-born of the Egyptians in the tenth plague sent against the Pharaoh (who refused to release the Jews from bondage), the Jews marked their doors with the blood of the sacrificed animal so the Angel would pass over their homes. The earlier meaning of the Festival of Matsos (or Matzo) came to symbolize the bread of affliction since the Jews did not have time for their bread to rise when fleeing Egypt.

Because spring was a busy season, many Jews could not travel to the faraway Temple in Jerusalem, the national center, the only place where the sacrificed lamb could be killed. Thus blood was no longer smeared on the doorposts, and Passover became, and still is, a home-centered festival. After the Romans destroyed the Second Temple (around 70 C.E.), the Pesach sacrifice was totally discontinued, but re-emerged in symbolic form as a roasted shankbone on the Seder plate.

Passover signals the beginning of spring and a celebration of freedom—a unique paradigm for a historically oppressed people. The eight-day holiday,[6] starting on the evening of the fourteenth of Nisan (calculated by the Jewish lunar calendar, which explains its variation from a fixed secular date), begins with a ritual meal called a Seder, the symbolic foods of which lead Jews to experience the past and bring the story of the Exodus into the present. Indeed, according to the Torah, parents have a duty to tell the tale to children; in every generation each Jew must feel as if he or she personally came out of Egypt.

In contemporary times, Passover has numerous connotations. The celebration of freedom, for example, brings to mind not only the Exodus, but the pogroms of Russia and Poland, the Holocaust, the Warsaw Ghetto uprising, the establishment of the State of Israel, the plight of the Ethiopian Black Jews (or "Falasha" [outsiders] as they are called by other Ethiopians), and the situation of today's Soviet Jews (to whom matzo is smuggled for Passover). All of these events become part of the tale and add new dimensions for families whose members may have lived through such acts and now relive them in memories evoked by the Seder. For example, Doris, a member of the family studied, commented upon her daughter-in-law's parents, who survived the Holocaust: "Sheri's family—her mother was in the camps—her father was in the camps—and they had gone through so much hardship and they can come out of that experience and still believe in

God, and still have so much religious faith. It's marvelous to see." Another family member, Tillie, who fled Poland before the Nazi occupation, remarked: "This, in essence, is the idea behind Passover—that you went out of slavery and tried to get into freedom, and what you had to pay for it. . . . It seems the more you are repressed, the stronger your roots come through."

Ruth Gruber Fredman, in *The Passsover Seder: Afikoman in Exile,* has pointed out the structural oppositions balanced by the Seder and argues that Jewish culture attempts to create order, placing it eternally in transition. Thus, the Seder becomes a means of expressing *galut,* an in-between state which illuminates "the experience of the individual Jew."[7] The ordering exhibited by the Seder can also be seen as being symbolic of the ordering of family. Like Seder, "family" connotes order. And, like Seder, families exhibit change. Just as the Haggadah does not explicate everything which must be done during the Seder,[8] mere family membership does not guarantee the rules and roles demanded for family participation, particularly because a family consists of individuals who constantly combine and recombine their experiences. In participating in the dynamics of this disordering and reordering, a sense of family emerges.

For instance, most of the people at the Kates's Seder have participated in Seders dating back to the last Seder held by Pearl Gershenowitz, my maternal grandmother. The memory of that Seder provides a point of reference for the current Seder members and a symbolic common link. But everyone who attended remembers the Seder for different reasons. For example, Pearl's daughter-in-law, Doris, whom I interviewed, sees that Seder as an initiation into the Gershenowitz family and as an introduction to a "real" Passover Seder.

> We always had Passover in our house but we never really had a Seder. . . . My father was more Canadianized, my mother was more European, so we just had Kiddush and we had someone read the four questions but we never had a full Seder, and we didn't start having a full Seder, I remember, until we went to your Grandmother's. Do you remember? Well, anyways, when your grandmother had the first Seder and Joel [Doris's son] was just a baby at the time and that was very, very memorable because we had the whole family together and we had a full Seder, and I didn't know what a Seder was until then.

For Brenda, however, it was the death of her grandmother that she associates with that Seder:

> My grandmother had a Seder and, um, that Seder I remember for different reasons because my grandmother was very sick and then, that was the last Seder she was here for. . . . I don't associate my grandmother with Seders that much, partly because she died when I was thirteen and partly because she really didn't have many Seders. She may have

had them before I was born, but I only remember one Seder at her place and that was just before she died. And I associate the Seder with the family all being together. But not as much as a Seder ... The Seder that my grandmother and grandfather made doesn't stand out as a Seder; it stands out for other reasons.

Pearl's daughter, Trudy, remembers the Seder not only because of its traumatic aspects but because she realized that the responsibility for the Seder would now shift to her generation:

The one that stands out in my mind the most is about the last Passover that I had at my mother's home before she passed on.... She'd been home from the hospital about a month and I was making dinner for everyone that was coming in from out of town, and for our family, when Mother said, "Next year we will have a bigger Passover and we will invite all my brothers and sisters and their offsprings." And I started to cry because I knew there wasn't going to be a next year, and she said, "Why are you crying?" and I said, "Well, it's the onions that I'm cutting." So that is the Passover that has stayed ... been outstanding in my mind ever since.

At that Seder, my sister Suzanne and I, both Pearl's grandchildren, were six and eleven years old. For us, Grandma's Seder also stood out in memory, although I am certain we did not know she was dying. Perhaps the Seder was highlighted in our memories because it became the model for subsequent Seders. Over thirty years of Seders have come and gone, but this *one* Seder is spoken of each year and has become part of Passover for all in the family who participated. Although the narrative may appear to function as a means of creating solidarity for the family, at the same time it also functions differently for each person who tells it; for those who did not attend Grandma's Seder, the telling is an introduction to the Gershenowitz family Seder.

The dynamics of a family can frequently be illuminated by its foodways, especially of the Seder. The Seder ritual has a break during which a festive and relaxed meal is served. For the Gershenowitz family, the "rules" for what may be eaten are based not only on prohibitions against *chometz* (leavened foods), but also on the family's notions of acceptability, derived from the foods served by Pearl. As is true for most Ashkenazic Jews, the foods recall Eastern European meals. Pearl, who immigrated to Canada from a small village in Poland, continued to prepare foods common in the "old country": chicken soup with matzo, *knadlach* (dumplings), roast chicken, beef brisket, potato *kugel* (pudding), and *tzimmes* (cooked carrots, prunes and apricots in a rich, thick, honeyed sauce). Thus, these foods are always served by the family. However, no one eats the *tzimmes* and every year someone mentions that it should not be included in next year's menu. A year later, *tzimmes* again appears and Pearl's family tradition is upheld.

The meals for the two nights vary, but some items remain the same. Gefilte fish (made from chopped whitefish and pike, formed into ovals), sometimes referred to as "Jewish fish" on Russian and Polish restaurant menus, was an economical dish in Eastern Europe, and is now traditionally served for Passover by most families. Available at supermarkets in jars packaged by Jewish food suppliers, gefilte fish is usually served cold and needs no further preparation. Pearl's daughter, Trudy, however, remembers her mother's painstaking cooking and thus boils the already cooked fish in a broth with carrots, celery, and spices, chills the fish, and serves it on lettuce with a slice of carrot as garnish. On the second night, tomato juice is substituted as an appetizer for either the fish or the chicken soup.

Beef brisket, prepared by Trudy or her daughter (trained to make it the "same" way), is served the first night, along with *kishka* (also East European in origin)—intestine stuffed with flour, fat, crumbs, and minced onion filling which is then roasted with the brisket. Brenda buys a standing rib roast for the second night, an innovation, but the roast is rarely cooked since so much food remains from the prior night's feast (except the *kishka*, which disappears immediately despite Brenda's dislike of it). The second night's menu also includes two capons to add to any leftover chicken.

Who prepares or brings certain dishes is supposedly open but nevertheless a pattern has been re-established each year. Doris brings chicken or turkey for the first night. Trudy, who stays at Brenda's home during Passover, prepares the fish and brisket, fills the silver salt and pepper shakers, cuts and arranges a pickle tray, and hardboils dozens of eggs. A fertility and springtime symbol, the egg (now often associated with Easter but whose ritual use is ancient) is served in a bowl with salt water as the first course. Salad, another appetizer and a contemporary, health-conscious addition, is always brought by someone of Brenda's generation. Great Aunt Lil, Pearl's sister-in-law, always brings a cake, usually a sponge cake made with matzo flour—a very traditional Passover dessert. Guests who do not prepare food bring Passover chocolate, small gifts, or freshly cut flowers.

Brenda's responsibility for food preparation has changed because of the vast marketing of Passover foods, especially in cities like Toronto, where large numbers of Jews live. In fact, some companies, such as Coca-Cola and Canada Dry, and many local dairies in Toronto, have their entire stock made "kosher for Passover" to simplify bottling and distribution during the holiday. Traditional foods, such as matzo, chicken soup, sponge cake mix, horseradish, and beet borsht, are packaged and available in the major supermarkets. Kosher butchers not only stock the standard items and meat cuts, but will cook chickens, *tzimmes,* potato *kugel, kishka,* and soup. Brenda orders all of these items already cooked; the brisket is one of the few foods actually made in the house. Nevertheless, neighborhood availability and what is served are of paramount importance to Brenda. She commented,

> I take for granted the fact that I can get all of these Jewish products, whether they're prepared or whether I have to prepare them and they're just the materials for preparing them. . . . And it's important for me to live in the kind of neighborhood where all of these things are accessible to me.
>
> I can order the traditional dishes and we cook certain things ourselves. Trudy does a lot of work . . . helping me prepare the way, ah, I was going to say the way my grandmother used to, but that isn't true. I mean obviously we have made certain changes even in the foods. But we do try to stick to the traditional things that we remember.

Tillie recalled how much things had actually changed from what was done when the family lived in Europe:

> You made all the food by yourself and . . . there was a limited range of food. Foods that you use now that are considered to be, oh, how should I say, kosher for Pesach, weren't considered kosher at that time. You had fish and you had meat, like, ah, geese, ducks, chickens, and, um, roasts, veal or beef. . . . You used fish, you used matzo, you used eggs and, you know, certain fruit you were allowed, and certain staples like carrots, potatoes, onions . . . a limited selection because they weren't sure whether it's right or wrong. They figured, you know, it's best not to use certain things so then you know you're doing the right thing.

She underscored that matzo was made by hand and not sold in boxes:

> All matzo at that time years ago was made by hand and it was round; it wasn't made on a machine, where it's put through, ah, on an assembly line way. It was made by hand. It wasn't packaged. It came, oh, you bought it by the pound and mostly it came in big wicker baskets that you bought so many pounds. Mostly it was a lot and, um, that's the way it was delivered to you. It wasn't packaged. And it wasn't square. It was round and it was all made by hand.

The situation Brenda finds herself in is radically different—and she is pleased to find herself living where Jewish stores are common. The older generation has not quite adjusted to these changes. Doris pointed out:

> The only thing about Seder or Passover that upsets me is the fact that some of the shop-keepers seem to take advantage—just like Christmas, it's too commercialized. And prices go sky high and the women, when you go shopping, get a little hyper, and you want to buy your fish or chicken or whatever—it's quite an ordeal [laugh].

Stan, not dependent on memories of past Gershenowitz Seders, is free to create his own role. He assumes responsibility for the foods on the Seder plate and for setting out the wine glasses, refilling the decanter, and leading the Seder. Passing pieces of the various Seder plate foods from hand to hand down the table, rather than distributing them on a dish, he consciously chooses to act as a pivot for the meanings applied to the Seder by the participants. All of these actions and attitudes of the various generations define appropriate behavior and create a notion of *communitas.*

The newest generation sees the Passover Seder from a completely different perspective from that of their parents (Pearl's grandchildren). The children are preoccupied with learning the basics of the Passover Seder: how to ask the four questions, open the door for Elijah, and steal the Afikomen. All the adults take responsibility for educating the children, but the roles accompanying grandmother, mother, and grandchild are not generationally restricted. The grandmother, Pearl, who passed away in 1954, is ever present in the minds of her children. But, as children of each new generation are born, the mothers also become grandmothers in their role as transmitters for a family tradition. Pearl's daughter, Trudy, is now the grandmother of my son Mikey. Trudy's daughter Suzanne, now in her late thirties, remained the child who asked the four questions until she assisted Mikey in learning this skill. That these generations overlap is exemplified by the joint responsibilities undertaken by both Suzanne and Mikey to insure that the four questions are asked. Until Mikey began attending Seders at the age of three, my sister Suzanne always asked the questions. The 1983 and 1984 Seders demonstrated that this phase was in flux. Mikey asked the questions with Suzanne in 1982, attempted to ask them himself with some help in 1983, and by 1984 learned not only how to ask them without assistance, but surprised the group by reciting them in Hebrew (which he became motivated to do after watching his visiting Israeli cousins do so the previous year). Thus Suzanne's role finally shifted from child to adult.

Areas of folklore which invariably function to bind the children together as active participants and the adults as an encouraging audience occur at places where the Haggadah lacks commentary, thus providing an open interpretative frame for certain portions of the Seder, such as explanations for Elijah's entry and the importance of the Afikomen. Each adult reveals his/her interpretations of the rituals. The following exchange about opening the door for Elijah the prophet illustrates how meanings for familiar themes arise. The family discusses who Elijah is, how he will arrive to announce the coming of the messiah, visit families on Passover, and take a sip of wine from a cup reserved especially for him. The children then are placed in charge of opening and closing the door and are joshed about the level of wine diminishing (someone will often jiggle the table as well). Stan points out, "This cup is for Elijah the prophet. When you opened up the door we think he was in the neighborhood and came in and had a drink. We didn't see him, but, you see, the glass was full before...." Another cousin interrupts: "Did you see him at the door?" Brenda notes, "You don't have to be afraid of him because he's a good prophet." Amy's grandmother joins in, "He's a good prophet, he's a friend." Mikey repeats, "A friend." Stan says, "So we think he came in and took a sip of wine." "You don't believe it, right, Amy?" asks Brenda. "I don't know," Amy responds. Stan points, "The glass was full before we started." "I don't know," Amy repeats, as Mikey stares at the wine goblet, and the service continues. Here, despite the lack of commentary in the Haggadah, all family members share in the recitation and acting out of an ancient story which is transformed into a family tradition in its own right.

Hiding the Afikomen is another family event that is not commented on in the Haggadah. The edition used by this family makes no mention of the activity but rather states, "After the meal, the Afikomen is distributed." The Afikomen, or dessert matzo, must be eaten before the service commences following the meal. During the dinner, as courses are served and cleared, the adults urge the children to steal and hide this matzo when Stan is not looking. Several adults whisper at one time: "Don't eat it, don't eat it." ... "Wrap it in a napkin." ... "Go hide it somewhere, go hide it together." ... "Under the tablecloth, in front of your seat." "Here?" "Yeah, underneath." ... "Lift up the tablecloth." "Hurry up." ... "Did you hide it?" ... "OK, that's all. OK, now you can go play." "OK, put your napkin on top of it so it won't be noticeable." "We'll call you."

After the children leave the room, the adults laugh at the obvious hiding place. "And the thing I like is ... you can't even tell it's there," Brenda laughs. "Well, children have so much faith. They don't question things, thank God," says Amy's grandmother.

This little interchange is a prime example of family participation in a food-centered ritual of their own making. Likewise, the ransoming of the Afikomen follows the family's tradition rather than any command in the Haggadah. Stan always calls everyone's attention back to the service, and then reaches ceremoniously for the Afikomen, now mysteriously missing. "Which one of you guys has got the Afikomen?" he asks. Everyone chimes in, "Oh oh; who hid something?" The children always claim that they don't have it and don't know where it is. Finally, the adults encourage them to make a deal with Stan, and ask him how much it's worth to him. Amidst much laughter and bantering, a deal is struck. This part of the Seder will often take twenty minutes, involves everyone, and is family folklore which adheres to an almost identical structure each year. (If the children have gone to sleep, an adult represents them.) Such folklore is shared, follows the childhood experiences adults recall, and, although it marks a "change" from the Seder ritual, it conforms to family expectations.

Because the bargaining event is not prescribed by the Haggadah, it serves as a point in the ritual where change may occur. For Stan and Brenda, the host and hostess of this Seder, it represents one example of a blend of family traditions now experienced by the group as a whole. As Brenda pointed out, "When the children steal the Afikomen at our Seder, they do get little presents for it, and I remember that as a child.... Stan doesn't remember getting anything for stealing it. He likes, though, combining this because he feels that this makes it nicer for the children." Here one family's tradition has been merged with another's through marriage. Just as Brenda has retained the tradition of gift-giving, Stan has brought elements of his childhood Seder to his new family's Seder. For example, instead of using parsley for the green vegetable on the Seder plate, he provides onion (acceptable since it grows green above the ground). Thus both continuity and change are promoted as one would expect with folkloric manifestations, and as the above examples demonstrate.

One might assume that the Seder plate, constituting a table of ritual foods which correspond in the text to the deliverance from Egypt, would be static. The foods on the Seder plate have acknowledged and deeply ingrained meanings. A piece of roasted lamb shank bone (although any roasted meat bone may be used) represents the Pesach sacrifice. A roasted egg, called "chagigoh," symbolizes a second animal sacrificed in Jerusalem. The first animal had to be entirely eaten before the dawn of the first day. Because the group was large, some only received a small bite, so a second animal (not sacrificed in the Temple) was used for the second night. "Charoses," a kind of fruit salad from the early Spring festival, consists of nuts, cinnamon, wine, and apples; it is often said to symbolize the mortar mixed by Jewish slaves for the Pharaoh's buildings in Egypt. It also represents the hope of freedom. Bitter herbs or "moror," usually a piece of horseradish, symbolize the bitterness of the Jews' lives in Egypt. Greens, often parsley, lettuce or watercress, dipped in salt water (representing tears) stand for the coming of spring and the hope of redemption.[9] The table setting includes a plate with three pieces of matzo, each wrapped separately within a folded cloth. The matzo has three meanings: (1) the bread which the Jews took with them on fleeing Egypt that had not risen (including the dessert matzo or "afikomen"); (2) the bread of poverty; and (3) the bread of the simple life in the desert. A wine decanter and wine glasses for each person are also set on the table. Participants drink four glasses of wine: one for Kiddush (thanks to God for the fruit of the vine); one after the first part of the Seder ends and before the festive meal is eaten; one after grace following the meal; and one at the end of the Seder. These glasses of wine are said to match the four-fold promise of redemption given by God to the Jewish people.[10] Lastly, an empty wine glass or cup is set for Elijah, the prophet. It is not filled until the end of the meal.[11]

As is obvious from this description of the background and meanings attributed to the foods which are displayed and discussed during the Seder, a Seder is multilayered like all ritual events. On the surface, it appears to be a "text," with historical commentary, liturgical readings, symbolic foods, and obligatory roles to be played by the *dramatis personae* of a family. However, scholars' assumptions about reducing events to "texts" or conceptions about common meanings for groups of individuals engaged in events have to be challenged when one examines the significance of the Seder and its foods as symbolic for the Jewish people at large and then narrows that examination to one extended family and the individuals which make up that family.

For example, in eight interviews in which I asked a question about the personal or religious importance of the ritual foods as signifiers, only two people mentioned specific foods. Doris initially said, "No," when I asked if there were symbols that were most important to her. After a brief pause, she continued:

> I guess when you think of the moror, the bitterness and everything, you realize how lucky we are here to be living in Canada, to be in a free country. . . . We can imagine what it is to be a slave but it must have been terrible for them, and to have survived all these things and now we live in Canada, we should really appreciate it 'cause we have a marvelous life here. We really do.

Stan singled out matzo because it identified him as a Jew:

> I think matzo is the most important because that's the most obvious. That's the one that not only we as Jews see but non-Jews are very much aware of it, and they're aware that there's a holiday going on. Because I remember, even at school, during the Passover period, that instead of having sandwiches, we would have hardboiled eggs and pieces of matzo with butter in them, and that was, again, very symbolic as something different was happening. So all of my non-Jewish friends would be aware that I was celebrating or partaking of something that was different from what they were used to. And they, of course, wanted to taste it, and that sort of made me special at that time.

I was surprised that Stan, as the leader of the Seder, did not remark about the other ritual foods. I asked, "Is there anything about the bitter herbs . . . ?" He quickly replied:

> Those things are intellectually symbolic, I think, rather than emotionally symbolic. The matzo's very emotional. The bitter herbs and the egg and the neck of the chicken, these are all very intellectual kinds of things and I guess have been created by the rabbis through the ages and . . . they're interesting symbols, but you don't *feel* them as much as you do the matzo.

Joel's comment about the foods in general point out their functional aspects:

> Well, the whole idea of the symbolism of the various objects, the fact that, you know, there's physical things there to point at, to keep . . . to draw people's attention to . . . to keep people interested. I mean, it's not particularly a very long thing, but you know it is before supper, during and after, and you know it's at night, people can get very bored, but I think it's good because you have the various things to look at and to describe and it keeps everybody involved.

Other participants shifted the topic to concerns about the Seder as a whole. Tillie, for example, remarked that some people "eat a fancy dinner," but do not think about the underlying idea—freedom. Trudy noted that the symbols stand for "what the Jews had gone through" and "everything that is going on today."

Common themes run through these comments, but particular references do not recur. Circumscribed meanings give way to individualized and personalized "texts." Because each Seder builds on past events, overall messages and individual memories create a different "text" for each participant. Food is perhaps more important for the memories it triggers than for its ritual qualities. Although the Seder represents a major past event for all Jews, Stan's recollections emphasize how much the Seder foods bring the individual's past into the present.

> I think Passover is probably the most symbolic of all the holidays . . . we celebrate as Jews. It's the one that . . . I remember as being the happiest when I was a child. We would have . . . Seders at my Grandparents' home or my Grandmother's home and . . . as a child I remember running around and . . . taking . . . bits and pieces of the special foods and it was a holiday that had the smell of cooking, it was a holiday that . . . had a lot of people around, and it wasn't focused on the synagogue, it was focused on the home more than anything else. And I think that was nice, and I remember meeting my cousins, and meeting my uncles and my aunts, and . . . having all sorts of good times. So to me it's one that . . . is filled with a lot of very pleasant early childhood memories, and those memories go back to, you know, when I was four or five years old. I remember crawling underneath the table as the Seder was being conducted and that . . . has nice memories for me. I remember playing with my cousins, and I remember the taste of various foods. I remember the taste of matzo, and I remember the taste of the charoses and as a kid we were allowed to have wine, and that was fun. Very nice and warm and very symbolic kind of holiday.

Like the foods, family relationships mark changes and make every Seder a different "text." But, under the surface, the changes are not merely a signal for the ever-shifting dynamic of folklore ritual. One's knowledge of how to effect changes within unstated family rules can function to define roles within the family. For blood relatives, incorporation in the family is automatic. Growing up within its confines and rituals, family members learn to fit in. Those who marry into the family must actively seek entry. Their success or failure may be determined by how well they understand and help shape family folklore.

Michael, who is Suzanne's husband, is younger than she by two months, but is not asked to assist in the four questions. His lack of participation is revealed in a traditional family interchange: Stan tells Mikey, "You can say it with Suzanne because she's young too." Suzanne replies (as she does every year), "I'm older than Michael" (referring to her husband). Brenda responds (also every year), "You say that all the time." Suzanne is a blood relative of the inner family circle. Michael has married in. He was often criticized because he attended only the first Seder night until his daughter was born. "For me, one night is enough, and I don't consider myself to be a hypocrite, and to me it was hypocritical to come two nights and spend that much time with something I'm not really that fond of and don't believe in that much." Yet Michael also said that Passover was his "favorite holiday because of the Seder—not for the Seder itself, but because the entire family gets together. . . ." Michael's aloofness from this family's Seder is due to his positive experiences with his own family. He has ambivalent feelings about his role in this Seder since his responsibilities are not clearly delineated, as they were in his "blood" family.

Amy, the child of a Jewish father and a non-Jewish mother, does not want to ask the questions although she has attended the Seders since she was a baby and is three years older than Mikey. Amy's reluctance may be due to her own sense of not fully belonging. Although family members encourage her and attempt to make her comfortable with the Seder ritual, they also are concerned about her lack of Jewish identity.

Alan, about to marry a cousin in the family, broke the "rules" by arriving in the midst of the 1984 Seder. He explained that he had to participate in his own family's Seder. Despite his somewhat intrusive behavior, he added to the Seder by bringing in a special prayer. In many families it is now customary to say an extra prayer for oppressed Jews. Often the prayer is for Soviet Jewry, although prayers for the Ethiopian Jews are recent additions. Seder leaders will pencil in a note in their Haggadahs to insert the prayer at a certain point. Stan commented that his father did not recite such a prayer, but he does: "That's my personal choice. It's not something that has been said 'do this.'" Alan instinctively knew that he could add a prayer to the Seder and brought one commemorating the forty-year anniversary of the Warsaw Ghetto uprising. Not yet particularly close to Alan at this point in their relationship, family members treated him with new respect for his attempt to fit into their ritual.

Stan considers himself part of this intensely matriarchal family. Again, past experiences are significant in shaping such behavior. "I guess from about age eighteen to twenty-five, I had a very poor relationship with my own personal family ... and when Brenda and I got married, the Hertz and Gershenowitz family seemed to adopt me, and ... they became very much my first family." One way Stan was able to effect this shift was by taking over the host and Seder leader role, and blending many of his own family's traditions with his new one in an acceptable way. When the generation preceding his was ready to give over the role of leading the Seders, Stan was ready and willing to take on the task. Amy and Mikey, even at their young ages, demonstrate the importance of one's acceptance of generational roles. Their budding knowledge of family lore and levels of participation make one child a guest and one child a central figure in the family.

However, the idyllic picture of a cohesive family, all sharing the same folklore, is modified if not shattered when we consider individual differences. Not only does one's generational and host/guest role color one's perception of and role in the event, but one's sense of responsibility for continuity of the tradition, one's level of participation, and one's personal experiences with Judaism and previous Seders are all motivations which decide the particulars of traditional involvement. Even the mix of family members on a given night can significantly influence the event. As well as focusing on the similarities in the content, as folklorists usually do, we must look at differences in the behaviors and performances of individuals as well as other, perhaps larger, social changes in the form of the event. In this particular setting, foodways (i.e., participation in the preparation and consumption of Seder meals) can be as important as the underlying ritual itself in the determination of *communitas*. Moreover, in this family, folkloric behavior actually defines who is in control, who the "guests" really are, and, ultimately, who is and isn't "family."

Notes

This article is an expanded version of a paper presented at the annual meeting of the American Folklore Society in San Diego, October 1984.

1. Steven J. Zeitlin, Amy J. Kotkin, and Holly Cutting Baker, *A Celebration of American Family Folklore* (New York: Pantheon Books, 1982): 2.

2. The results of that fieldwork project appear on videotape as *Passover: A Celebration* (B & W, 28 min.), 1983, distributed by the Folklore and Ethnic Studies Program, University of Oregon, Eugene, Oregon. For details of the fieldwork and videotaping processes and the problems inherent in studying one's own family, see Sharon R. Sherman, "'That's How the Seder Looks': A Fieldwork Account of Videotaping Family Folklore," *Journal of Folklore Research* 23 (1986): 53–70.

3. The Passover Seder commemorates the deliverance of the Jewish people from bondage in the land of Egypt, their exodus into the desert, and the journey to the Promised Land—an event which occurred over three thousand years ago. Each year, Passover is celebrated by Jews with varying levels of religious observance and, more than any other holiday, is enjoyed by both religious and secular Jews.

4. Beatrice S. Weinreich, "The Americanization of Passover," in *Studies in Biblical and Jewish Folklore,* ed. Ralphael Patai, Francis Lee Utley, and Dov Noy (Bloomington: Indiana University Press, Indiana University Folklore Series No. 13:1960): 342.

5. See Hayyim Schauss, *The Jewish Festivals: History and Observance* (New York: Schocken Books, 1962 [originally published in 1938]): 38–85, for a detailed description of Passover's origins as well as different observances in various places through time.

6. The Torah specifies a seven-day observance (Exodus 12:15; 13:6). An exiled people, the Jews added an extra day to ensure correct observance for many holidays since people were notified by bonfires lit on mountains and the possibility for error was great. Because a reliable calendar exists, Reform Jews and all Jews in Israel celebrate for seven days. Conservative and Orthodox families, having followed an eight-day holiday for centuries, continue the ancient practice. Thus, they have two Seder nights, whereas Reform Jews and those in Israel have one.

7. Ruth Gruber Fredman, *The Passover Seder: Afikoman in Exile* (Phildadelphia: University of Pennsylvania Press, 1981): 34. In analyzing the metaphoric and symbolic characteristics of the Seder, Fredman also presents the Seder plate as one that summarizes oppositions to achieve balance or ordering.

8. One would assume that, at the least, continuity would be exhibited by the Haggadah, since it is written text. All participants at a Seder read from individual Haggadahs placed before them. Haggadah means "telling" and the booklet contains directions for how to organize the Seder plate, and is a blend of legends, prayers, commentary, questions, and songs set in an order for following the ritual. Parts are from the Mishnah and parts from the Talmud. Although Haggadahs vary in translation and tone, the order is constant. Thus, even if as many as five different versions are used at one table, readers will be able to recognize the similarity between the portion of the text being read aloud by another participant and the portion in their own Haggadahs. As the evening progresses through four glasses of wine, variations in the texts may lead to questions and laughter about the differences. Scholars assume the Haggadah and the Seder were instituted after the destruction of the Second Temple, with the Haggadah added to the prayer book, but much of it was recited as early as the days of the Second Temple. In the thirteenth century the Haggadah appeared as a separate volume and new editions continue to appear every year, reflecting changing times and interpretations.

9. Greens were commonly dipped once in a tart sauce at regular meals and after washing one's hands at banquets (which, like Passover, also began with wine).

10. "I will bring you out; I will deliver you; I will redeem you; I will take you to me for a people." The number "four" is a constant throughout the Seder: four glasses of wine, four questions, four sons, four matriarchs of Israel, four promises, and four Pesach symbols.

11. Several explanations have been offered for the existence of the cup of Elijah or "fifth" cup. Elijah is said to have gone, living, to Heaven in a chariot of fire. Many tales are told about his magical feats while on earth. Popular belief is that Elijah will return and

announce the coming of the Messiah and lead the Jewish people to a new deliverance as Moses did in ancient days. At a point late in the Seder the door is opened for Elijah to enter. Opening the door was once done at the beginning of the Seder so any traveling or hungry Jew could join the ritual, but as Jews began living in areas with non-Jews (often hostile ones), opening the door was shifted to the conclusion of the Seder. Another explanation is that a fifth cup of wine was disputed by the Talmudists. "Let Elijah decide" was the solution offered and the fifth glass became his. In the family studied, any extra chair or place set by accident is always referred to as Elijah's in-jokes throughout the year.

3

A Halloween Brunch:
The Affirmation of Group
in a Temporary Community

Nancy Klavans

At least three observations about contemporary social life appear to hold
true for significant numbers of people in our society: Community life may
consist of a series of temporary encounters with other individuals likewise
part of our mobile society. Extended families, once the norm, are being
replaced by single-parent families, often located far from their home communities and traditional families. But families with small children generally
experience at least one common bond at some period in their existence,
the phenomenon of school-centered communities. In them, young families
especially find in fleeting moments of festive interaction, especially in food-
centered festive events, a way of creating, if but for a little while, community of common purpose and vision; understanding how such events are
shaped and how their menus and food-related behaviors symbolize and
communicate powerful images of family and community sheds light not
only on an interesting and widespread set of phenomena but also on an
important and deeply rooted impulse in human nature. While folklore
scholarship has tended to focus on more or less permanent, often isolated,
communities, stable groups in which activities and celebrations recur in
recognizable patterns over relatively long periods of time, temporary communities such as the Parents' Association of the Bala House Montessori
pre-school, in which I have participated for the last three years, also merit
examination. Although ephemeral in the sense of changing membership,
they endure in the sense of overall organization. In such communities food
often plays a central role in creating a sense of connection with the past
memory of the group. Tastes, smells, sights, and even tactile sensations
provide a direct link through which people can reaffirm a sense of *communitas*. Food-related events provide the prime vehicle through which a sense

of tradition, continuity, and community are performed and transmitted to new members.

Although a more permanent organization (than that of the parents and students) of teachers and staff exists at the school in Bala Cynwyd, Pennsylvania, the Parents' Association exists to support the educational environment, creating a sense of belonging and community beyond the day-to-day school experience through a variety of traditional, food-centered festive events: a Parents' Potluck, a Halloween Brunch, a Valentine Potluck, a Spring Concert, and a Family Picnic. While the brunch appears to be an enactment of traditional community involvement, the context of this food event is a community, the memership of which is constantly changing although its belief systems (as evidenced by this Halloween Brunch) remain fairly constant. The Bala House Parents' Association is part of an academic community, the belief systems of which center on the education of preschool children by a particular method with particular values attached. Examining the Halloween Brunch and the changes it has undergone over the last six years reveals how a strongly symbolic, if largely unself-conscious, menu evolved, one that presents an idealized vision of family values and community integrity. Furthermore, the persistent desire for a high degree of member participation in the brunch demonstrates a traditional means of community formation and bonding.

It's ten o'clock on a crisp Saturday morning, the last day in October. Nancy B. unlocks the parish hall door of St. Asaph's Church and begins to unload the mixing bowls, skillets, and other cooking utensils from her car trunk. Three other members of her committee—Dick K., Richard C., and I—soon join her. Our cars contain cooking utensils, dozens of eggs, flour, milk, paper goods and decorations. We transport the boxes of supplies into the parish hall and await further instructions from Nancy B., looking to her for guidance since none of us has ever worked on the Parents' Association's Halloween Brunch before. We view her as an old hand because she assisted last year's chairperson.

Nancy B. directs the team to the church kitchen where we set up the work area—the stainless steel bowls on the work table, ready to receive dozens of eggs for scrambling, four skillets on the stove with spatulas and whisks on a nearby counter, and two cutting boards on the kitchen table ready to slice the dozens of breakfast loaves.

The set-up crew arrives at 10:30. Andy, Carolyn, and Ann stand around awkwardly, unsure what they are supposed to do. Nancy B. directs them to set up the chairs and tables first and then to decorate the parish hall. After some discussion with her about the actual placement of the furniture, the power of tradition asserts itself, and they settle on the configuration used at the previous year's event, setting the twelve long tables, a hundred chairs, and four long benches in four long, narrow rows. Carolyn, with the help of Ann, puts up the decorations, transforming the parish hall from a sterile brown and white room into a golden-hued, autumnal country scene where ghosts and skeletons might lurk at every corner. They drape paper streamers across the doorways and over the rafters of the high vaulted ceiling, tape cardboard pumpkins, scarecrows, cats, and witches to the walls, and cover ten of the long tables (those to be used for eating) with orange table cloths. The remaining two, to be used for serving, are covered with a special cloth decorated with Halloween motifs. A small table near the entry also receives a special cloth and the stacks of paper plates, cups, and napkins, each imprinted with a pumpkin and witch pattern. The traditional icons of Halloween are all in place.

At 11:00 the kitchen crew springs into frenzied action. Nancy B. whisks together dozens of eggs, milk, nutmeg, salt, and pepper. Richard mixes up a gallon of pancake batter and begins making the flapjacks. I fill the 75-cup coffee maker and start it perking. Then I begin to scramble the eggs, putting the finished batches in warming trays to await the hungry throngs.

At 11:30 the first guests appear in the entryway to the parish hall—two small girls, one dressed as a pumpkin, the other as a ballerina, each carrying a loaf of hot homemade pumpkin bread. Their mother and father follow with two jugs of cider, but they wear casual party clothes rather than costumes to this event. Other guests follow in rapid succession. The children wear a variety of costumes ranging from commercial ones representing Shiray, Princess of Power, and He-Man, to homemade ones representing cats, rabbits, pirates, and witches. The parents, in general, are not in costume, with the exception of a couple of self-expressive clowns and a witch. However, they are all carrying their contributions to the brunch. Some bring the hot, homemade breads, others the fruit salad and juices requested by the food committee. Others have decided to ignore the request and bring a special dish of their own choosing—quiche, kugel, and Haitian chicken pie, for instance. The set-up crew transfers all donations to the kitchen, slices the breads, and arranges them on serving trays with the homemade muffins. They combine the smaller containers of fruit salad in a large stainless steel bowl and place it on the buffet table. They store most of the milk and cider in the kitchen so it will not be consumed too fast. Meanwhile, Nancy B. and I madly scramble eggs to create a stockpile. Richard C. and Dick K. are turning out dozens of pancakes with the same intent. The smells of an old-fashioned country breakfast begin to permeate the kitchen and waft out into the parish hall as we complete the preparations for the Sixth Annual Halloween Brunch of the Bala House Montessori Pre-School Parents' Association.

The preparations nearly complete, a steady stream of guests now arrives. At first they mill around, unsure what they are supposed to do. But then fathers congregate, discussing the latest sports scores and the state of the economy. Mothers chat about after-school programs and how to pick a children's dentist. The children admire each other's costumes and play tag among the tables. A semicontrolled chaos seems to reign. Finally, at a cue from Nancy B., a single family breaks away from the group and moves toward the buffet table. Others, seeing this, gather their children and begin to fall into line. It is as if some inaudible dinner bell has rung signaling that it is time to eat.

The set-up crew directs traffic around the buffet table. They make sure that each person begins by collecting plates, utensils, and napkins, and then proceeds down the food table in an orderly fashion. In addition, they oversee the amounts and kinds of foods chosen. When an overexuberant six-year-old puts three muffins on his plate, Ann G. suggests that he come back for seconds after everyone else has had their firsts. As the trays of scrambled eggs and breads dwindle, the crew runs them back to the kitchen for refills.

Meanwhile, Richard C. and Dick K. are frantically flipping pancakes to keep up with the demand. The children stand expectantly in front of the griddle, almost drooling at the sight of the hotcakes browning before their eyes. As the cakes are pitched onto the serving platter, they eagerly snatch them up, hardly pausing to pour on the syrup. Richard comments that they could have used an extra "flapjack cook." "Why, when I was in the army, we turned these babies out by the thousand," he says.

As families come to the end of the buffet line, the parents pause looking around for vacant spaces at the tables, so they can all sit together. As their children want to sit next to classmates, compromises often must be worked out on the spot. Soon all are comfortably arranged around the tables. They pause from time to time to chat about the quality of the food or to replenish their plates. The general consensus is that this meal is the "best ever," that everything is "great as usual."

By 12:45, the feast is over. Although a few latecomers are still getting seconds, everyone else is stuffed to the gills. Children are becoming restless, returning to their pre-meal games of tag. One of the parents suggests that all the youngsters should be taken outside before the entertainment program begins. Two parents organize a procession, leading the children outside to the grassy meadow. There, they form a giant circle, marching around and around while proud parents madly snap photos.

Inside, the set-up crew, aided by some of the adults who choose to stay inside, quickly clean up the debris and take down tables and chairs to make space for the entertainment. Some years the Parents' Association has hired a magician or clown. This year it has arranged for a nature show put on by the local Academy of Natural Sciences. The woman from the Academy begins setting up her display of wild animals. She has brought a snake, a ferret, and an owl to teach the children about the differences between scales, fur, and feathers.

At one o'clock the children are marshalled back into the parish hall and instructed to sit quietly on the floor. The woman from the Academy presents her animals one by one, while her young audience sits in rapt attention. The adults stand in the background, chatting together in lowered voices and generally making sure that order is maintained. Meanwhile, Nancy B. and her committee are cleaning up the mess in the kitchen. They neatly package leftover food in Ziploc bags, ready to be sold at the end of the brunch. They divide up the eggs, flour, and other raw ingredients amongst themselves. Finally, they scrub and dry the utensils, setting them in neat rows to await their owners.

The cooks at last allow themselves to sit down. As the intense pressure of the morning drains away, they relax. Nancy B. asks her crew how they feel the event went and a lively discussion ensues. As always, the food donations were a little out of balance, too many eggs and not enough baked goods and juices. I suggest making a written record of the whole event before all is forgotten including data on quantities of food used, as well as organizational issues such as ways to deal with "greedy brunchers." Although everyone agrees that this is a great idea, no one actually volunteers to do it.

By 2:00 p.m. the event is over. The woman from the Academy packs up her animals. The children reluctantly say goodbye to their friends and are led away by their parents. Several guests pitch in to help the set-up crew vacuum up the parish hall, straighten up the furniture, and put away the decorations for another year. Finally Nancy B. and her kitchen crew pack up their belongings, run a last sponge around the kitchen, and lock the parish hall door behind themselves. The Halloween Brunch is over for another year; peace and solitude return to St. Asaph's Church.

The event has changed in a number of ways over six years, and those changes suggest the role that food plays in maintaining a sense of continuity and tradition in this community. The Bala House Parents' Association organized the Halloween Brunch in 1981; it grew out of a recognition that the Bala House families lacked a sense of connection with the school.[1] In the Spring of 1982 the Association planned a Magic Brunch; parents were asked to donate food and to help staff the event. The food committee decided on a "typical country farm breakfast" of scrambled eggs, french toast, bacon, sausage, creamed chipped beef, and home-baked breads. According to Pat L., their thought was that this type of traditional American fare would appeal to a broad spectrum of people. (No one was much concerned about attempting to identify just what a "typical country farm breakfast" might indeed be or have been.) As an added attraction, the committee hired a local magician to entertain the children.

The brunch was such a hit that the organizers decided to follow up with another similar event. Recognizing that the spring was too late in the year to drum up enthusiasm for the school, they decided to plan a fall event. As Pat tells it, the first holiday in the school year to provide a theme worth celebrating was Halloween. So the committee created the concept of the Halloween Brunch by combining the best elements of the Magic Brunch and traditional Halloween celebrations. Interestingly, new Bala House parents often erroneously assume that the event grew out of a fear of trick or treat tampering and a consequent need to develop alternative celebrations.

The first Halloween Brunch maintained many of the elements of its spring predecessor. The menu remained much the same, except for the addition of "Dutch Babies" (a popover-like pastry) and the removal of the chipped beef, deemed too "breakfasty" by the food committee. Pat, the chairperson for that year, decided to move the starting time from 9:00 to 11:30. She felt that the later time would be easier on family schedules and also more respectful of the Jewish Sabbath.

None of the food items, it will be noted, reflected a traditional Halloween theme; the committee depended on the decorations to provide the appropriate ambiance. Real pumpkins and harvest corn were scattered amongst cardboard representations of scarecrows, witches, and black cats. The committee encouraged the children to wear costumes, also an attempt to enhance the focus on the holiday. However, none of the traditional Halloween games, such as bobbing for apples, were played. Instead, Pat hired outside entertainment, as had been done for the Magic Brunch. But it is clear that the focus of the event was on cooking and eating together, with entertainment secondary.

This first Halloween Brunch became the model for the Halloween Brunches which have followed. Each year the core menu has remained basically the same. A dish may be added or removed if that year's participants so desire, yet the central image of a "typical" home-cooked country breakfast is maintained. Each year, the time of day remained constant. When the committee discussed changing the starting time, they reached the same conclusions as their predecessors, that 11:30 a.m. to 2:00 p.m. is best for all involved. Each year the cardboard scarecrows, witches, and pumpkins are pulled out of their plastic garbage bags. Some have been repaired several times, and the committee replaces those that are not salvageable with equally friendly new characters. Each year, the committee consistently has chosen a "passive" activity, such as a magician, clown, or lecturer, which requires a quiet, seated audience for the event. The norm seems to have been to focus on cooking and eating and to avoid postprandial activities that might require a high degree of effort by the adults.

Thus, over the past six years, the Parents' Association has developed a model for a food event. The central focus of the Halloween Brunch is the cooking and eating of a special meal. The menu is a symbolic representation, a projection, of a nostalgic Norman Rockwell-type of home-cooked country farm breakfast with only a small portion of the foods served being traditional items in the actual daily diet of the participants. It may seem surprising that the Parents' Association has chosen to incorporate the cooking and eating of these particular symbolic foods into an annual Brunch menu since these items are not part of the cultural baggage of the participants. Approximately 40% of the families are Jewish. Another 20% are racially or religiously intermarried. Eighteen percent are Protestant; 10% are Black; 5% are Catholic, and 5% are Asian. A final 2% falls into such other religions as Sufi and Muslim. A more heterogeneous group would be hard to find.

A glance at typical breakfast/brunch menus of each of these groups clearly demonstrates their diversity. An Ashkenazic Jew might favor bagels, cream cheese, and lox for breakfast. A Protestant with Scotch/Irish background could prefer hot cereal with milk. On the other hand, a Black whose parents came from the South is probably more accustomed to fried eggs and grits. An Italian Catholic might eat a simple roll with preserves. By comparison, a Korean's breakfast could resemble a dinner with rice, kimchi, fish, and vegetables. None of these traditional menus blends with each other or with the country breakfast developed by the food committee.

Yet the Halloween Brunch food committee did not respond to the diversity of the school population by asking each family to contribute a dish which reflected its ethnic or religious background. Instead, the committee has attempted to establish a standardized menu type, one which evokes images of a stereotypical "American" home-cooked country breakfast with the family cooking and eating together. The menu is symbolic of an idealized vision of family. Over the years, the stable items of this brunchy/breakfast menu have been scrambled eggs, hot homemade breads, pancakes, and bacon and sausage, foods that for the most part must be prepared on the spot, emphasizing the togetherness of the group. To further enhance the sense of a family's working and feasting together, the committee has encouraged people to join in the cooking of the meal at the Parish Hall.

Each year, however, several Bala House families do bring to the Halloween Brunch foods which are part of their traditional repertoire, asserting alternative visions of family. A woman born in Haiti has cooked a special chicken pie for the last three years. It is filled with chunks of chicken, sweet potato and onions and flavored with cinnamon, ginger, and brown sugar.

Although the committee has never asked her to bring her pie, it appears at the Brunch each year and is always very popular with guests. A Jewish mother has donated bagels, loxspread, and cream cheese for several years. Again, her gift, although not requested, is always appreciated by everyone and leftovers are rare. Similarly, members of the food committee have added such items as the "Dutch Babies" and apple pizzas and deleted others such as french toast. These changes reflect their own food preferences and their need to put a personal imprint on the Brunch. However, Bala House parents have always taken active steps to maintain the country breakfast theme and the group involvement in cooking, suggesting unity and cohesiveness within what is otherwise a diverse group brought together only by the educational purpose of this ephemeral community.

For that reason, the underlying theme of the Brunch has persisted, despite efforts by chairpersons to make changes. For example, the chairperson for the most recent Brunch was a new parent. Prior to this year, the brunch committee had had at least one member who had participated in the organization of the previous year's event. This year's chairperson had only been told about the event by people who had attended it. She was unaware of the food traditions which had evolved in connection with this event. Not having shared the experience before, she was unaware of the underlying (if unarticulated) assumptions for the Brunch and the idealized vision of family its traditional menu projects. The menu she developed consisted of cold mini sandwiches, waffles, bagels and cream cheese, and fruit salad. The previous year's chairperson tried to convince her to add scrambled eggs, arguing that they had always been a hit and that people had enjoyed the group involvement in cooking them. At first, the new chairperson resisted. Finally, she acquiesced to the pressures from old parents by adding a hot precooked egg dish to the menu. However, she had not responded to the additional expressed need for a group cooking experience. Two days before the event was to take place, Richard C. called the chairperson and told her that he was planning to cook pancakes at the Brunch as he had the previous year. Somewhat taken aback, she nevertheless complied with his plan. The pancakes were the most popular food item at that year's Brunch. Several parents commented that they had enjoyed helping to make the flapjacks almost as much as eating them. Clearly the homemade country breakfast theme with its emphasis on cooking and eating together is central to the Halloween Brunch experience of the Bala House Montessori Pre-School even though this theme does not seem to blend with the cultural experiences of Bala House families. In choosing those particular foods for their first Brunch, the original committee was motivated, according to Pat L.'s statement, by the desire to appeal to the broadest possible range of people. But why would such a menu have that appeal? I think it is clear that the combination of food items drawn from an inventory felt to be traditional and representative of "American" and "old-fashioned" values coupled with the experience of shared cooking articulates very clearly the theme underlying the school experience itself. The family is seen as a positive value, parents and children participating together in discovering the world. In doing so, they hit upon a symbolic menu that establishes and maintains a sense of *communitas* among Bala House families because of its emphasis on a vision of family values.

Sharing a common vision of what education should be has created the shell of the community in the first place, but it is coming together to cook and eat a meal that has joined these diverse individuals into an affective if temporary community in the larger sense of the word. Over time, a tradition has grown out of compromises as the various members of the community groped toward an effective way of symbolizing and performing their idea of the community. Conscious choices made about the time of day for the event, the nature of the menu, the type of food preparation, and the specific food served have brought the event by fits and starts to the status of being an effective performance of community despite the lack of continuity in membership. Three themes have persisted. The first is personal involvement. Families contribute their time to bake at home or cook at the event. They break bread and share food as a way of establishing and maintaining their sense of community. Changes in the menu reflect the desire to enhance the food experience for everyone. The second theme is nurturance. Over time, the families have developed a group norm concerning the value of wholesome, nutritious (and symbolic) food. The final theme concerns the low value which the community seems to place on Halloween as a traditional venue for itself. The decorations and costumes were the only vestiges of the traditional holiday. None of the foods traditional to Halloween were served, nor were Halloween games played.

This brief examination of a changing event in a temporary community provides us with some interesting insights into the ways communities and their traditions are created and maintained if not always fully understood or articulated by the membership. Food is a key component in the transmission of traditions to new Association members. By partaking in the feast, each person is enculturated into the group norms of personal involvement, nurturance, and low calendaric holiday value. By partaking in the Halloween Brunch, a sense of group identity is established, maintained, and remembered over the years even though the participating membership is constantly in flux.

Notes

1.   Pat L., personal interview.

4

"Soup Night":
Community Creation through Foodways

Lin T. Humphrey

Soup Night, a contemporary small group festive gathering, began in my kitchen in Claremont, California in 1974.[1] It grew out of my perceived need to spend time with friends in a less formal, less time-consuming format than the formal, sit-down, reciprocal dinner party. Although this had been the main avenue for social exchange among most of our friends, many of the women, including myself, had returned to jobs and interrupted careers, and we did not want to spend our weekends preparing fancy dinners and keeping track of reciprocity. After a successful New Year's Day Hoppin' John celebration in which we managed to feed close to a hundred people from one large pot of black-eyed peas and rice, I initiated Soup Night, or Soup, as it is frequently called. As "chief kitchen person"[2] I invited the people, arranged the table, made the soup, and actively participated in the consuming of the food and the conversation that accompanied it. Out of this has grown a sense of community and group identity based on the sharing and consuming of food once a week. The balance and tension between individual and shared power, the limits of hospitality and reciprocity, the flexibility and portability of the event, and the need for *communitas* and commensality in a modern, urbanized society maintain this food-centered event and create a viable, recognizable community of participants for whom Soup expresses values and social identity.

The people who compose the community are not the same ones who started it; only a few of the original "soupers" are still active in the group. There are, however, several constants. The main foodstuff is soup; participants bring bread or wine or both; we provide bowls, wine glasses, spoons, knives, butter, napkins, bottle openers and corkscrews (although in truth, many of the bowls, glasses, spoons, and openers are gifts from various members of the group). My husband always serves the first bowl of soup to guests (except for the year he spent in Oklahoma when I took over the task). And there is a toast that is always made before everyone settles down to eating and talking. Since this event takes place in my home, since the participants are, for the most part, good, and in some cases, intimate friends, and since I initiated and maintain it, the idea of objectivity in my analysis of it is absurd. Yet these very problems, conflicts, and biases provide a basis for an intense esoteric view of this community.

The Soup Group has few of the traditional ties that bind groups together such as kinship, economic dependency, work or neighborhood affiliations. Generally speaking, the members are liberal in both religion and politics, concerned about the environment, and about individual health and fitness. More than half of those who usually frequent Soup were born and educated outside the state of California. Many, but not all, are teachers at all levels from kindergarten to university. Others are artists, designers, lawyers, chiropractors, office managers, occasional students, and sheriffs. Many do not live in Claremont but come from 20 or 30 miles away. There are regulars who have been coming every Thursday night for thirteen years; others come by once a month or so. "Going to Soup" becomes a password which designates those who belong to the community. The group maintains itself even during the summer through a series of salad potlucks that rotate from house to house depending on individual schedule and whim. This flexible community is balanced on a subtle hierarchy maintained by the tension between hospitality and power and a mutually understood but largely unspoken value system and code of behavior, both of which can be and have been broken. Within the experience and within the food consumed can be seen the structure, function, values and world view of the community known as "The Soup Group."

Having established that there is indeed a group of people who not only view themselves as a community bonded together by sharing food, but name themselves after the food that they share, let us look at the food involved in a typical Soup Night. In "Deciphering a Meal," Mary Douglas defines a meal as "a mixture of solid food accompanied by liquids."[3] A quick glance through any number of cookbooks confirms that soup, indeed, consists of blending "soup liquids with your favorite meats, beans, vegetables, and fruits."[4] Douglas (1972) goes on to say that "Meals properly require the use of at least one mouth-entering utensil per head." We eat our soup with large soup or table spoons, one per person. Soup is physical food; the eating of soup together constitutes a physical meal; and the process satisfies the physical need for sustenance. According to Charles Camp's typography in his dissertation, "America Eats: Toward a Social Definition of American Foodways," Soup fits into his Type Three category: "The foods prepared for these events are not the sort prepared for the everyday world, and the foods themselves serve as the reason for special gatherings."[5] He goes on to say that structurally such a semi-public food event in which a single individual is responsible for the event but in which this person also participates can be delineated as "A = A + B + ."[6] Even Mary Douglas gives credence to the one-dish meal if it preserves the minimum structure of a meal—"vegetable soup with noodles and grated cheese" (1972). Peter Farb and George Armelagos (1980) also assert that soup is a meal which fits the pattern A + 2b (central ingredient together with two [and usually many more] un-stressed ingredients). But Soup is primarily a meal because the participants define it as such. Furthermore, the food is so important that it names the event, Soup Night, and the people who attend refer to themselves as "The Soup Group" or as "Soupers."

Soup, however, is a very common, economical, ordinary food which, in most cultures, can be dressed up or down. Why is the soup served on Soup Night to the Soup Group special? Charles Camp argues that food is used along with other signs and symbols to execute implicit and explicit social strategies; thus the same food served at different occasions will have different intentions and different meaning and values (Camp n.d., 6). On a more practical level, soup serves well as the main foodstuff for an indeter-minant number of people. It can be, and usually is, inexpensive; the ingredi-ents seldom cost more than ten or twelve dollars. A twenty-quart pot will hold enough to feed as many as 35 or 40 people, and when the crowd is smaller (the average attendance is about 20), there is plenty for seconds or even thirds or to give to departing guests to take home afterward. Soup is also relatively easy to prepare, especially on a grand scale, for there is space and time to make and correct errors in seasoning, etc. On the other hand, this need for space and time may be seen as impractical in a rushed, fast-paced, urban society. For the Soup Group and for the cook, the very fact that making and consuming soup requires one to stop rushing around is both an implicit and explicit value. Thursday afternoons are sacred times for me, time set aside for making soup. I refuse committee appointments or meetings that conflict with that time. The afternoon is devoted to chop-ping, slicing, simmering, and thinking about soup. To paraphrase Claude Levi-Strauss, "Soup is good to think."

When one thinks about the physical aspect of soup, it becomes a metaphor for the event of Soup Night itself. Roger Abrahams suggests that "the currencies of exchange of primary importance in culture are ... food, sex, talk," which include values, meaning, an ettiquette, a decorum system, symbolic objects, and actions that "carry the most profound, if everyday, cultural messages."[7] Soup is a mixture of many and various ingredients: vegetables, meats, liquids, cereals, and seasonings blend together to make something other than what each ingredient is by itself. It is a food of

Figure 4-1. Lin T. Humphrey Stirs the Soup for "Soup Night" in Her
Twenty-Quart Kettle
(Photo by Theodore C. Humphrey)

harmony and cooperation, almost always warm and aromatic. Furthermore, the increase in quantity, the large "mother" pot full of food for all-comers is the symbolic center of the event. Mary Douglas writes in the Introduction to *Food in the Social Order* that food can be given more meaning or the meaning can be changed not just by altering the quality of the food served but by changes in the quantity of food available; thus the greater the quantity of food, the greater the investment in cost, time, thought, and space (p. 15).

The community created by and around Soup Night is also flexible in size. The number of people who attend varies from as few as ten to as many as forty or more. Part of the fun, the freedom, and the tension is in not knowing who will be there. As far as can be determined, there are no exclusionary barriers to Soup. People come because they are friends with others who come; certainly one would not come if one hated everyone there. Ted and I have never told anyone not to come, and Ted in particular tends to invite everyone he meets. People who come and do not enjoy themselves usually do not return. Somehow in this process freedom and hospitality are compromised. Hospitality is not the sole responsibility of the host or hostess, but an action wherein many of the participants seize power. The door is always unlocked and the porch light is on; returning participants let themselves in. If someone knocks or rings the doorbell, whoever is handy lets him or her in. Over the years, this has occasionally led to strangers' being escorted in when actually they were looking for another address. Usually people greet each other with hugs, especially if someone has not been around for a while. People are invited formally once by either Ted or myself or by other guests; after that they are free to decide whether or not it is their "cup of soup." Friends usually feel free to bring along another friend, although sometimes they will call in the afternoon to let me know that some one new will be there. This may be a ritual of politeness or a way of noting the presence of someone unfamiliar to us and to the event itself.

Guests begin to arrive about 6:30 or shortly thereafter. Early birds often bring a bottle of "good" wine to share before everyone else comes. Most participants have a glass of wine before dinner and check on the kind of soup simmering on the stove. Wine glasses, open bottles of wine, and openers are handy on the main table. Bread is taken to the kitchen to be warmed. At seven, give or take a few minutes, when the house seems sufficiently crowded, Ted shouts, in his loudest voice, "Soup's On!," and most people pick up bowls stacked on the kitchen table and line up. (Although this may suggest soup lines during the Depression, most of the participants are too young to remember this except in books and films.) Participants crowd around the main table, which will seat a tight thirteen (no significance to the number, although we sometimes joke about it), sit on the floor and the furniture in the living room around a round coffee table, stand in the kitchen; or if it is warm enough, sit outside on the patio. Bread and butter (depending on what people bring) are available at both tables, and everyone is free to move around at will. Part of the feeling of free access is in the way the soup is served. After Ted serves himself and sits down, anyone who comes late or who wants more simply helps him/herself. Often a good-hearted "souper" will offer to get a bowl for another person, but in general each person is responsible for his or her own soup. Spoons, knives, glasses, and paper napkins are already on the main tables. In this curious, complex coming together of food and food-eaters, it is sometimes difficult to determine who is in charge. The lines of responsibility and power between host and guest are quite blurred. Strangers brought by other people may go half the evening before meeting both my husband and me. Certainly the open door, the nonspecified seating arrangement (with the exception of the seats reserved by custom—no place cards—for host and hostess), the access to food, utensils and beverages, and the free movement from room to room and table to table encourage, if not create, this division of power. A very important factor is the actual responsibility of the guests to provide important parts of the meal: i.e. the bread and the wine. Bread and wine, incidentally are not mandatory or inclusive; guests often bring dessert, cheese, crackers, or occasionally come empty-handed, promising to make up for it next time. The understanding and the acceptance of this shared power and responsibility is in part what holds this group together. Otherwise the limits of hospitality and reciprocity would be too overburdened for the event to continue.

Contributing to an event gives participants some power in shaping the event. In *Consuming Passions: The Anthropology of Eating,* Farb and Armelagos state, "The important metaphorical associations a society has are usually with the staples. In the Near East and Europe [and in America], the staple is bread," our so-called "staff of life."[8] The power and responsibility for bread rest almost entirely on the shoulders of the other participants. We eat whatever bread is brought to the house. When little or no bread turns up, some of the guests may make a quick "bread-run" to the store, but more often, we simply share what is there. Invariably, the next week we will have far more bread than can be consumed in one evening. I save most of what is left over, especially if the loaves have not been opened, in the freezer and bring it out the next week. Occasionally someone will bring actual "home-made" bread, but most often it comes from local bakeries or grocery stores. There is a definite hierarchy of values given to the loaves of bread; dark bread, those made from whole grains, large round, brown loaves, fancy cheese or braided bread inevitably are eaten first, with some grabbing and finally sharing of the last small portions. Most bread arrives at the table, warm from the microwave, but uncut. We simply pass it around and tear off hunks or ask someone to pass a certain kind. Loud verbal praise is given to those who brought especially good bread, and a common question resounding around the room is, "Who brought the big loaf of pumpernickel?" The preference for dark, whole-grained bread is probably the result of the emphasis on healthy foods that influences nearly everyone who comes to Soup; this appreciation for healthy food (i.e. no fat, no sugar, whole grains, fresh vegetables) is one of the values held by the group as a whole. Camp affirms the idea that there is more to bread than good food when he says there are "symbolic and religious elements in the breaking of bread among friends or fellow worshippers which has little to do with the recipe from which the dough was made or the kind of oven in which it was made" (Camp 1978).

An equally important substance for which guests are also responsible is wine or other beverages. As with the bread, it is often "feast or famine"—everyone brings wine or no one does. I also will set on the table any wine left over from the week before; unfortunately, what is left is what no one wanted to drink in the first place. Here again judgments are made about the quality of what people bring. Most wine-bringers bring an inexpensive bottle of California wine that they themselves like. Most people prefer white, but in warm weather they have trouble getting it chilled before coming to Soup because it is something they usually pick up on the way. Good reds are actually rarer and much appreciated. Some guests bring a large bottle every other week or so, depending on specials at the local stores. Participants set the bottles on the long dining room table where openers are handy. Sex role transitions and accommodations appear here. Some women hand bottles to men to open; others pride themselves on their mastery of the wine cork. Once on the table, the wine, like the bread, belongs to everyone, and some people rush around to insure getting a glass of the "good stuff" which they or someone else brought As a whole, we are not wine connoisseurs, but the tastes run generally to dry chablis, French Colombards, and hearty, dry reds, while quite a few of the women profess a fondness for white zinfandel or other so-called "blush wines." But not everyone drinks wine. A few bring beer which they stash in the refrigerator in the kitchen; some drink mineral water, apple cider, or diet soda. The point here is that the wine is important to the meal and it is almost completely in the hands of the participants, other than the host and hostess. Unopened bottles find their way into our wine rack from which they may emerge the next week. We tend to drink the opened bottles during the week, or use them for cooking. (Wine is almost always one of the ingredients in the soup.)

Bringing together bread and wine in a Western country inevitably raises the question of religious symbol and ritual. Indeed, what ritual we do maintain does involve the wine, but the degree to which it is overtly religious seems insignificant. Douglas notes that ritual performs several functions: it focuses attention by framing; it enlivens memory and links the present with the relevant past; it aids perception of an event; and it controls and modifies our experience of the outer world.[9] The main ritual at Soup is quite simple, a toast given at the beginning of the meal in a call-and-response mode by my husband and me. In order for this ritual to be effective, it is necessary that we be seated at opposite ends of the main table—these are the only two seats "set aside" during the event. When nearly everyone is seated and has managed to get a glass of something to drink, a spoon, a knife, and a piece of bread, but before too much soup has actually been eaten, Ted raises his glass and says, "To friends who are present," and I respond, "And those who are not." Glasses clink, we usually raise our glasses to "those at the lower table," and we drink. This is not the first drink of the evening, as most guests have consumed a glass of wine or two before dinner, but it is important. At that moment there is a unity of focus that does not occur at any other time during the evening. The toast began at the same time that Soup began. It came from our realization and recognition that friends come and go in many ways. About the time Soup started, a good friend of mine, a former dance teacher who was important to many of the women in the group, died. "Those who are not" includes those who will never be at Soup or anywhere else again, but it also signifies those who simply are not present for various reasons, those who used to come but come no more, those who have moved away, perhaps those yet to come. It is all inclusive within the limits of friendship. Thus, Soup is a celebration of friendship, of community which transcends the here and now. Farb and Armelagos suggest that ritual provides comfort, security, and the reassurance that there will be no surprises (1980, 217). For those who come to Soup it is a moment of contact, recognition, and appreciation. I am not suggesting that all those who share the toast understand its meaning. We don't talk about it; we just do it. After the toast is the time for announcements, subsequent toasts, invitations, and applause. Toasts are made by anyone present to anyone else who has won an award, celebrated a birthday, written a paper, published a book, bought a house. Participants also use this time to invite people to other social or civic events. If any cards or letters have come to "the Soup Group," they are read and passed around. Thus we move quickly from the spiritual to the secular.

One way of looking at this event suggests the more primitive idea of "potlach." We—the "chief" or "big man," my husband, aided and abetted by "the chief kitchen person," me—create, control, and maintain a network of friends in a loose pattern of allegiance. But allegiance to whom or to what? We are not plotting a political coup in the city of Claremont. It may be an unspoken allegiance to a way or life or a set of values that Soup represents. Certainly there is a great deal of ego-satisfaction when twenty people praise my soup and express what a good time they are having in our house. I enjoy the prestige of being known as "the Soup Lady" and the reputation of being a good cook, but suburban Claremont, located 35 miles from Los Angeles, is not a rural community where wives are ranked on the basis of their culinary skill or clean houses. Nearly all the men and women who come to Soup are college educated, professional people whose values do not center on domestic traditions. Soup may be seen as looking back at older values or a former lifestyle, lost in many modern urban communities. Because Soup Night takes place in a modern, post-industrial suburban location, the group experience is not like that in pre- or nonindustrial tribal life. A tribal or "family" feeling is created among individuals who are not blood-related by down-playing status. The emphasis is on contact and a feeling of community. Since Soup Night is not regulated by seasons or weather cycles, it is not a "natural" celebration. Instead it conforms to the so-called academic calendar, ceasing during school holidays and summer vacations. Occasionally it is cancelled so that my husband and I can go to various academic conferences.

Of course, there are some Thursdays when I would prefer not to have to spend the afternoon making soup or when there is something else going on that I would like to do instead, but there is a balance between pleasure and duty that Soup seems to satisfy. The enjoyment of sharing my house and soup with friends is balanced by spending Thursday afternoon not just making soup, which is creative fun, but in straightening the rest of the house, arranging furniture, and setting the table. Sometimes, once the soup is made and the table set, I have considered simply crawling into bed with a book and glass of wine, letting the event happen without me. Both Ted and I experience some Soup Nights in which we feel alienated and left out; we look at each other and nonverbally say, "Who are these people and why are they here?" Of course, these feelings are not common or we would stop having Soup. Furthermore, there are some people who come or have come to Soup that we do not like. And some of them do not like each other. But on Thursday night, we are not the sole owners of the house. It belongs to the Soup Group, which is large enough and complex enough to include ex-husbands and wives who are not speaking or, occasionally, several individuals that other guests may not enjoy particularly. However, the participants manage to maneuver and mingle so that there are very rarely unpleasant confrontations or outbursts. Part of the control is the reverse of what I just said—even though we have turned our house over to a community, because it is still a "private" home, no one can ask anyone else not to come or to leave. Neither Ted nor I have ever exercised that power; one of the basic tenets of the evening is that it is open to anyone who likes it.

Nevertheless, I know there is subtle weeding-out that takes place under what seems to be a self-selecting process. Soup does not suit everyone, yet many participants have stated that it can and does meet varied needs. If one is tired and depressed, it is all right to come by, have a bowl of soup, and go home; if one wishes to celebrate a birthday or anniversary, Soup provides a built-in party; if one is sad and needs comforting, there are people who will freely dispense hugs and advice. When Soup Night first began, most of the participants did not have extended family groups to which they belonged. Soup was often expanded, moved, and modified to cover Thanksgiving, Christmas, and Easter dinners. As the group has changed, several of the members have brought their mothers, brothers, and sisters to Soup, and the need for Soup to provide holiday meals has diminished. On the other hand, several people have told me that sometimes Soup is "just too much." Indeed the mood and noise level at Soup Night is jovial. Implicit in the freedom and flow are rules, codes, and structures that are understood and enforced by the "in-group" who assume the responsibility for making Soup work and the community continue. It is not a one-person show.

The shape, consistency, ritual, and the needs of all the participants create and maintain the etiquette and protocol of Soup Night. Since these rules are not written down or delivered orally, since there is no code for proper conduct or prescription for a successful Soup, the rules must be implicit in the behavior of the participants. As an insider, I have internalized, and perhaps created, the proper behavior, so it is difficult to sort out the appropriate and inappropriate ways to behave. Often we are aware of these only when they are violated. Anthropologists who have studied less industrialized societies are able to discern meaning in the structure of a meal by looking at the seating arrangements, the time span, and the interaction of the participants. For example, Tony Whitehead, in looking at how food behavior reveals culturally perceived needs, states: "The timing, seating arrangements, and dispensing protocol of a meal reflect ideas regarding role allocations, gender orientation, social order, status, and control."[10] Richard Mirsky, in his study of food habits, goes even further and claims that "Food sharing events have been interpreted as occasions when the members of a social unit join together to express symbolically and to maintain social cohesion as opportunities for the establishment of social prestige through demonstrations of superior wealth and property, as elements in systems of property distribution which tend to minimize individual differences in wealth, and as expression of friendship or covert hostility."[11] This does not apply to the small group festive gathering in a modern suburban setting. There is agreement among most food scholars that food events which involve sharing food within a small group are important in maintaining social cohesion. Jack Goody, quoting Robertson Smith, says that "the act of eating and drinking together is the solemn and stated expression of the fact that all those who share the meal are brethren and that all the duties of friendship and brotherhood are implicitly acknowledged in their common act."[12] Understanding these "duties" determines the behavior code at Soup.

The unwritten rules of Soup Night are not handed down arbitrarily from on high. The protocol actually begins with the cook who is subject to the expectations of the community of soup eaters. The decision concerning the kind of soup to prepare is complicated by group considerations: who hates parsnips? who is allergic to oysters? are the vegetarians likely to be there? how hot can I make the curry? This may be complicated further by the knowledge that it is someone's birthday and thus special consideration should be given to the honored person. Of course, the ultimate decision may be based on what is easy, whether time is a factor, or what is cheap this week at the store. Thus power and responsibility must be compromised before the soup is made. There is also an important liminal period preceding Soup. The afternoon is a solitary time, devoted to cooking and watching soap operas on television. At various times well-intentioned friends have dropped by to lend a helping hand. Although they are treated politely and usually given a cup of coffee or iced tea, it is no doubt obvious that they are neither helpful nor welcome. To prepare for twenty or thirty guests, solitude is best. The half hour right before Soup is, for the cook, one of the high points of the event. With Soup made, table set, door unlocked, and drink in hand, I can sit down (often the first time all afternoon) and read until the first guest arrives. In Claremont, at least with this group, hardly anyone is ever on time, let alone early. Six-thirty means anytime between 6:30 and 7:00. As the days lengthen in springtime, guests arrive later. If someone comes early, he/she often sits alone in the living room, drinking wine while I run around showering or grating cheese. Sometimes a close friend may come by early in order to have a quiet, private conversation before the others arrive. But there is no punishment for being early; we laugh. This is a community of friends, of family. The rules are family rules. Dress codes are nonexistent. If someone arrives dressed up from work or on the way to a fancier function, the other guests notice, especially if a man arrives wearing a tie, but for the most part the emphasis is on comfort; after all, many people end up sitting on the floor. As already noted, the door is unlocked. Newcomers may knock and be let in, but most people simply walk in and greet those already there. There is, however, one written rule on the outside of the front door, a request that no one smoke in the house. Smokers smoke outside on the patio or on the front steps, but there are fewer than three people who come to Soup that smoke anywhere. Since we have three cats and a Scottish terrier who run around the house, friends with allergies or who do not like animals have to work out the frequency of their participation. It is possible to simply avoid the cats and dog. Children are another issue. Most of the Soupers have grown or at least teenage children. Even back when my own and others' children were younger, Soup has been an "adult" event. My own son and daughter never have and still do not like homemade soup. As preteens, I think they were embarrassed to see their parents and their friends' parents laughing and joking and drinking wine. There are exceptions, times when friends of my children would be there, but they usually spent all evening in the bedroom or went out for walks or to run around the neighborhood. Now when a few of the children come home from college, they come to Soup and are accepted as part of the group. The group has never banned children, but no accommodation has been made for them. At present, a younger couple, who have been coming to Soup for several years, even before they were married, have a one-year-old daughter whom they have brought all during the first year of her life. Most people, their own baby-producing years well behind them, enjoy holding her for a little while, but generally the parents come and leave early. They are aware that Soup Night is geared for adults.

There is no limit to the number of bowls of soup anyone may have, but we very rarely run out of soup. If someone comes by about nine o'clock, he/she may have to scrape the bottom of the pan and add a little water, but more often there are several quarts left over and some participants take it home in coffee cans or plastic butter dishes. There is no mother-figure insisting that you clean your bowl. Some people drink a lot of wine or beer; some drink only a little or none at all. Only one person in the history of this event ever got so drunk that it was obvious. He stood up, threw up and went home; the remaining Soupers pitched in and cleaned up the mess. Table manners at Soup are casual, informal to a fault. Farb and Armelagos state that "under special conditions . . . Western people consciously imitate an earlier stage in culture at a picnic, fish fry or campfire— . . . [they] still tear food apart with their fingers and their teeth, in a nostalgic renactment of eating behavior long vanished. Today's neighborhood barbecue recreates a world of sharing and hospitality that becomes rarer every year" (1980, 208).

The making and serving of coffee has developed into a small ritual over the years. One of the regular Soupers started making the coffee at the end of the meal several years ago. In the past year, because of personal and business commitments, he was not present at most Soup Nights. It took months before we finally realized that the "coffee-maker" was not there and that someone else had better take over that job. At first Ted or I did it, reasserting ourselves as providers. Recently, a friend who is now married to the ex-wife of the former coffee-maker has assumed the job, primarily because he likes coffee after a meal. When the former coffee-maker comes to Soup, the job is returned to him. About 9 o'clock, hospitality begins to wear a little thin. Most participants depart between 8:30 and 9:00 because Friday is a working day. Two hours of good food and good company are sufficient for supper. Occasionally a few linger on. The conversation, facilitated by the wine, creates intimacy and intensity that they are reluctant to break. Sometimes several guests will leave together and go somewhere else to dance or just talk some more. Lingering is especially tempting when one is sitting in the hot tub. But at 9:00, Ted and I are tired. We flip the lights off and on, turn off the jets in the tub, push people off our bed, and send them home. If only Ted is tired, he may simply crawl in bed, leaving me to sit and talk as long as I like. By 10, we are usually reading in bed, exchanging information and opinions gleaned at Soup. The behavior code of Soup, then, fits Camp's rubric: "The social organization . . . is ordered by the selectivity of participation . . . who may or may not be involved, and relationships—the determination and assumption of formal and informal roles with regard to the event. The social rules governing the determination of participation in turn give shape to the meal and establish the significance of the occasion" (Camp n.d., 5). Those who choose to come to Soup both set, accept, and enforce a necessary, but flexible and unwritten, etiquette and protocol of Soup Night.

Soup, wine, and bread make a simple supper. By themselves, eaten alone, they fulfill the requirements of a meal, but little else. Soup Night imbues these foodstuffs with meaning and power, and they in turn explain and reinforce the values and identity of the Soup Group. If bread and wine create communion, what does this communion mean? In one collection of essays on foodways and eating habits, the editors assert that "once we have associated food with social experience, and have attributed meaning and significance to preparing or serving a dish, then food becomes symbolic. Experiencing food with others often results in a transference to food of assessments and valuations of those experiences" (Jones, Giuliano, and Krell 1983, 41–42). The bread and the wine are bonding devices; sharing the food is an acknowlegement that one is willing to share oneself. Because the bread and wine are provided by the participants themselves, each becomes an active part of the event, inviting others to share what he/she has brought to the meal. Instead of merely taking soup from the host, they are reciprocating at the same time they are receiving. Thus, the communion is a communion of good and equal fellowship. The aspect of communion is emphasized early in the event with the ritual of the toast. The act of eating together is both powerful and symbolic. Eating a common food, in this case soup, creates a communion of common values. In addition, this eating event extends the boundaries of the core community. Newcomers are invited to become members through the simple act of taking part. In taking part, they may become part of a network. This past fall, a new couple came to Soup. The husband was a new faculty member at the college where my husband teaches, the wife, an unemployed children's librarian. They apparently enjoyed Soup and were soon present at spin-off occasions such as birthday celebrations at local restaurants with some, but not all, of the Soup Groupers. In addition, she became part of a women's Saturday morning breakfast group and also participated in Sunday morning bike rides with four or six of us. A couple of months ago, they decided to separate. The Soup community is supportive of both; both still come to Soup. Certainly one of the motivating forces behind why Soup works is the human need to belong. Fieldhouse asserts, "Food readily becomes an expression of the search for belongingness."[13] His earlier contention that "Recurrent exchange and sharing [of food] is a feature of societies where community solidarity is maximal" (Fieldhouse 1986, 75) says something about the intentionality of Soup. Soup was conceived as a meal for the coming together of friends once a week in order to maintain contact and intimacy at a time when work and other obligations did not allow such contact to happen naturally. Mary Douglas states, "Meals are for family, close friends, honored guests. The ground operator of the system is the line between intimacy and distance.... The meal expresses close friendship" (Douglas 1972, 256). The assertion that Soup is a meal, not a party, is an extremely important distinction. In spite of divorces, dislike, aggravation, and frustration with the world and with each other, the people who come to Soup Night believe on some level that they are friends, good friends. They call on each other when cars break down or when they need help moving heavy furniture; they share good news and bad. In a town of 32,000 people, surrounded by 8 million others, the Soup Group bind themselves together through the act of eating. "Eating is symbolically associated with the most deeply felt human experiences, and thus expresses things that are sometimes difficult to articulate in everyday language" (Farb and Armelagos 1980, 111).

Soup Night is a time, a place, a meal, and a community. The tension between individual power and the concept of hospitality establishes the invisible but viable limits for behavior during this small group festive gathering. Hospitality is generally thought of as a part of a reciprocal exchange. Giving away food unilaterally would make an unbalanced and, hence, unpleasant relationship. The constant guest becomes a beggar (Douglas 1984, 10). But my guests must bring and pour their own wine, provide and serve their own bread, ask for butter or knives to be passed around the table, and freely share with others. I am relieved of nearly all the duties of being a hospitable hostess. When people need things that are not visible on the table, I tell them to look in the kitchen in various places. We become, at least for part of the evening, a family, with each member responsible for his/her own happiness. This engenders a feeling of freedom and cooperation not generally possible at a more formal dinner party. According to Paul Fieldhouse, "The act of eating together indicates some degree of compatability or acceptance; food is offered as a gesture of friendship.... Offering to share food is to offer to share a bit of oneself; to refuse food when offered is easily seen as a rejection of friendship" (p. 82). The tension between hospitality and power is also evident here. When participants refuse to have soup, pleading nonhunger or having eaten elsewhere, there is consternation, not just from my husband and me, but from other guests. Often participants may come by early, before they have to be somewhere else, and eat a solitary bowl of soup while everyone else is sipping wine—a way of taking part in the gathering as much as possible. Or someone may come by late, after everyone else has eaten and sit and have a bowl of soup while everyone else winds down. Neither of these activities is considered rude or unorthodox. Group hospitality keeps the evening going and accepts the responsibility for social ease and enjoyment. Participants let others in, greet them at the door, help clear the table, load the dishwasher, and mingle with whomever they wish. These are the acts of family and friends.

Unlike traditional communities, the participants at Soup Night cannot rely on kinship networks to hold the group together, nor are they tied to each other by neighborhood or work affiliations. Other soup nights have been started in other parts of the country—New Paltz, New York, Little Rock, Arkansas. There is even a similar group in Claremont whose members are part of the local Unitarian Society. The survival of these and other communal activities depends on the needs of the participants. The Claremont Soup Group continues, its existence broadening beyond ethnicity Susan Kalčik's argument that "shared foodways are so symbolically powerful that they can unite members of a group separated geographically—even those separated by death."[14] Here's "to Friends who are present, and those who are not."

Notes

1. See my "Small Group Festive Gatherings," *Journal of the Folklore Institute* 16 (1979): 190–201.

2. Mary Douglas provides this interesting term in *Food in the Social Order: Studies of Food and Festivities in Three American Communities* (New York: Russell Sage Foundation, 1984): 17.

3. *Daedalus* 101.1 (1972): 61–81.

4. Julee Rosso and Sheila Lukins, *The Silver Palate Cookbook* (New York: Workman Publishing, 1979): 43.

5. Unpublished Ph.D. diss. (University of Pennsylvania, 1978), p. 327.

6. "'The Funeral Bak'd Meats Did Coldly Furnish Forth the Marriage Table': A Semiotic Analysis of Food Events," Unpublished paper (n.d.): 15.

7. Roger Abrahams, "Equal Opportunity Eating: Structural Excursus on Things of the Mouth," *Ethnic and Regional Foodways in the United States: The Performance of Group Identity,* ed. Linda Keller Brown and Kay Mussell (Knoxville: University of Tennessee Press, 1984): 19–36.

8. Peter Farb and George Armelagos, *Consuming Passions: The Anthropology of Eating* (Boston: Houghton Mifflin, 1980): 108.

9. Mary Douglas, *Purity and Danger: An Analysis of the Concepts of Pollution and Taboo* (London: Ark, 1966): 62–64, 67.

10. Tony Larry Whitehead, "Sociocultural Dynamics and Food Habits in a Southern Community," in *Studies of Food and Festivities in Three American Communities,* ed. Mary Douglas (New York: Russell Sage Foundation, 1984): 104.

11. Richard Mirsky, "Perspectives in the Study of Food Habits," in *Foodways & Eating Habits: Directions for Research,* ed. Michael Owen Jones, Bruce Guiliano, and Roberta Krell (Los Angeles: The California Folklore Society, 1983): 129.

12. Jack Goody, *Cooking, Cuisine, and Class: A Study in Comparative Sociology* (Cambridge University Press, 1982): 12.

13. Paul Fieldhouse, *Food & Nutrition: Customs & Culture* (London: Helm, 1986): 82.

14. Susan Kalčik, "Ethnic Foodways in America; Symbol and the Performance of Identity," in *Ethnic and Regional Foodways in the United States: The Performance of Group Identity* ed. Linda Keller Brown and Kay Mussell (Knoxville: University of Tennessee Press, 1984): 13, 37–65.

Part II

Regional Specialties: Work and Play

Introduction to Part II

While the essays in this section examine events characteristic of different regions of our country, they are bound together even more by the idea of working and eating together as two of the most powerful modes of creating community. Participation is the key to this powerful and continuing impulse that lies behind so many "performances" of community. They survey also the wide variety of food events used to create homecoming, the return to the community where the symbolic power of food in community festive food events is perhaps the strongest. Although the Morrison community barbecue examined by Theodore Humphrey has only recently been "officially" merged with the reunion of the community's high school classes, it has been from the beginning an event to which its sons and daughters have returned, and was created to "return" in another sense to a time of remembered communal closeness. Eleanor Wachs's and Kathy Neustadt's clambakes likewise are events symbolically anchoring participants to home. Carol Edison's two Utah celebrations, Koosharem's "Old Folks Day" and Fountain Green's "Lamb Day, " are traditional events at which the community's residents celebrate themselves with foods strongly suggestive of the community's history and traditions. Being involved in these events, as Edison notes, whether "donating a salad or pie, working on the committee that cooks, serves, and cleans up, or simply attending the event as a former resident or as one of the honored senior guests, makes everyone an important part of the celebration. The result of participation in the group-run event," she notes, "is likely a renewed sense of individual membership in the community; the preparation and presentation of food at this event presents a symbolic display of community-held values that helps define the community's unique identity" and clearly suggests the nature and importance of homecoming celebrations throughout the country—and the roles that foods play at them.

Working together and homecoming are likewise strong ideas in the two articles that deal with an archetypal food event of the New England region, the clambake. But two such contrasting clambakes! Their history, their menus and the methods of preparation of the foods are quite different. Yet, as Eleanor Wachs and Kathy Neustadt point out, their motivations and functions are similar and, indeed, closely parallel those of the other festive events studied in this volume. Neustadt studies a century-old clambake that identifies a Quaker congregation—and serves to raise funds as well, "a kind of summer Thanksgiving, 'bigger than Christmas,' some say—and the major source of funds for the Allen's Neck Meeting. It is also a time of reunion, renewal, and good eating," as well as group participation and homecoming, common functions for such festive events. Wachs notes how "Robert Scheurch, the family patriarch, [once] watched a clambake underway on Peddock's Island" and thus began the tradition of the Johnston Family Clambake. Just as he began the Johnston Family Clambake after watching one, so too did Calvin Pauley "see it done" and begin the younger tradition of the Morrison Community Barbecue, analyzed by Humphrey.

Working together to produce an event clearly draws the participants together in a true community. The nature of the community's work outside the festive occasion, whether directly experienced or remembered, is also a subtext of all of the essays in this section. Conversation focuses on the pleasures involved in working hard together and shares memories of earlier times when such hard physical communal labor was a necessary part of everyone's life. The appeal of such events is surely a combined pleasure, part memory of an earlier (idealized) time, part the direct enjoyment of working together complete with all the traditional teaching, learning, and evaluation of skills that such events entail. A common value is the value of hard work, the finest appetizer in the world, as everyone's father used to say. No "fast foods" here, these are the "real thing," created directly by the sweat and toil, the intelligence and sense of tradition of all of the participants. Thus, whether they are the foods of the traditional Mormon Sunday dinner served to the "Old Folks" at Koosharem, Utah, or "booya" created by fraternal organizations in St. Paul, Minnesota, the clams, tripe, sausage, and lobster of a clambake, the pit barbecued beef, goat, pig, or lamb of the West, or Bud Gardner's sugar cured ham, they are powerful foods and symbolize each community's sense of itself.

A major focus of this section, then, is how social meaning is created in the nexus of homecoming, shared work, and traditional foods. Anne Kaplan argues that "booya is unquestionably meant to be a social event, where the focus is on eating, drinking, playing games, and talking" even though the underlying purpose is to raise money for the groups hosting the event. Barbara Fertig and Amy Skillman move us into more traditional work contexts, which, while hardly free of the "modern" age, nevertheless play on an older mode, a romantic harkening, perhaps, to a time when community-based work was necessary to the economic as well as social life of society. In showing neighbors who get together to transform pig to pork through "cutting out" and "curing," processes that make symbolic forms out of natural ones, their essays also clearly show how the shared work of both processes created social events that demonstrate a well-defined sense of community. The time spent before the actual work of butchering or hamming begins comprises a time of visiting, of traditional exchanges and behaviors that affirm the community in that context. The stories, the reminiscences, the sharing of coffee and breakfast, and the church suppers, for example, that feature Bud Gardner's hams, all contribute to this sense among the participants and support the notion of food, talk, and work as essential components of community creation. The literal nourishing quality of food is enhanced not only by the cultural acts of processing, curing, and cooking but also by the social events of its preparation and consumption that, as Amy Skillman notes, "provide a catalyst for community identity and cohesiveness."

5

"To Toast the Bake":
The Johnston Family Clambake

Eleanor Wachs

A colonial New England account tells of Governor William Bradford's sense of humiliation when, in 1622, the colonists, short of food, had to feed their guests a one-dish meal—lobster. In fact, lobster was such common fare that the residents of the Plymouth almshouse, given so much of it, often complained.[1] The riches of New England, particularly the harvest of the sea, eventually a backbone of the region's economy, astounded the colonists and its chroniclers from the earliest days of settlement.[2] The plentiful foodstuffs, in particular corn, lobsters, clams, and the ubiquitous cod, substantiated the claim that New England's shores and farmlands were truly bountiful.[3] Colonial documenters often comment about these riches. John Winthrop writes, "If we have corne enough we may live plentifully." In 1630, Francis Higginson remarks, "The abundance of seafish are almost beyond believing, and sure I should scarce have believed it except I had seen it with mine own eyes...."[4] He continues, noting "an abundance of lobsters, and the least boy in the plantation may both catch and eat what he will of them. For my own part I was soon cloyed with them, they were so great and fat and luscious."[5] Another observer, John Pory, comments: "Lobsters are in season during the four months, so large so full of meat, and so plentiful in number, as no man will believe that hath not seen.... Mussels and clams they have all the year long ... if ours upon any extremity did enjoy in the South Colony they would never complain of famine or want...."[6] Food historian Reay Tannahill notes:

From the Indians, the settlers discovered not only what was edible, but how to cook it. They learned about the seacoast clambake. A pit was dug and lined with flat stones on which a fire was lit. When the stones were white-hot, the embers were brushed away and a layer of seaweed placed on the stones. On top of this went alternate layers of clams and ears of maize, interleaved with further quantities of seaweed. The pit when full, was covered with a blanket of wet cloth or hide, which was kept moist throughout the hour or so of cooking time. The clams and corn emerged tender, moist, and delicious.[7]

Over the centuries, the status of lobster has changed from a food for paupers to a gourmet treat. This well-known crustacean, the *Homarus americanus,* along with the milky white clam chowder and the corn of Squanto's legend, has served as a foodways emblem for the New England region.[8] From the original bake of the region's Native Americans to the clambake affairs catered for the employees of Massachusetts' high tech firms, the clambake is still a popular way to celebrate the rich bounty of New England.

In our time, the three ingredients—corn, lobsters, and clams—comprise the traditional principal ingredients of the New England clambake, a foodways ritual method of preparation inherited by the colonists from their Indian neighbors. The local clambake, one must bear in mind, is only one of the many regional foodways events related to the sea. Chowder feasts, oyster shucking contests, harvest home dinners, strawberry and apple festivals, represent other popular festivities widespread in New England.

The Johnston family of Hough's Neck, Quincy, Massachusetts are quite certain that their annual family clambake will continue despite the popularity of catered clambakes and the presence of severe environmental pollution in the Greater Boston harbor area. This event has been a part of their family tradition since 1907 when, as a young man, Robert Scheurch, the family patriarch, watched a clambake underway on Peddock's Island. Mr. Scheurch so instilled in his daughter, Carol Johnston, the importance of carrying on this summertime tradition that she now presides over an event shared with family, her Hough's Neck neighbors and her co-workers at a health maintenance organization.

Like most places in the Greater Boston area, each community has a noble past. Hough's Neck, a neighborhood of Quincy, Massachusetts, the home town of John Quincy Adams, was originally owned by Atherton Hough, a follower of the Puritan John Cotton. Hough, an assistant to Governor John Winthrop, acquired the land which bears his name in 1635. In the seventeenth and eighteenth centuries, the land was probably farmland. With the appearance of streetcars in the 1870s, the area became a summer resort. Smaller farms stood alongside summer bungalows. The residents of Boston and nearby Dorchester walked the Hough's Neck beaches for the invigorating and restorative sea air. Hotels and beach homes sprang up on this one mile wide peninsula and each season brought its summer theatre schedule and Illumination Week.[9] Fishermen from all over still come to the

Neck's well-known flounder beds to fish, and clammers still pluck clams from its shores, despite the severe pollution in the area caused by the inadequate waste treatment plant on Nut Island, which pumps raw sewage directly into Quincy Bay.

Being a peninsula, and thus cut off from the well-populated city of Quincy, Hough's Neck achieves the hamlet-like atmosphere of a tightly knit community. Its inhabitants call themselves "neckers." When an interracial conflict occurred in the area several years ago placing Hough's Neck in the city spotlight, a *Boston Globe* reporter described the community this way:

> Hough's . . . Neck is a place where no one lives more than a few hundred yards from the ocean; where many people leave their doors unlocked and women think nothing of visiting neighbors at night alone; where children filet flounder caught by tourists at 15 cents a fish; where the nights are seldom disturbed except by odor from the sewer treatment plant on the Nut Island, part of the peninsula; where you must virtually wait until someone dies to buy a house, typically a four-or five-room winterized summer cottage selling for $60,000; where people eagerly join in raising $10,000 to educate a widow's three children or $5,000 to send youngsters to baseball camp in the summer.[10]

When Carol Scheurch and Bob Johnston first married, they settled in Framingham, a bedroom community west of Boston, until they returned to Hough's Neck with their children. They have two children, a college-student son and a daughter who lives with her husband and child in a separate apartment in the Johnston home. The apartment was used by Carol's father until his death in 1983. Carol is a nurse-administrator in a large HMO in the Greater Boston area.

I heard about the Johnston family clambake when Brenda enrolled in a folklore class I taught at the University of Massachusetts-Boston in 1982. Expressing interest in the clambake, I was first invited in 1982 and again in 1984. Both times that I attended the clambake, I interviewed Carol and Bob Johnston and several guests, recorded interviews, took numerous of photographs and had a delicious clambake meal. My interest in the event was well received by the hosts and the guests of both bakes. The 1982 bake differed little from the one held in 1984. However, Carol's father died in 1983; thus, the 1984 bake marked the passing-on of a family tradition.

Carol and Bob Johnston host the family clambake, which officially begins for Carol when she checks the summer tide calendar and selects the best date for the two-day bake. As the time approaches, she collects a pool of money from expected participants for foodstuffs. At the bake itself, little or no exchange of money takes place, although a few later invitees might hand personal checks to the hosts. The procurement of foodstuffs takes place over several days. Carol does the ordering: twenty racks of clams from a large Boston seafood distributor; fruit and fifty ears of corn from a local market; forty-five lobsters from a lobsterman, a relative, who delivers them on the morning of the bake itself.

The Johnston home is a modest, white and blue aluminum-sided house that is deceptively small from the outside. A narrow hallway leads into a rectangular shaped combination dining and living room area. The two areas share a large picture window displaying a panoramic view of the Johnston's beachfront, the site of the bake. In the background is the Boston skyline, approximately twelve miles across Quincy Bay. The large window is the centerpiece of the room: one naturally looks out at the beautiful, constantly changing scene of city lights, small boats on the bay and splendid summer sunsets. The picture window is an important place for Carol and others since they can look out from the window and observe the activities beginning when Bob and his helpers dig the clam pit.

The small kitchen, where the chowder is made, is off the living room, and has two entrances; one makes for easy access to the dining room area where in addition to the kitchen, most of the food preparation takes place. The other entrance leads to the kitchen, which leads to a steep staircase to the second floor where one walks through a small bedroom onto a deck providing another beautiful vista of the bay and skyline. These rooms—the kitchen, dining area, living room, deck, grassy yard on the side of the house, and the beachfront—are the areas used for the preparation for the bake and for socializing.

On a July Friday at dusk, several cars turn into the Johnston driveway. Fifteen of the bake's forty participants arrive to begin the food preparation. On this night preceding the clambake, three important tasks, divided by gender, need to be accomplished: digging the clam pit, preparing some items of the clambake menu, and gathering rockweed, an essential ingredient of the clambake's success. The women work in the dining room and kitchen areas and later gather rockweed, while the men congregate on the ocean backyard to dig the clam pit.

On Friday night, Carol begins the preparation of the clam chowder, made according to a traditional family recipe. The chowder is served late in the morning on the following day to abate people's hunger while the feast is baking in the pit. Carol organizes the work for the women participants, while Brenda, Carol's daughter, assists. The women spend about three hours peeling and cutting potatoes, dicing onions, chopping salt pork, and preparing the clams for the chowder. Five women surround the dining room table up to their arms in onion skins and potato peels. Soon the clams, which have soaked in cold water, salt and cornmeal to remove trapped sand, are steamed and ready to be opened by the women. Everyone is told that the black slip around the neck of the clam has to be removed by cracking open the clam shell, pulling out the clam from the shell, and holding the slippery clam belly while pulling off the black slip to leave the mushy clam intact for the chowder. Some nibble on the clam necks as they work. Twenty pounds of clams have been purchased for the chowder; another twenty arrives the following day; each guests eats between a pound and a pound-and-a-quarter of clams.

Carol Johnston works mostly in the kitchen overseeing the chowder preparation, continually walking back and forth to the women at the table, offering suggestions on how best to prepare the ingredients for the chowder and to share in the constant joking and lively conversation. Soon the elements for the chowder are finished and refrigerated. The next morning, they will be combined and will be cooked slowly with butter and evaporated milk under Carol's watchful eye. Carol explains, "One time, it spoiled on us, so after that we never put anything together. We're afraid it will spoil, so we keep it separate."[11]

While dicing and peeling and cutting, the women socialize, bantering good-naturedly about the messy tasks at hand. This time is also used to talk about the latest events in their homes and workplaces and to share expectations about the next day. At this time also they initiate newcomers to the tasks at hand. Much of the talk around the table consists of chatter about the importance of working together to make the bake come about. Much of the conversation consists of chiding one another about the individual performance of their culinary tasks. Jokes are made about the need to join a potato peeler's union. Some agree that they deserve an extra cup of chowder for their efforts. Comments are made comparing the clambake preparation to a quilting bee in which many help in a shared enterprise, in contrast to the daily food preparing the women accomplish alone for their families. The time, too, is spent reminiscing about previous bakes at the Johnston home. Carol recalls one time when she forgot to cook the potatoes for the chowder. Her nephew made her aware of the *faux pas.* "Auntie Carol," he said, "these potatoes are really hard. Did you cook them first?"[12] A quick "zapping" in the microwave, Carol recalls, remedied the mishap.

Next, the women work on large fruit baskets, scooping melon balls of honeydew and cantaloupe and putting the balls and other summer fruit into carved out watermelons. At the same time, four women remove the silk and shucks of fifty ears of corn, leaving the innermost green shucks intact to prevent overcooking in the pit. Next, the corn is placed in wooden crates ready for the next day's steaming in the pit.

While the women are working in the kitchen and dining rooms, Bob Johnston, five men, and one woman, begin digging the clam pit on the beachfront. Their progress is repeatedly checked by the women, who watch the activity from the large picture window. Bob first tries to find the bake pit of the previous year in hopes of making the laborious job easier.

No longer is the pit dug on the morning of the bake because it takes several hours to dig. (At the 1984 bake, he corralled a young boy to spray paint a marker on a huge rock directly above the pit so the following year's search could be eliminated.) In 1984, four men and one woman dug the pit. Once the pit is dug it is lined with flat, hard rocks: soft rocks would explode or break under the extreme heat of the bake. Driftwood picked up by the men on the beach the previous evening will be the fuel. Bob and his helpers dig a second pit near the first one but closer to the tidemark. A fire preventative, it will be filled with the burnt coals raked from the bake pit after the stones are heated and before the food is put into the bake pit.[13] Robert Scheurch explained how to dig the pit to his granddaughter, Brenda: "Well, you get up early, and you dig two holes. Dig one above the high water mark and another one, as tide goes out, dig it below the high water mark. You dig it fairly deep, probably knee deep, depending on how many are coming to the thing. And dirt you have to throw, you throw away from your bake pit but handy to it."[14]

In addition to friends and delicious chowder, an essential ingredient for a successful Johnston family clambake is rockweed. Rockweed is exactly what the name implies: an elastic grayish green and slimy weed (genus *Fucus*) that grows wild over the rocks near the shore line. It has small nodules which fill with steam and explode when under the intense heat of the pit. The steam from the nodules accounts for the succulent taste of the food. At one time, this weed grew all over the Hough's Neck shore line and was plentiful for the taking. But because of the Neck shore's serious environmental and pollution problems, rockweed is now rare in the area. These days, a half-hour ride to Hull, Massachusetts to the home of a friend (who has been "blessed" with this special natural substance in his backyard) is necessary to the bake's success. Having arrived at the Hull backyard, Carol organizes a team of rockweed pullers. They follow her down to the small dock, down the ladder to the shore, and over to the slippery rocks covered with the weed. Walking around in the slippery mud, they gather the rockweed, filling thirteen plastic trash bags and then dragging them back to the station wagon.

Gathering the rockweed becomes an adventure; much is made of the unpleasant task. New initiates ("virgin pullers") are encouraged to participate. The time sequence for getting rockweed changed with the two bakes I attended; in 1982, the rockweed gatherers yanked the weed off the rocks on the same day as the bake; in 1984, the trip to Hull was an event of Friday evening. But for Carol, the event had changed in a more fundamental way. She recalls that "when I was a kid ... you'd go to the islands [in Quincy Bay] but we just happened to have friends in Hull that live on the water, that have a lot of rocks in front of their yard; in front of their house is the beach . . . so it's easy to get. It's just a half-an-hour ride down. Also, we don't have a boat anymore. My dad always had a boat. . . ."[15]

After the rockweed pullers accomplish their mission, they stop by a local pizzeria to pick up the ten pies needed for the late evening meal. After a pizza dinner in the Johnston living room, almost everyone goes up to the second floor deck to relax and reminisce about past bakes and to talk about their expectations of the upcoming bake, to laugh and joke about the rockweed gathering because it is regarded as such an unpleasant and dirty task. As Bob Johnston recalls, "You need three experienced people and one novice every year. We generally try to keep the horror story about the rockweed a secret from the rest of the people. . . . It's really not that bad. It's just a matter of going and gushing around in the mud and the sea and the flats . . . and we just fill up the bags."[16]

Anecdotes about the work fill the conversation, revealing attitudes about the purpose of the bake to its participants. The event has a structure, a beginning, middle, and end. Some participants are there from start to finish; others come only on Saturdays when much of the work has been accomplished. But, whatever role one plays, all comment on the hard work. "The hard work makes it worthwhile," Bob Johnston says:

> You know, you talk about magic time, when the work goes on, when that bake is opened. It really is magic. It's super. It's a special time. And if you're here, even if you don't know what it's all about and can't understand how hot rocks can do all that . . . that's right . . . when the bake is opened it's a very special moment. . . . And you feel like you've been to something. What usually happens is that the people that come and are here for the opening of the bake, start going back and asking the people who were here, what happened, how did this work, how did it come together, what did you do? Because it is so special. It's not just, "let's have lobster and clams."[17]

The bake day's events begin around nine on Saturday morning when Bob Johnston lights the kindling in the bake pit to heat the rocks, a process that will take several hours. Shortly after noon, the rocks are judged to be sufficiently heated. Bob and his brother-in-law put on goggles and put wet towels around their heads and faces to protect themselves from the excessive heat of the pit. Using rakes, they quickly pull out the charred coals of the first pit and push them into the second pit nearby, then cover the second pit with sand. Because of the intense heat, the men must work quickly and efficiently during the fifteen minutes it takes to complete the task, the most difficult and dangerous aspect of the clambake preparation.

The pit is now ready for the bake. Most of the participants have now arrived by this time, and many help lug the food down to the bake pit in one of two ways: by carrying the crated food down the steep incline of thirty or so feet down a wooden staircase located in their next-door-neighbor's backyard, or by putting the crated food on a platform attached to a pulley that can lower it to the beachfront below.

The rockweed is dumped out of the garbage bags onto the hot rocks by Bob and four other men, a task that ties this event historically to its pre-colonial days. The pit is now ready to be filled with clams, lobster, and corn. The clams, previously washed and bagged in cotton pillowcases, are thrown into the pit. (One summer when I attended the bake, the clams were forgotten until the last minute. A flurry of washing and bagging saved the day.) The clams are covered with a layer of rockweed, then forty ears of corn are layered in, followed by another layer of rockweed. Moments later, Bob counts the live lobsters and then tosses them into the pit. A batch of rockweed covers the lobsters and the entire pit evenly, the whole thing now covered by a canvas tarp about the size of a double bedspread. Finally, the pit men rake sand over the tarp, and the food lies buried four feet down where it will bake for about two hours.

As soon as the bake is covered, an important Scheurch-Johnston tradition occurs: the toasting of the bake. All the participants are asked to come down to the covered pit to form a circle around the pit area. Those who do not come down to the beachfront watch and participate in the toast by observing others from the Johnston's living room window. Everyone holds a glass of beer or soda and Carol begins the toast. In the past, including the first bake I attended at the Johnston's, Mr. Scheurch, a rather sedate, quiet gentleman, probably not given to long-winded speeches, had led the short toast. He was adamant about the toast's importance: "You gotta have a drink before you can eat; you gotta toast the damn thing or it never works. It don't come out without it."[18] The heir apparent to the bake toast is Carol. "I guess it's usually me since my Dad died. It's usually my Dad.... He used to watch us quite carefully at first, but then he figured out we could do it. The first time I toasted the bake, he said, 'I hope you did it right.' ... It's like, almost like the spirits aren't gonna come and make the bake good if you don't toast it.... I'm sure he didn't really believe that, but it's what he used to say."[19] Raising her glass, Carol shouts, "This is to tradition and families and friends and good times and hard work. To The Bake!"

As the men are building the bake pit with the successive layers of food, Carol is "building the chowder," one of many essential tasks readying a successful clambake. All the ingredients are, as we have seen, prepared the night before, but the chowder itself is not made until Saturday morning. Chowder making is serious business in New England. Chowder tasting festivals are held annually, and chowder afficionados know where the finest chowders are served. A "Necker" knows, however, that Carol's chowder is the best anywhere in the neighborhood. While the recipe is not exactly kept secret within the family (Carol is quick to tell you that evaporated milk is her special ingredient), the several hours she spends on Saturday morning standing over the kitchen stove perfecting and tasting the chowder are not translatable into a conventional recipe format. She has taught both her son and her daughter how to make the family chowder. "They were brought up on it," she said to me as I watched her swirl a wooden spoon through the rich chowder. So it is the experience of repeated tasting that is the genuine secret ingredient. Only the ongoing tradition of eating the chowder on a regular basis results in a full knowledge of its preparation—and its power within the group.

While the bake is steaming under its layer of tarp and sand, the clambake participants mingle, enjoying Carol's famous chowder. During the time that the bake cooks, the forty or so guests inhabit several rooms of the Johnston house, the beach, and the front and back yards. The gender division persists. The women talk among themselves about children, relatives, family life or their shared work place. The men discuss sports and politics. Most of the clambake participants are middle-aged adults. The children talked about are conspicuous by their absence.

Once Bob gives the call that the bake should be ready, uncovering the pit begins. Several guests go to the bake spot on the beach. The sand is removed and the tarp pulled back from the pit a bit so that Bob Johnston can sample an exposed lobster claw. Once his experienced palette pronounces it done, the men and women assembled help remove the rest of the sand and tarp, and then remove from the pit the lobsters, corn, and clams. The rockweed is discarded in the trash cans. Bob counts the lobsters along with the corn; the steaming pillowcases, filled with clams, are laid on the beach. A line forms, the participants passing the food from one to the other to the platform and pulley, which once loaded are hoisted to the house level. The crates of food are put on the picnic tables near the side of the house. The scooped-out watermelon baskets brimming with fruit prepared the previous evening are brought out to the tables. The guests serve themselves: one lobster, an ear of corn, a dozen or so clams—to start with. Portions are big; appetites are big. Everyone is encouraged to indulge.

The feast is soon in full swing. People find seats at the picnic tables or on a lawn chair or on blankets spread out all over the Johnston yard, soon filled with eaters. Rules of propriety are momentarily suspended; most of the food is eaten with one's hands. The eaters begin to satisfy their immediate hunger; informal judging begins, this bake being compared to previous ones. Which lobster is most succulent? Which corn the sweetest? Which clams the tastiest? Two days of cooperation, work, and fellowship are devoured in less than half an hour!

Celebrations like the Johnston Family Clambake are often instruments for creating community, fellowship, and intimacy through the process of continual interaction among participants.[20] Throughout the two-day event, several situational contexts endow the participants with a sense of community, of belonging. Throughout the bake, most work is done in groups, often divided by gender. Aside from raking the pit, most work is done at a leisurely pace, leaving time for joking behavior. The jokes, however, often center on how well or poorly a participant is performing a particular task; those who feign work are ridiculed and urged to join in more fully. Small groups prepare the food. Communal effort transports pit ingredients from beach and rock to the pit. Teamwork among the men raking the hot pit promotes efficiency and is essential to avoid mishap or injury. In much the same way, teamwork among the women assists in the safe gathering of rockweed. Community also develops during such times between periods of work as Friday night when participants are milling about, drinking and anticipating the bake day. Most importantly, the roles that Bob and Carol play create a sense of fellowship. While both command the successful execution of their respective parts of the bake, they do so in ways to encourage new participants to learn quickly one or two steps in the preparation process. They fit everyone to a suitable task, even if it is a small chore like finding firewood on the beach or dicing salt pork for the chowder. Beyond the knowledge they share about their family tradition, their hospitality, friendliness, and good spirits assure a successful bake and promote a sense of community among the participants.

The very structure of the event itself promotes communal bonding. The inherent or deep structure of the bake is a continual "building up" and "building down" of the physical environment and the foodstuffs. Just as Bob and his helpers dig the pits and add the food in order to "build the bake," so Carol, in her own words, "builds the chowder" to make her perfect recipe. Even the participants contribute to this metaphoric construction project: they build their plates with lobster, clams, corn, and fruit, the metaphor being part of every bake.

The Johnston clambake is replete with such symbolic meanings, typical for events of this type. In recent decades, several innovations have occurred in the form of clambakes. It is popular, even fashionable, for example, to order a large wastebasket sized tin, filled with the usual clambake ingredients and sausage from a specialty clambake shop on Cape Cod. But for the Johnstons, the style of such a clambake would be very disappointing. It would be too easy, with little effort, and without the crucial element of fellowship. For the Johnstons and their guests (a few of whom, former Neckers, return to the old neighborhood just for the bake), the event stands as an historical/regional symbol. It is an event that goes on despite the major physical changes in the local environment. The persistent beach and water pollution often closes the beach to swimmers and the huge luxury condominiums being built on the Quincy waterfront have dramatically changed the skyline of this formerly blue-collar area. "Well, we used to dig our own clams," states Carol, when asked about how the bake had changed over the years. "We'd go out, take a boat out to the rocks out here and get the weed and the only stuff we'd go out for was the lobsters and the corn. The clams you dug yourself, made the chowder. It was the same thing but the family did all the work." The bake retains these essential menu components, yet the family has made accommodations. For Carol Johnston, who dearly loved her father, the bake's initiator, the bake is also a personal symbol. The continued reenactment of the clambake since her father's death in 1983 reaffirms the legacy of the bake for her and is a way to reaffirm her father's spirit, love for the water, and the lifestyle he led as the long-time commander of the Quincy Yacht Club. Some of the other participants, former and current neighbors, for example, find that the bake holds many personal memories. These participants talk of the old "Neck" in conversations as the bake is being prepared. The event serves as a nostalgic link to their pasts as former members of the community. Carrying on of the tradition by the Johnstons symbolizes an earlier, perhaps idealized, time for the "Neckers" and introduces newcomers to a sense of the neighborhood's history and traditions important to the Johnston family and friends.

Furthermore, the Johnston clambake is a rejection of attitudes toward the contemporary urban world of high rises, concrete, anonymity, and impersonality. Certainly, the bake serves, literally and figuratively, as a way in which its urban participants may be in touch with their physical environments and use and manipulate them to their own advantage. The physical act of working on the beach helps link the participants to a shared regional cultural heritage. As cultural geographer Carl Sauer notes, to be in touch with the beach environment is a way in which we can all return to the "primitive act and mood" where man first lived.[21] Furthermore, the participants have the license to break many rules of propriety concerning food.

Not only does the bake link the participants to their immediate pasts, it also links them to the historical past of New England, especially to the Yankee and Native American traditions which preceded them. Enactment of this traditional event provides the opportunity to be as self-sufficient as one can get these days living but twelve miles away from the major metropolitan center of Boston. The Johnston clambake reminds all concerned of the bountiful shores of the region, of the value of cooperation between members of a small community, and of the power of the traditional knowledge necessary for demonstrating this time-honored tradition. The combination of hard work, cooperation, fellowship, family lore, and conserving of tradition in the midst of a changing urban environment makes the Johnston family clambake a meaningful celebration.

Notes

I would like to thank Carol and Robert Johnston for letting me into their home to document their clambake and to Brenda Cuneo for introducing her family tradition to me. I am also grateful to Linda Morley and Ted Humphrey for their suggestions and comments during the writing stages of this article.

1. David Arnold, "The Lobster: A Delicacy Man Knows Little About," *The Boston Globe,* 20 August 1984, pp. 41–42; Waverly Root and Richard de Rochamont, *Eating in America: A History* (New York: William Morrow & Co., Inc., 1976), 29, 51–55.

2. Richard M. Dorson, *America Begins* (Bloomington, Indiana: Indiana University Press, 1950).

3. Jay Anderson, "The Bountiful Yeoman," *Natural History* 91:10 (1982): 38–46; Sally Smith Booth, *Hung, Strung and Potted: A History of Eating Habits in Colonial America* (New York: Clarkson N. Potter, Inc., 1971); Sarah McMahon, "A Comfortable Subsistence" (Ph.D. diss., Brandeis University, 1982).

4. Dorson, p. 74.

5. Dorson, p. 75.

6. Dorson, pp. 80–81.

7. Reay Tannahill, *Food in History* (New York: Stein and Day Publishers, 1973): 265; Helen Newbury Burke, *Foods from the Founding Fathers: Recipes from Five Colonial Seaports* (Hicksville, New York: Exposition Press, 1978): 23–31; Richard Osborn Cummings, *The American and His Food* (New York: Arno Press, 1970).

8. Wilbur Zelinsky, *The Cultural Geography of the United States* (Englewood Cliffs, New Jersey: Prentice-Hall, Inc., 1973): 122. Zelinsky writes, "In keeping with the basic criterion for defining a culture area, New Englanders have been keenly aware of their identity, though probably more so in the past than at present; and they usually have been readily labelled by outsiders by virtue of pattern of speech, religion, behavior or thought." No doubt, foodways as well contribute to the regional identity of a culture area.

    The study of how a particular food becomes symbolic of a particular area is an important aspect of the study of foodways. For an excellent discussion of how a food item becomes symbolic of a culture see: C. Paige Guiterrez, "The Social and Symbolic Uses of Ethnic/Regional Foodways: Cajuns and Crawfish in South Louisiana," in Linda Keller Brown and Kay Mussell, *Ethnic and Regional Foodways in the United States: The Performance of Group Identity* (Knoxville: University of Tennessee Press, 1984): 169–82.

9. Dorothy T. Laing and Ruth H. Wainwright, *The Hough's Neck Story and Atherton Hough, A Puritan's Progress* (Hough's Neck, Mass.: Hough's Neck Community Council, 1981): 11–26.

10. Jerry Taylor, "10 From Hough's Neck Going on Trial in Attack on Sailors," *The Boston Globe,* 20 August 1984, p. 35.

11. Carol Johnston, Interview with author, Quincy, Mass., July 15, 1984.

12. Carol Johnston, Interview with author, Quincy, Mass., July 15, 1984.

13. Brenda Cuneo, "Lobsters, Steamers, Chowder: A New England Party Tradition," Acquisition Number 082–21, U/Mass-Boston Folklore and Oral History Archives, pp. 4–5.

14. Ibid.

15. Carol Johnston, Interview with author, Quincy, Mass., July 15, 1984.

16. Bob Johnston, Interview with author, Quincy, Mass., June 23, 1982.

17. Bob Johnston, Interview with author, Quincy, Mass., June 23, 1982.

18. Cuneo, p. 5.

19. Carol Johnston, Interview with author, Quincy, Mass., July 16, 1984.

20. Hortense Powdermaker, "Feasts in New Ireland: The Social Function of Eating," *American Anthropologist* 34 (1932): 236–47. See also Linda T. Humphrey, "Small Group Festive Gatherings," *Journal of the Folklore Institute,* 16:3 (Sept.–Dec., 1979): 190–201.

21. Carl Sauer, "Seashore—Primitive Home of Man?" in *Land and Life,* ed. John Leightley (Berkeley: University of California Press, 1963): 320.

6

"Born among the Shells":
The Quakers of Allen's Neck and Their Clambake

Kathy Neustadt

At 7:30 a.m., as the mist burns off the surrounding cornfields, a small group of people begins to gather in the stand of trees where Allen's Neck and Horseneck Roads meet. Peter Gonet arrives first. He parks his pick-up next to the stone wall and hops out to survey the now-empty and quiet scene. Everything is in order: The summer's growth of long grass has been cut back, tables and benches have been laid out on the cross-beamed stumps, the firewood is stacked and dry next to the weathered but intact concrete slab, the rock pile is ample, and the rockweed dumped yesterday is still fresh and moist under the old tent canvas. Best of all, there's not a chance of rain.

Within a few minutes, Peter is joined by his cousin, Burney, his girl-friend, Cathy, Burney's wife, Julie, and Julie and Burney's infant daughter, Corey. Neighboring kids come strolling in to be conscripted, willingly, to help build the fire. Willy brings the kerosene and heads back to pick up his grandson and the other supplies from his store, despite his bad back. As newcomers arrive, yawning and stretching, they form a line and begin passing the melon-sized rocks from the pile by the side of the road to the wooden cribs being constructed on the concrete slab.

Gordon starts unpacking the sausage, butter, and tripe from his van while his brother-in-law, Karl, helps to cover the long tables from the enormous roll of brown paper. Their grandchildren, recently arrived from various parts of the country for the occasion, begin to prepare the food. The sound of their banter as they get reacquainted replaces the chirping of the birds, and they cut and season and twist first sausage, then tripe, and

Figure 6-1.   Building the Bake

Out-of-town and local members of the Parsons and Erickson families form a line to pass rocks from the pile by the side of the road to the clambake structure, where Julie Brown and husband Burney Gifford finish the third of four levels of wood and rocks. *(Photo by the author)* later fish into small brown paper bags. They load the bags into the weathered wooden trays brought out of the small hut at the back of the grove and stack them next to some trees, out of the way.

Pies and brown bread begin to arrive, some of them warm from the oven, and are cut by some teen-aged girls sitting along the tables back by the "cookshack." Paula sits with the brown bread, cutting with care and spreading the pieces evenly around the paper serving plates. The rustic old pie rack is carried out of the shack and soon begins to fill up. Some of the younger boys start to congregate nearby, talking, laughing, their eyes riveted to the rack and its succulent treasures. Two boys drag out the old sign and carry it to the road where they lean it against the stone wall.

Vehicles come and go with great purpose. Raymond drops off the fish and heads down to the beach with the clams—the missing ten bushels are on their way from Maine, he reports, due in around 9:30: he'll be back. Ila backs up the Peugot, and she and her daughter unload its contents onto the handicrafts table—homemade aprons, quilts, and potholders, dried ornamental flowers, and wooden toys. Jewel-colored jams and jellies, perfect vegetables, and Muriel's famous Jim Dandies are spread out across the adjoining food table. Cathy takes off in her pick-up for Tiverton to buy the corn, which is just being picked.

Karl's three-week-old great-grandson is passed from relative to relative, until he falls asleep in his basket under the trees. Corey, after helping with the kindling and twisting a bag or two of sausage, sits with the grapes Julie has brought for her and eats and plays. Both of her grandmothers, Elsie and Norma, stop from time to time to give her a hug as they go about setting up their table. Some of the older men take time out to regale Lewis Coles, the minister, with stories of years past and the way things "used to be done." And as the fire is being lit in one part of the grove, over by the food table, nine-year-old Zachary Smith is challenged to take his first taste of raw tripe.

Away from the tables, back in the trees, the corn is being partially husked, the sweet potatoes hacked into pieces. Onions sit waiting in aluminum pots, surrounded by mounds of corn silk and leaves. The stacks of trays grow higher and more numerous, as these preparations are nearly completed. Now that Burney has tended to it, the fire is burning evenly and hot, and the red flames flare high into the air. "I call this the altar of burnt sacrifices," Lewis jokes. "Reminds me of the primitive religious rites."

Down on the beach, a group of men and a few women kneel in the white sand around two rowboats, filled with water and clams. "I think there must have been a secret society down here, and women weren't allowed," laughs one of the out-of-town Gifford women, "because then we'd have known how much fun it was." One by one, they lift out the clams and

Figure 6-2.   On the Beach
Eric Tardif carries a rack full of clams from the rowboats,
where they have been rinsed and picked over, to the pile
of racks waiting to be transported back to the clambake
grove.
(Photo by the author)

inspect them, tossing all cracked, smashed, and open ones into one bucket and all good ones into another. After the "good" buckets have been emptied into the wooden racks, the racks are stacked in the back of Raymond's truck, and he drives them back to the waiting fire.

The narrow country roads which edge the lot are lined with cars as people holding tickets and silverware begin to arrive. The stillness of morning gives way to the din of midday and the renewal of friendships, strung from year to year in this small grove of trees. The scene is suddenly filled with bright colors, floral prints, and the sheen of pearls, and the gaggle of guests flocks to the sale tables: everyone seems to be carrying potholders and loaves of fresh baked bread. Meanwhile, a group of men in work clothes starts to form around the fire: Peter and Burney, Burney's father, Allen, Raymond back from the beach, Ralph Macomber—Fat Mac, as he is called—the burly sawyer from Acushnet; a few young newcomers who must earn their right to walk into fire, and a few old men who have done their service and earned the right to watch. Julie, her hair tucked up into a baseball cap, wearing a flannel shirt, jeans, and heavy boots, unceremoniously joins them.

A little before noon, a hush descends over the grove, and workers and guests alike begin to form a circle around the fire. Slowly at first, but with increasing speed, Julie and the men step into the fire and with the long-handled pitchforks, pick up the ashen logs and smoldering sticks that are the last remains of the three-hour fire and move them off the slab. Next, moving forward and backward in a dance choreographed by intense heat, they pull the rocks toward them, and Raymond, shielded by his worn fireman's coat and rubber boots, runs down the middle of the slab, where the heat is most intense, pushing the coals and cinders aside until the slab is clear. The rocks are tossed back into place, and, wielding a homemade wooden tool, Fat Mac, shouting orders and red-faced from the heat, remolds the bed to its proper size and shape.

Almost before the silent crowd can take a breath, the sweating crew begins pitching rockweed from the nearby pile onto the rock bed, still white with heat. The sound is like spitting oil, the smell is heavy and pungent; a thick smoke billows upward. Appearing and disappearing through the steam, the workers carry the trays filled with food to the slab and stack them blindly, but carefully, on top of the rocks and the rockweed. Here a tray of gray, striated clams, there a flash of bright orange sweet potatoes; neat rows of brown bags in brown racks, white corn peeking through the brilliant green of tender husk; the silver-foiled pans of stuffing glisten on the top. "Let's go," says Burney, and the parade of men carrying canvases aloft begins. Tarp after tarp is lowered and draped over the food. As a last gesture, the edges are sealed with leftover rockweed.

For the next hour, as the food cooks, people mingle and chat. Snatches

Figure 6-3. The End of the Rake-Out

When the last remnants of wood have been removed, the ashes cleared away, and the hot rocks replaced, rockweed is piled on to produce the steam necessary for a "proper clambake." Food racks will be stacked on top of the rockweed, covered by several layers of tarpaulin, and allowed to cook for one hour.

(Photo by the author)

of conversation, postcards of life: "Stephen, hi. Mrs. Ford. I'm just stopping by for my annual hello. Is your mother here today?" "Yeah, she's on the first table. You haven't met my wife before, have you?" "Last year, for one brief moment. Hello." "So, how are you? Is David still around Boston?" . . . the chatter of reunions overlapping each other, sentences being finished from years past, being started for years to come. "Well, see you next year," they all finish up.

Before long, a new circle has formed around the steaming food, this time to hear Lewis deliver the prayer. His quiet voice drifts in and out of hearing, ". . . the larger family back together again . . . ," drowned out from time to time by the wind and more secular voices. "Heavenly Father," he intones, "we thank you for drawing us together in this gathering of family and friends. We thank you for your providence of nature, from farm and from water, and we thank you for your friendship and fellowship that has developed over the years. We ask that everyone may be blessed by this gathering, and that we may be together again next year. We pray through Jesus Christ, Our Lord."

While the crowd stands still in silence, Ralph Macomber steps forward and pulls up an edge of the tarpaulin mound, reaches into one of the bottom trays, and stands back, holding a single, steaming clam in his hand. He removes the gray morsel from its shell, pops it in his mouth, looks once around the circle of expectant faces, and pronounces in his booming, resonant voice, "It's good."

As if a spring were released, everyone is suddenly in motion. In reverse order now, the bake is opened: the tarps are pulled off, the bottom trays of clams pulled out first. Guests scurry back to their seats while men carry trays of food from the fire to the serving tables. Women and children move the food from the trays to serving bowls and baskets, and rush off to their assigned tables to "wait on" while the food is still hot. Around the eating tables the waiters and waitresses go, then back to the food source, then out again with more food: each table a living, feeding organism with its own distinct style of service.

Before the hour is over, more than 600 people will consume 26 bushels of clams, 200 lbs. of sausage, 165 lbs. of fish, and 175 of tripe; 75 dozen ears of corn, 3 bushels of sweet potatoes, 100 lbs. of onions, 30 trays of stuffing, 15 loaves of brown bread, 50 lbs. of butter, a dozen large watermelons, and more than 50 homemade pies. Before another hour is past, the remains of that meal will be swept up and taken to the dump, serving dishes washed and put away, tables and benches taken up and carried back to the cookshack. Everyone will go home, sated and tired, and in the empty lot the birds will be heard again. The only sign that anyone has been there, a few charred pieces of wood and some warm, melon-sized rocks.

It's been going on like this since 1888. Every third Thursday in August, the members of the Allen's Neck Friends Meeting have joined together with their friends, relations, and neighbors to produce their clambake. Starting out as a simple picnic for the Sunday school, the clambake has become a central event in the larger community's festive calendar—a kind of summer Thanksgiving, "bigger than Christmas," some say—and the major source of funds for the Allen's Neck Meeting. It is also a time of reunion, renewal, and good eating.

It is in the clambake that the people of Allen's Neck also express and celebrate their identity: as Quakers, as Yankees, as farmers and fishermen; in touch with their environment, ecologically and historically, and connected to each other. The success of the Allen's Neck Clambake is due in large part to their artful manipulation of the elements which make up their world, the production of a symbolically powerful and aesthetically rich experience for themselves and the people they serve. It is the purpose of this portrait to show that for the Allen's Neck community putting on their clambake, they are, in the deepest sense, what they eat.

Allen's Neck consists of a tiny strip of land just east of the Rhode Island border and southwest of New Bedford, along the Atlantic coast in southeastern Massachusetts. Originally the home of the Wampanoag Tribe—Acushnets, Appconegansets, and Acoaxets—the area was settled in the mid-1600s by the English immigrants to the colonies of Massachusetts and Rhode Island. Among them, with names like Allen and Slocum, Howland, Smith, Tucker, and Gifford, were Quakers seeking refuge from the religious persecution of the Puritans.

Although according to the map a part of the town of Dartmouth, Allen's Neck constitutes a kind of human ecosystem which includes parts of neighboring Westport, as well as nearby Russells Mills. "It's something about this square mile," Julie Brown says, gesturing across her in-laws' farm on Horseneck Road where she and her husband are building their house. "There are a lot of people that really feel right, here. It's really special . . . really different."

In the symbolic center of the "square mile" is Bald Hill and the Allen's Neck Meeting. The meeting house, which was built in 1873, is one of a half dozen in the immediate area. Ila Gonet, the treasurer of the Allen's Neck Meeting, figures their current membership at 80, "but about 35 or 40 working members." Sunday mornings in the summertime, when the popular Sunday School is closed, there are even fewer: a group of 20 or so women and a few men mostly in their 60s, 70s, and 80s. In the peaceful low-lit stillness of the simple meeting room, it is often difficult to imagine that this is the group which generates the loud and boisterous crowd of 600-plus that descends upon the small plot of oaks just down the road.

Following the course of the Gurneyite or Orthodox Friends, most of the local Meetings are superficially indistinguishable from other liberal Protestant sects: they have "ministers" who conduct "church" services complete with sermons, pastoral prayers, hymn-singing, and an offering. Under pressure from some of the younger members during a short-lived "generation gap" in the early 1970s, a time for silent prayer was set aside during the Allen's Neck service, but it remains a somewhat uncomfortable silence regularly broken by requests to sing favorite hymns.

Allen's Neck Friends consider theirs to be "a community meeting," catering to the needs of the local residents, and they are pleased with the great popularity of their Sunday School, which is attended by many non-Quakers from their midst. The clambake is like the Sunday School in this respect, the ranks of workers being swelled by friendly but unconverted neighbors. "I think it's very gratifying for our Meeting to know that people care enough to work for us that day," Barbara Erickson explains. Or as her brother-in-law, Gordon Parsons, says, "It's pretty ecumenical down there—I don't know what we'd do without them."

Fertile soil and easy access to the ocean have greatly shaped the history of the region. Farmed from the beginning of their settlement, Dartmouth and Westport continue to make up part of the largest remaining agricultural region in the Commonwealth. Once largely poultry farms, today dairy farms predominate. In a move toward specialization, nursery businesses have begun to develop in the area: two very large companies and one moderate but growing newcomer have peppered the landscape with plastic tunnel greenhouses. Across the road from each other, Julie and Ila both carry on herb businesses; nearby, there is a small nursery which raises mums.

Otherwise, traditional farming for a living is growing steadily more difficult. Families continue to own their farms—a few have grown over the years through a merging of family holdings and most have diminished through necessity or disinterest—but few can claim to make an annual income equal to the price being paid for an acre or two of their now-prime residential land. Against the larger drama of the demise of small farming in America, local farmers—or their more urbanized, less tradition-bound heirs—are yielding to the pressures to sell. As a result, developments and condominiums have started to appear in the area, all the while that Boston and Providence sprawl ever closer.

Fishing is not without its own saga. At the time of the White settlement, the well-stocked rivers, streams, bays, and sea made fishing an obvious and rewarding enterprise. But today, between government regulations and man-made pollution, the bounty has been greatly affected. The clams for the clambake, for example, have to be brought down from Maine: the local supply is not dependably sufficient or safe. And mackerel, the traditional fish component since the Bake's beginning, no longer live in these waters in any abundance.

The pollution of the water off New Bedford with highly topic PCBs is only one of the factors affecting the larger patterns of fishing. When Raymond Davoll first started lobstering in the late 50s and early 60s, there were 4 or 5 boats fishing out of Westport; today there are close to 30. Offsetting this kind of competition for a diminishing commodity is the rise in the prices paid for the catch: Raymond remembers his grandfather's stories of selling lobster along the beach in the summertime, off the back of a horse-drawn wagon, for 4¢ a pound; today, some 25 years later, he can expect something in the range of $2.60 a pound.

The whaling industry, which originated on the islands of Nantucket and Martha's Vineyard, took hold in the New Bedford area as early as the mid-1700s and continued down into the 1920s, albeit in much degenerated form. Mary Davoll's father, Raymond's grandfather, was a whaler around the turn of the century. "As I have understood it," Mary tells, "when he wanted to marry my mother, her father took a dim view of whaling and made him give it up." When a man was done whaling, he often settled down on a farm. The demise of whaling represented the first of several major economic depressions in New Bedford, and according to many concerned citizens, the city's growing dependence on the fishing industry as an economic base is capable of bringing on another one.

Whaling also brought the Portuguese to the area, first as seamen, then as immigrants, and New Bedford, through the years, has become a center of Hispanic immigration of several cultures. Another even larger draw for foreign-born immigrants was the mills of New Bedford and Fall River, which attracted large numbers of Poles and Acadian workers from French Canada, as well as the English, with their long tradition of textile work. Over the years, the original urban immigration has filtered out to the rural areas, including Dartmouth and Westport.

"A lot of Portuguese people made their way out to farms," says Allen Gifford. "They were the next ones that took over when the old Yankees petered out on the farms. The Portuguese bought them all, 'cause they were interested in doing that." Many stories about clambakes highlight the good feelings between the two groups, focusing particularly on the generosity of the newer Portuguese residents toward the "birthright" Quakers.

At the same time, the influx of "outsiders" has not been completely free of tension. Jokes about the "greenhorns," quite specifically referring to Portuguese newly arrived in America, are common, if not particularly venomous. Since many of the "old-timers" are by now of mixed heritage, talk like this is often prefaced by statements like, "I'm part Port-a-geeze myself, so it's okay." People also talk about the arrival of the hard-working Portuguese as being a good thing for the community overall, an antidote to a situation which one person described as having been "old Yankee—like this," clenching his fist. According to the internal social history, the original families were starting to intermarry: it was time for some new blood.

Another influx which has been met with a less hospitable reception is that of the gentrifiers, the people from the city who are not farmers but want to live in the country. Scornful of their organic interests, old BMWs, and desire to barter, the old-timers make it clear to the newcomers that true membership in the community could possibly take generations. In this exchange, the much touted Yankee spirit has sometimes been perceived to be cold and unfriendly. The new welcome sign between Route 88 and Central Village, signed "Westport Newcomers' Club," seems at once wry and hopeful.

The substantial summer community in the general vicinity creates additional fodder for tension surrounding membership. Interestingly enough, even the presence of "summer people" has a long history, and at fêtes like the Allen's Neck Clambake, the ticketholders are sometimes second- and third-generation participants. A few years ago in Westport Point, an area considered by the farmers to be tourist-infested and citified, a sign saying "Skewks go home" was posted by some irate local people and triggered a short-lived but heated discussion in the local papers of the nature of the "community."

The term "skewk," according to Julie, is reputed to be an Indian term—making it, therefore, truly authentic—"It was a bird that used to come here from other places, and it would come in and kick out the old birds: not necessarily kick them out, but they'd take all the old nests that the birds had before, and they'd move into the nests for the summer. And they were obnoxious birds, from what the Indians said; the Indians didn't like these birds. And then in the fall, they would head off and leave." To which Burney adds, "leaving everything a pigsty." Many of the older people, particularly, are uncomfortable with this expression of animosity, and with the suggestion that such a rift within the community exists, but "skewk" has become a common idiom among the younger generation.

Feelings are as varied and complex about the term "skewks" as they are about the presence of the people incurring the name, and the larger issues of tourism, progress, and change. Without sentimentality, the people of Allen's Neck appear to be acutely aware of their past and their possible future. Evident among them is an active interest in the aesthetics and form of farming, and they work consciously at being "students" of farm culture.

The depth of knowledge which Allen and Elsie Gifford or Muriel Silvia display in talking about the Shakers and the Amish, for example, exhibits not only their extensive reading about these groups, but their pilgrimages to the others' farms and communities. Elden Mills, "a young preacher, recently out of the cornfields of Indiana" when he came to the Allen's Neck Meeting in 1919, characterizes the people of Allen's Neck through his long years of association with them by their "erudition," and it is undoubtedly this mixture of thought and action to which he refers.

Of their own local history—religious, civic, economic, cultural—people are equally able and eager to speak. They read all of the books written about them and by them and transform the literary materials into an integral part of the traditional knowledge and cultural heritage. For example, *Turtle Rock Tales,* J. T. Smith's privately published booklet of reminiscences, can be found in many neighboring households, and his daughter Barbara Erickson still gives them out to interested readers. The Allen's Neck Friends all own the *Allen's Neck Friends Meeting Cook Book,* which was a fundraising publication with an introductory piece by "Gram" Gladys Gifford and Marjorie Macomber on the history of the clambake—that's how everyone came to know so well when, where, and why Clambake got started.

The Allen's Neck Meeting also has its own library, which is a substantial historical resource overseen by Ginny Morrison, who has recently retired from her professional librarian's work; already one graduate student has used the Minutes of the Meeting as a major source of data for a dissertation on the famous Quaker philosopher/teacher Rufus Jones. Ginny is also the unofficial cataloguer of the myriad articles which have appeared over the years about the Allen's Neck Clambake, although most households have their own copy of one or another of the many clippings.

The *Christian Science Monitor* has published more than one article over the years, and local papers like the *Standard Times* regularly send out a reporter to capture the local color. An article by Raymond Sokolov that appeared in *Natural History Magazine* was later reprinted as a chapter in his book, *Fading Feasts: A Compendium of Disappearing American Regional Foods,* published in 1981, which featured on the cover a picture of the steamy, clam-filled Allen's Neck Bake being opened. Because they are used to reading about themselves, the people of Allen's Neck have become critical readers, and they recognize what good copy the clambake makes.

The clambake, like images of whales and nautical gear, has come to represent New England summertimes in the popular imagination. Pictures of the bounty of the clambake illuminate tourist brochures and inspire feature articles in *Yankee* magazine. At least one how-to clambake book has been printed, and magazines and newspapers throughout the summer are littered with similar hints for favorite pre-bake chowder recipes or hints on using charcoal and aluminum foil as clambake shortcuts. The *New York Times* will have a lead article in "The Living Section" on clambaking in Maine, while *The Boston Globe,* in search of even more exotic angles, will report on how transplanted New Englanders do clambakes in Texas.

Culinary historians have credited coastal Native Americans with the invention of cooking in pits and above-ground earth ovens using coals or heated rocks as the source of heat and water-holding seaweed to produce steam. A more recent culinary past is also accessible, that of the clambake pavillions which flourished during the earlier decades of this century. Clambake pavillions were commercial establishments where people could buy tickets and dine in "family style." More than a dozen of them stretched between the New Bedford/Fairhaven area and Dartmouth-Westport: most of the ones built along the water were lost in the hurricane of 1938; others closed during the years surrounding the Second World War. Currently there is one clambake pavillion nearby in Rhode Island, which serves clambake to corporate groups using gas heat for fire and metal ingots for rocks.

The pavillions guaranteed that clambake was a familiar meal, and that partaking of it was considered a special occasion. Commercial "clamboils" were also a popular form of festive eating: 55-gallon drums filled with rockweed and food, which could cook during delivery, would arrive ready to serve a party of family and friends. "Clamboil" is also the term used by Allen's Neck natives to distinguish prepared meals including clams from the true clambake—because, of course, there's a proper way and an improper way to put on a bake, and there's no telling what you might find in a supposed clambake these days—anything from linguica and hot dogs to chicken and hard-boiled eggs!

Besides the Allen's Neck Sunday School, many community groups used to have clambakes as an annual summer event: the Grange Hall and the fire station; more recently, the congregational church in Padanaram. "Do you remember the stone church in Adamsville?" Gram asks. "I can remember going over there. They sold 1500 tickets, but after that they stopped because it cost so much to hire the help." A lot of the other local bakes folded over time for this same reason: they couldn't find enough people to tend to all of the tasks and details that a good clambake requires.

Raymond Davoll and Robert Wordell, a plumber from Little Compton, began moonlighting as bakemasters in the mid-70s in response to this need, assisted intermittently by a stable of helpers which includes Burney and Peter and now Julie. Acknowledged as the masters of their trade, before the season is over, Raymond and Robert will have put on more than a dozen different clambakes: a few small parties; a couple of summer-crowd functions; the Democratic Bake; and usually a big one over Labor Day weekend at Sakonnet Point—although they've recently been outbid by someone planning to use charcoal briquets. They also do the two at the Russell's Mills fire station, where Raymond is the elected fire chief, one in mid-summer and one after Labor Day.

The characterization of the clambake as a "disappearing regional food-way," made by Sokolov and others, is complicated by the evidence. Although public commercial bakes seem to have diminished, semi-private organizational clambakes, particularly as fundraisers, have become more prevalent. At the same time, the private party *cum* clambake is becoming increasingly popular: Burney and Julie had a clambake as their wedding reception, and although some of their elders still wonder whether this is quite proper, a trend has been set and others have followed. The clambake as a meal has been revived through redefinition, and the spectrum of clambake as an event has been broadened.

This, then, is the larger context in which the Allen's Neck Clambake exists. By looking closely at the Clambake—its organization, the food preparation, the building of the fire, and the service of the meal—a coherent system of meaning begins to emerge. From the annual decision to hold a clambake to the method for stacking the wood to the humble squash pie, every procedure has a history, every item, a memory; and taken together, they constitute an organic, integrated world view. The Clambake serves as an expression of this communal vision that recalls, reinforces, and helps to recreate the community each year, anew.

For the people of Allen's Neck, the natural elements of the Clambake are the natural elements of their environment; the skills required to put on a bake draw on activities learned out in their fields or down in their ocean; the attitude and manner that people bring to the tasks are reflections of what it means to be a Friend in a small community. The traditions of Clambake, like the shape of their houses and barns, have been weathered by time and made venerable. Even change is familiar: like the end of the mills and the demise of whaling, a necessary part of organic life.

In this way, the Clambake is an event inextricably bound up with the overall cultural pattern, values, history and aesthetic of the Allen's Neck Friends, expressing and reifying their farming and fishing culture, Yankee traditions, and Quaker values. According to one member of the Meeting, the Clambake is a religious experience for them, "our most holy day." It is a sacrament of season, a blessing on abundance, a performance of family, and a fleeting but intense celebration of themselves.

Each year the minutes of the Allen's Neck Meeting record the decision that a clambake will be held that year and that the Clambake Committee will be "same as last year;" no names have ever been recorded, no hierarchy set down. So in the spring, when the Committee is called to a meeting, a handful of people show up, almost tentatively, not quite sure whether they're supposed to be there, but knowledgeable in their areas of expertise. "If an emergency came up," Ila points out, "we could do it without a committee meeting because the same people have done the same things right straight down. And if one person has to give it up for some reason, they turn it over to somebody else, their son or their daughter or their friend."

In early July, some 225 notices announcing the Clambake are mailed out, and within a week all 500 tickets are sold and a waiting list of more than 200 is formed. The people buying the tickets are generally from outside of Allen's Neck, people who have moved away but come back for a visit, or summer people; the people who work on the Clambake are the "birthright" community and their returning kin, and the Allen's Neck neighbors. The enormous popularity of the Allen's Neck's Bake, which is a natural function of generational increase further complicated by media coverage, has become somewhat problematic. On the one hand, people delight in telling of the great distances travelled by ticket holders and the long-distance friendships that are established; on the other hand, they are uncomfortable with turning people away and seeming exclusive. It is essentially the same problem which lies behind issues of tourism and influx of new residents.

In early August, the neighborhood begins to buzz again with Clambake activities. The minister makes the announcement in Meeting: don't forget to bring in your baked goods and hand-made items for the sale tables. Gordon calls the butcher about the sausage, tripe, and butter. Raymond takes care of the seafood; Willy puts in an order for sodas and the ingredients for the dressing through his store. Hettie and Ila contact their lists of women making pies and brown bread. Because Ila's son Peter is the bakemaster, he'll be tending not only to the paper goods, corn, and watermelon, but to anything else that is left over. "Same as last year."

In the same way that Allen's Neck people don't generally presume to speak for each other, they all know their own jobs but not much about anyone else's. This becomes particularly clear during the week before the Bake, as the pace starts to pick up. Unheralded, a small crew of men goes to get rocks from the quarry. The heads-of-tables line up their waitresses. No one is quite sure who does it, but the grass gets cut. (It's Willie Morrison.) The table and bench posts have been repaired (Cliff Allen). When the work of Clambake becomes public again late Monday afternoon before the Bake, a core group of families arrive with their out-of-town "company" to help unpack the cookshack, set up tables and benches, and bring dishes out of storage to be cleaned.

On Wednesday, the day before the Bake, more new faces join their grandparents, siblings, and cousins in the rockweed run. The image of a group of people standing in the glistening blue ocean flanked by the steep, grassy knoll and the horses beyond is a rich one. There is much laughter and banter as they work, bent over in the water, hacking at the rocky anchors which hold the slippery weed. Laboring together guarantees a way of knowing each other, and the Yankee ethos of sweat and toil makes manifest its reward of peaceful joy during these times. After the dump truck makes its way back to the bakeground, loaded high with rockweed, brakes squealing, there is nothing left for people to do but go home and wait—and pray for no rain.

The same spirit informs the day of the bake, people working together willingly, joyfully. Work crews for building the fire, preparing the food, setting up the sale tables, and serving the meal form without being officially signalled, without being told, what Norma Judson describes as being "divinely directed, when you don't depend on human organization." It's a style which she recognizes is hard for the outsider to understand, but for the rest, it's simple: "Everyone feels responsible, without saying. I mean, it is an absolute responsibility to be there and to contribute. Very Quakerly."

As the day of Clambake dawns, the activities become more focused: there's the fire and the food. Each of these is worked on separately, usually by different people. For the most part the men tend to the fire, the women to the food. On almost every level, the fire is at the center of the Clambake: it is where the action takes place, where the food is turned into a meal, and where all of the "shows" are performed. When community members discuss the production of "a proper bake," they focus primarily on the materials, skills, technique, and knowledge that the building and burning of the fire require.

But what is "a proper bake," after all, but the successful manipulation of some rocks, wood, and rockweed? Gathered by hand by small groups of men and some women, these elements represent the physical world of Allen's Neck: the same rocky soil that gave birth to ubiquitous stone walls, the trees that surround their farms and give them their special sound, the ocean that reaches out before them. Using tools that are either old farm instruments pressed into annual Clambake duty or are hand-crafted to the special requirements of clambaking, men combine and rearrange the elements of earth and air and water and fire. The combination of heat and moisture which transmutes the food into meal by cooking becomes a kind of allegory for the special alchemy of that place.

The men who become Masters of the Bake are the same ones who have mastered their environment, learned the elements, and made their commitment to the place in other aspects of their lives. It is no coincidence that Peter Gonet and Burney Gifford, who have come back to the farms

Figure 6-4.   Gathering Rockweed
Members of the Allen's Neck Friends Meeting, their
neighbors, and visiting relatives gather at water's edge
during low tide on the day before the bake to pick a
truckload's worth of rockweed.
(Photo by the author)

intending to stay in the area, are serious clambakers, or that Raymond, as master of masterbakers, is such a well-respected seaman. The community recognizes their talents and depends on them, not only to make a clambake proper, but, on the symbolic level, to hold the physical world together and keep Allen's Neck intact. The knowledge of the fire is closely connected in this sense to the ordering of the universe.

At the same time, but on a different plane, the food of Clambake constitutes another sense of order and identity. When articulated, the menu is valued because it is traditional, because it has not been changed over a hundred years. What lies beneath that appreciation and what emerges in the stories the women tell is the texture of the meal as memory, as pleasure revisited, the past revived. Ila dreamily recalls her mother's story about her father and the other men catching mackerel off the shore while the women waited the bake for them. The squash pie she plans to make for this year's Clambake inspires Mary Davoll to tell—in almost poetic form—of the self-sufficiency of her family's farm when she was a girl three-quarters of a century ago. By baking the pies and putting up jams and jellies for the sale tables, the women are transported back through generations of the same activity, are put in touch with each other and a world of women's work and culture which hardly exists anymore.

Common Crackers for the stuffing, Johnnycake Meal for the brown bread, home-baked pies are all "old-fashioned" foods which are almost impossible to find anywhere else, at any other time. Once common, they have become rarefied; once everyday, they have become specialized. They represent a way of eating that is valued because it is both traditional and nourishing. At one time, of course, everything came from their own soil, their own fields: onions, corn, sweet potatoes; from the water, the fish and the clams; from their pigs, the sausage; and from their cattle, the tripe. The food, which is now purchased and brought in—the onions are canned, and the fish sometimes frozen—retains its nourishing quality, its sense of bountifulness, because of these historic and symbolic roots.

"Waiting on," as the service of the food is called, is organized among the women, although male family members are sometimes pressed into serving the tables and routinely carry the trays full of corn, clams, and watermelon. Kids join in as soon as they are able, following their mothers around, carrying platters of food. It gives them something to do, but more than that, it invests them in Clambake itself, so that they will want to come back each year to do more work and new work. As with everything else that is happening that day, people have to find their niche, learn their skills by participation. As Florence points out, "No one tells you anything, you just do it."

The work that goes into the fire and the food becomes rewarding because it is made both personally and communally valuable. In the process, the Clambake becomes a kind of indigenous and organic educational system, a process and method for communicating traditional knowledge. The people who work the Clambake learn what one has to know to perform "a proper bake," but they learn, beyond that, about their world, about their past, by touching it, working with it, listening to and learning its stories. Since every component of the Bake represents a piece of history or an artifact of culture from that community, the transmission is subtle and slow: "It just gets in you over the years," Peter says.

After the details have been explained, the techniques described, the traditional methods and materials traced backward, what the people of Allen's Neck want to tell are those stories. Many of them are public domain and popular: about the one time the Bake didn't cook but no one took their money back; about the couple from Iowa (or Florida or Ohio) who bought tickets but ended up serving, for the fun of it; about the year that it rained and the Holy Ghosters, the local Portuguese brotherhood, so graciously invited the Clambake to use their indoor eating facility just down the road. And the year that they were without a minister, and Jimmy Murphy from down the road—"Father Murphy" they call him now—gave the blessing. Sounding almost biblical in tenor, Karl Erickson recounts the "thing you can hardly say was true because it was so implausible": the time that rain fell in sheets across the road as the clambakers watched in dry amazement, feeling like Chosen People.

Many are private and individual, often humorous, vignettes that evoke the textures of the past: Gram's memory of riding to Clambake in her father's first car, the Rambler, which had to go up hills in reverse; the image that Elsie has of young Burney sitting on the back of his father's water truck, eating peanut butter sandwiches because he didn't like the taste of clambake. "People say, 'Why is the Clambake held on Thursday?'—there's a good reason for it," and accomplished oral historian Willy Morrison proceeds to tell about the marketing habits of the local farmers. "They went to town on Wednesdays, and on Wednesdays they could bring back your sausage and your tripe and the stuff that you just didn't make on the farm. So simple—Wednesday was city day. It was city day still when I was growing up."

In a community where silence is valued and emotions are rarely articulated, stories are intended to illustrate what Clambake really is and really means, to show its essence. As they accrue, they can be seen to communicate deep emotions about a rich past. Not nostalgia, since that implies a longing for things passed away, but an appreciation and reverence for what has come before, as the foundation for what is now present. It is not just a life that was simpler, less "regulated," less heavily trafficked that is being described, but a world where there was an integrity of thought, deed, and faith: Clambake is both a microcosm of this world and a symbol for its ideal image.

What many of the stories seem to be trying to capture is a message about the goodness of people, particularly as they are inspired by the Bake. Like the year one of the kids had a hurt back and was brought to Clambake in a body cast: his friends took turns playing with him in the back of the station wagon so he wouldn't miss the fun. And don't forget that Julie and Burney rediscovered each other at the Allen's Neck Clambake, first as neighbors and later as sweethearts. Florence Smith, who as ticket seller has learned to say "no" to the most baroque of pleas, will admit that she always let that one little man with the cherubic smile in without a ticket, because "he just had faith."

Together, the group constructs through a vision of the perfect community, laboring together, serving themselves by honoring their neighbors, breaking bread with, in some respects, their enemies. It is a vision not far from reality. In ecumenical harmony, the neighbors are all there working, no matter where they go to church on Sunday. The "skewks" eat their meals voraciously but in peace, and forgive their hosts' trespasses, as they forgive those trespassing against them. Generations work together without friction and with respect; indeed, Clambake is a ritual meant for growing up in, and every age can find an appropriate task. There is a flow between the work of men and the work of women, a bridge between their worlds which is necessary to the production and fertility of the Bake. The themes are of harmony which is permanent and ever-changing, and of connectedness with nature, humanity, and divinity.

Norma figures that she can see Clambake for what it really is because she's a "newcomer." Perhaps she can, because she expresses some of what is normally only intuited: "We are going through a type of ritual that we look forward to and live for from one Clambake to the next . . . and I think the ritual of Clambake sustains the tradition. The ticket holders are surely well fed, but it's the workers that are nourished. And it's a wonderful feeling, because I know that on the third Thursday of every August through eternity, I am going to have a child there, a grandchild there, or a great grandchild there, and on, and on, and on. And it's an unspoken thing—I've never really said this before—but I would dare say that everyone would agree with me."

Notes

I would like to express my deep gratitude to the members of the Allen's Neck Friends Meeting and to the community as a whole for allowing me to work on this project with and among them. They have tolerated my being underfoot with unfailing patience, bemusement, and good humor, and I dedicate this chapter to them as my first readers. As an academic project, the study of the clambake has provided me with exciting intellectual insights into the process of folklore, of tradition and innovation, the dynamics of festivity, and the complexities of community. More importantly, however, my own personal life has been greatly enriched by getting to know these people—and their clambake—better.

7

Hog Killing in Virginia: Work as Celebration

Barbara C. Fertig

Unlike the hog butcherings that most country people recall so fondly, this one is a modest celebration, even as hog killings go—no flurry of advanced preparations, nor any concluding feast of fresh pork to memorialize either the bonds between the workers or the prodigious richness of the meat. The setting is historical, the shore of the James River in Virginia where American hog raising began. English pigs arrived with the first English settlers of Jamestown, and generations of Virginia hogs destined to be cured to the area's distinctive dry-salt "country" taste have fed on acorns from the abundant local oak forests.[1] The best-known brands of Virginia country hams are cured nearby, both in Surry and in Smithfield, a few miles east, and some of the men who take part in this backyard event also raise hogs for the Gwaltneys, the Edwards, and the Luters, the best known packers of Virginia country hams.

Some of the festive events that we might have expected are missing from this contemporary hog killing. Here, on the James River in the 1980s, there is no music, no dancing, no open-fire roasting of fresh pork such as one might still find in a Cajun *boucherie* in which the pig is transformed on the spot into *boudin* sausage to provide an immediate feast for the family and invited guests.[2] There is one communal meal, served to family members on Saturday, but its contents owe little to the hog. Paved roads and pick-up trucks have lessened the need to provide communal meals for participating neighbors, although the rounds of coffee shared by the men who come to kill hogs on Friday provide a residual version of this social time. There are also two occasions for sampling the new meat, and these are highlights in the second day's proceedings, but the celebration itself appears to reside in the shared labor of transforming the natural pig into the cultural pork. This labor, in which every family member (and every friend as well) finds his or her own niche, binds the laborers together as one performing machine, and might be compared to singing in harmony or ensemble playing.

In fact, it is the work itself that is celebratory and festive—the harmony of working hard together and bonding with old times and old ways, reaffirming family and neighborly ties, and creating a communal opportunity to exercise direct control over at least one small piece of nature. This event is much more than just a job to be done, and just as clearly, it is no longer a necessity. Indeed, this backyard butchering takes place within a few miles of some of the world's most sophisticated machinery for accomplishing the same job in minutes rather than days. But the neighbors who come by to lend a hand, and the family that hosts the killing, are pleased to take this time out of busy lives and proud of their performance and its results.

Eight o'clock on a January morning in Southeastern Virginia: we are standing outside the kitchen of Mr. and Mrs. James Holt, whose farm lies about halfway between the village of Surry and the island in the James River where the Jamestown settlement once confined their pigs. James Holt says his family has been in Surry County since the early 1860s; Doris Barnes, one of Holt's sisters, says much longer than that. But they "don't rightly know for sure." James was six months old when the family moved into the house (a white clapboard I-house) in which they continue to live, but Doris points out that he was one of the youngest of several children. Certainly the Holt family is widely known and respected in the community. Wallace Edwards, the premier hog packer of Surry County, whose business is producing fine Virginia hams, sausage, and bacon, says that "James is known to everyone in Surry as somebody who does things right; everyone can see that his fields are always neat and well-tended. Back when we slaughtered for the business, we always bought James's hogs. He's known for good quality livestock."

It's cold on this January morning, the traditional kind of weather needed for backyard hog butchering. There isn't enough sun to mitigate the sharpness of the wind. The only relief, until the hard work of hog killing starts, is to wrap my hands around a mug of Mrs. Holt's coffee, strong and good, and stamp my feet, like the dozen or so neighbors who have shown up early on this Friday. Some are here because they have brought their own hogs to the Holt killing, to take advantage of the assembled manpower and equipment. Others, like hog grower Billy Savedge, have already slaughtered for the year, and are here because they enjoy working alongside their neighbors, or know that their particular expertise is needed. (In Billy's case, both pertain.)

Billy's son, a commercial airline pilot, will also lend a hand wherever it's needed. (Billy himself is a recreational pilot, keeping a plane at the end of a peanut field.) His son says he never misses a local hog killing if he can get the time off. Getting time off is an issue for many of these men, some of whom sport the logo of the nearby Surry nuclear power plant on their peaked caps, who supplement farming with wage work. James Holt, as host of this killing, must coordinate several schedules to find a day that accommodates all his neighbors. He must also consider the routines of his own family members: both the men who are working with him today, and the women who will spend the following day converting his hog carcasses into table meats must sandwich the event between the work week and Sunday morning services. He performs this service, as he has for years, because it is an important event to his family, and because his neighbors want to be included.

We're joined by Wallace Edwards. He can't stay for the killing, but has stopped in for coffee and a round of talk with his neighbors. Dick Edwards is recounting how a hot air balloon stampeded his hogs, causing injuries that will make his herd virtually unmarketable. The men explore the vagaries of insurance, and swap information on breeding, feed, and farrowing crates. Everyone is waiting for Holt to declare that the water in his scalding tank has reached exactly the right temperature. He follows his father's tradition, putting long-needled pine sprays in the water to augment the action of wet heat in loosening the pigs' bristly hair. The round-bottomed tank, long enough to hold two hogs snout to tail, abuts a plank table on one end. On the table James Holt has set out scrapers and metal hooks with handles. In southeastern Virginia, oyster shells are traditionally used as bristle scrapers, but Holt uses his father's equipment, in this case serrated metal rings attached to a handle.

"My daddy killed hogs to sell to the lumber companies, back around 1925," says Holt, by way of explaining his highly efficient setup. "There were oak forests all around here in those days, but they took out all the trees and now they're gone out of business." These days, a demand for regional delicacies has put profit back into pig raising in southeastern Virginia.

When the water in the tank has reached the proper temperature, Holt rakes the fire from under it and banks the coals around a small recirculating system attached to the tank. Mrs. Holt reminds us that we know where the coffee pot is, and disappears through the kitchen door. Four of the men, one carrying a rifle, another a large knife, set off for the holding pen that Holt has arranged on the far side of his "washhouse": a three-crib barn with a fireplace that stands opposite the smokehouse on the far side of Holt's yard.

Among the men who remain around the scalding tub, the conversation shifts from news, gossip, and joke-telling to reminiscences of former hog-kills and other earlier ways. Holt tells about Christmas among his eleven brothers and sisters when the family was materially poorer and a pair of hand-knit mittens was sufficient token of the spiritual warmth they exchanged. Someone else picks up the theme and soon the older men are remembering simple toys and simple pleasures from the past. To some extent they appear to be expositing for the benefit of the younger men, who rejoin by remarking on their elders' inability to live any simpler a life than their children in the consumerized present. A pattern is thereby established that will characterize the men's conversation as they work together: a thread of reminiscence is established and elaborated by individual anecdotes, then cut, before it becomes emotionally overcharged, by wry humor. During the morning's work all of the men will have contributed some slice of memory, and almost everyone will have made a definitive, deflating crack that returns the conversation to the present, and to their shared attitudes on politics, economics and family values. And as they work they demonstrate their cohesiveness not only in attitude but in kinetic and proxemic relationships as well.

The first three hogs have been shot in turn and their throats cut after death to bleed them and begin the process of lowering their body temperature. They are brought across the yard on a flatbed truck and unloaded, one at a time, into the scalding tub. A hundred-and-eighty pound hog carcass is difficult to maneuver; three or four men, using hooks to get a purchase on the carcass, must move together, staying out of each other's path, or risk dropping the hog and contaminating the meat. From this point until the carcasses grow rigid and are easily handled, the men will move together eleven times from flatbed to gallows in a somewhat graceless but efficient choreography.[3]

Holt directs the sequences from his position at the scalding tub, while he turns the floating hog with a long, sturdy pole and tugs at the hair until it comes away easily. With the help of a pole-wielding assistant he then levers the carcass up to the surface where men standing on the plank table can hook into it and drag it out of the tub. Many hands now grab at the bristles; the carcass is literally snatched bald before the skin cools; then knives and scrapers are used to shave the hog carefully, thoroughly, until it is a glistening white. (All hogs—red, black, or spotted—have white skins, and begin to look more or less identical as they pass through the various slaughtering operations. Just as in the commercial abbatoirs, the work of processing a pig on the Holt farm takes place on a disassembly line, hog after hog progressing from station to station where a team of men perform the operation that each does best.[4] An unvarying sequence in the killing

Figure 7-1. The Second Hog of the Morning is Wrestled from the
Scalding Tank
At left, James Holt, host of the butchering, guides the
carcass with a stout pole. The first hog to come out of
the tank rests on the plank table. Note the scrapers near
the carcass, used by the Holt family for more than sixty
years.
(Library of Congress photo; photo by the author)

process is carefully observed so that, at the end, each man will know where his own hogs are in the general order.)

The men who cleaned it will now hang the carcass by hooking the gambrel stick over a structure they call a gallows: a pole, set on a series of wood tripods, higher from the ground than the length of the longest pig. Here the last team deftly eviscerates the carcass, taking great care not to puncture internal organs that might contaminate the meat. Neighbor Earl Stewart does all the cutting; Rob Jacobs, who is married to Holt's daughter Marsha, stands ready to lend Earl a hand and perpetually sharpens knives for him.

As the first Holt hog is gutted, Mrs. Holt pops through the back door with an enamelled basin to collect a liver for lunch. She acknowledges that her doctor has advised her not to eat organ meat; this one liver (which completely fills her frying pan) will be a special treat; the others will be set aside for scrapple. A discussion of organ meats and treats ensues; everyone agrees that they have gone out of favor. The older men remember meals of "haslet hash"—lungs stewed with onions and potatoes—and the younger express relief at not having such dishes in their diet.[5]

Before noon all eleven hogs are decapitated, eviscerated, and fitted with stretchers—sticks that hold the cavity open. They will hang on the gallows to cool, looking like so many bleached union suits on a laundry line, until late afternoon. The men clean scrapers, knives and hooks and assist Holt in draining and disassembling the scalding tank. The scraping table is taken apart and, with the tank, stored in Holt's equipment shed, a large prefab metal structure. The hog bristles are raked up and removed; the ground hosed. Holt instructs the other hog owners regarding the hour, later this day, when they will assemble to move the carcasses into the smokehouse for the night; to the rest he announces that the "cutting-out" will begin the next morning promptly at eight.

James Holt's yard is a little damp, and, of course, eleven carcasses hang beside the smokehouse; otherwise there is no evidence of all that hogs and men have been through this morning. Holt's sense of order is as palpable in the follow-through as it is in the midst of activity. Throughout the hauling, slipping, bumping and shouting along the disassembly line, he has remained calm, deliberate and alert to every movement made or required to get the job done. Every other man defers to him and listens to his instructions as if hearing them for the first time, and whatever their own styles of working might be, they respect (and perhaps enjoy) his meticulous approach. On Saturday one of his daughters will remark, with wry humor, "Here comes Daddy; now you *know* you've got to get it right." The essence of hog killing at James Holt's is, indeed, getting it right. Wallace Edwards, who has a fine sense of the history of the region's hog culture, assures me that I'm witnessing "how it's *supposed* to be done, the old, country way."

Saturday is colder but brighter; the sun bounces off white hog carcasses and makes the men squint as they work. Holt has prepared for the "cutting out," as the process of transforming pig into pork is called, by setting up the plank table in front of the smokehouse door. Inside the smokehouse the carcasses have been hanging overnight in the same order in which they were killed. As each in turn is wrestled through the door and heaved onto the planks, the owner is identified and the first cut determined by how he wants the backbone treated. Holt and his family use pork chops and a variety of loin roasts, so his carcasses can be cut in thirds horizontally through the backbone. One neighbor wants a "whole loin roast"; the carcass of one of his pigs is cut carefully from shoulder to tail, leaving both sides of the tapering loins attached to the backbone. Another neighbor loads a smaller carcass in his truck without any cutting; it will be used whole for a pork barbecue.

Once again tasks are assumed by the men with greater expertise; the younger men hold the carcass while Billy Savedge and Dick Edwards make the basic cuts with axes and cross-cut saws. Everyone joins in the trimming of the larger cuts; Rob Jacobs begins his second day of keeping the knives sharp both here and in the washhouse, where the Holt women will whittle the large slabs of meat into table cuts, sausage and fat cubes for the lard kettle.

The men who are taking their own carcasses home have lined their truck beds with heavy plastic sheeting. Further processing of their meat will be done in their own homes, although they may come back to the Holt place to use the sausage grinder. As Holt's carcasses are cut into manageable pieces he sets aside hams, bacon and shoulders. The rest of the meat—ribs, side meat, belly and back—is taken in tubs to the washhouse and dumped in piles on a table running nearly the length of the long, shed-like room. One end of the shed is all fireplace, and the fire warms the room about half way to the outside door at the other end. On the long outside wall are windows, and the work table is pushed against this wall both to take advantage of the light, and also because the room is too narrow for the women to be able to use both sides of the table. Nancy Rorrer, one of Holt's daughters, hands me a knife. If I am going to take up space, I might as well be useful.

In the center of the yard Holt has set out the lard kettles, supported on a few firebricks. Kenny Rorrer, Nancy's husband, is preparing a small fire under one kettle. Several of the grandchildren hover and are sent to gather twigs to feed the fire. Ken explains to me that the fire is fed only with these

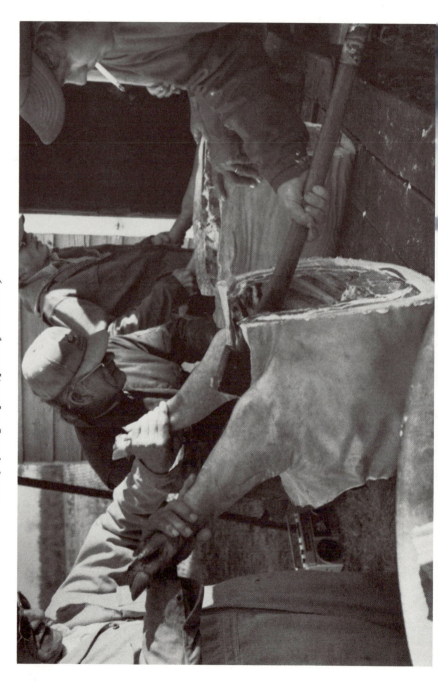

Figure 7-2. **Billy Savedge Holds the Front Quarters while James Earl Holt Uses an Ax to Split Them** Further down the table Dick Edwards and Earl Stewart work on the disassembly line. *(Library of Congress photo; photo by the author)*

small sticks so that it will not flare up and scorch the fat. By the time he has heated the first kettle, and kindled a fire under the second, Rob emerges from the washhouse with a tubful of one-inch cubes of pure white fat. He dumps the tub into the heated kettle and Ken begins to stir with a long-handled, oar-shaped paddle. The fat hisses and growls as it strikes the hot iron, and Ken stirs rapidly, coaxing the mass of cubes into swirls of movement so that nothing sticks or scorches. His job will become easier as the fat liquifies, protecting further tubfuls from contact with hot iron. Ken remarks with evident pride that this has become his traditional task since joining the family, although he is still apprenticed to James' sister, Hilda Scott, the family expert in matters of rendering and of much that is accomplished in the washhouse.

As he stirs, Ken also moves the fire with a rake, keeping it to the windward of the kettle. The heat blows toward the kettle now, and is less direct, another safeguard against scorching. Under Ken's supervision, the children are allowed to feed the fire with the sticks they've gathered. Doris Barnes warns them, "Play with fire and you'll wet your bed, you know. That's what *we* were told when we were children." Spirits undampened, the children intersperse fire-watching with horseplay, although one or two of the older children seem intent on learning from Ken, and are allowed to help with the raking and banking of the coals.

The younger cousins enjoy the freedom to run and shout that the Holt farmyard affords them, but occasional minor scrapes and grievances are taken to the washhouse to be settled by Holt's three daughters, Nancy, Marsha Jacobs, and Jackie Scarborough, or by great-aunts Hilda and Doris. The washhouse is also a good place to warm hands and feet, to store and retrieve toys and precious miscellany found in the farmyard, or just to check in with mom, so that the door is often open, to the discomfort of whoever is working at the near end of the table. The women are therefore in the habit of alternating positions, declaring that they are "freezing their butts" and moving to the fireplace end of the room. Since everyone near the fire is "frying" the same part of their anatomy, they move down the line, each spending some time in the comfortable zone halfway between fire and draught.

Each new crack about anatomy invokes a small round of gleeful sexual innuendos that trade on the thorough knowledge of each family member about the habits, personalities, and situations of all the others. The day's talk in the washhouse, carried on amid the comings and goings of men and children, and necessary attention to other tasks in yard and kitchen, explores the lives of family members present and absent, catches up on illnesses and cures, vexations and celebrations, and dwells generally on relationships among them all. When the men, who come to deliver meat, sharpen knives or warm themselves, join the conversation, it is usually with a quip or good-humored barb, although no one's wit is quicker or sharper than Nancy's. No man, not even Earl Stewart, who comes in at one point to use the sausage grinder, is able to escape without a round of feminine chuckles to speed him out the door.[6]

The main business in the washhouse is the cutting of side meat and trimmings into cubes: pure fat for lard, and mixed lean and fat for sausage meat. The fat cubes exit rapidly into the kettles in the yard, and soon Kenny sends one of the children into the house to summon James's nephew, James Earl, who has just finished with the cutting out, to stir the second kettle. James Earl, his wife Carolyn, and Ken will alternate at the kettles until the last cube has given up its weight of lard. Meanwhile the sausage meat piles up in plastic-lined tubs. Finally one of the grandchildren is sent to inform Holt that it's time to set out the grinder, which Billy Savedge brought over earlier in the week. The electric-powered commercial grinder is Billy's contribution to community hog processing and an innovation this year. Until he found this "good buy" on a used machine, sausage grinding went on for hours.

Although room is at a premium in the washhouse, a smaller table is set up midway between door and fireplace for the grinder after a trial run in the yard proves impractical. Nancy feeds the cubes into the funnel and Marsha catches the ground sausage meat in a basin, then empties it onto a well-scrubbed section of the worktable. While the sausage is being ground, Jackie, Doris, and Hilda are occupied with trimming and cleaning spare ribs and roasts at either end of the table. In order to escape the extremes of temperature they must maneuver past Nancy, Marsha, and the grinder, and more anatomical jests are forthcoming. At this moment Earl Stewart arrives to use the grinder, and is welcomed with high humor, despite the intensified crowding. Nancy and Marsha take up knives and spareribs until he is finished, then go back to grinding until all the sausage meat is processed and ready to be seasoned.

The Holt family prefers to flavor their sausage with a commercial seasoning containing a healthy amount of cayenne pepper. Each packet of spices seasons a given weight of meat, and Doris asks that her batch of sausage not exceed the manufacturer's specifications. The correct amount of ground meat is weighed out; then Marsha empties a bag of spices into it and kneads it well while Hilda explains that she is not only mixing in the seasoning but helping to distribute fat evenly through the leaner meat. When Marsha decides that the mixture feels right, Hilda rubs a pinch between her thumb and fingers, and concurs. Nancy and Jackie remark that it also looks right to them. A small amount is sent by child messenger to the kitchen to be cooked up and tasted. The first batch suits Doris fine, but isn't spicy enough for the others. Mixing, frying, and tasting proceed until the proportion of spice to meat is nearly double and the flavor is bracing, but still fresh and sweet. When the washhouse brigade declares the seasoning perfect, Mrs. Holt fries up a generous round of miniature patties to be shared with everyone on the premises.

"*This* is what we do all this work for," says Nancy.

"This, and the slice of fried ham next Christmas morning," says Marsha.

In the house Mrs. Holt has had a busy morning. Her helpers include James Earl's wife, Carolyn, and Betty Martin, who explains her presence as "just a friend of the family who got hooked years ago and wouldn't miss this day for anything." Together they have produced a noon meal for the work force: fifteen adults and assorted children. The meal is served in two seatings so that work can proceed uninterrupted in yard and washhouse, and also because Mrs. Holt's generous dining room table is so covered with food that it just can't accommodate everyone at once. The menu includes beef stew, navy beans, snap beans, scalloped apples, cornbread cakes fried in lard, whipped potatoes, sweet potato pudding, bread and butter and iced tea. During dinner we have a chance to visit with Sadie Anderson, James's older sister. Her fading eyesight and a hip injury limit Sadie's participation, but, like Betty, she has no intention of missing this occasion. When the first shift has finished, the table is quickly reset and more steaming bowlfuls are produced. As we return to the yard Betty presses more hot and crispy corn cakes upon us.

When dinner is over, Holt places a sturdy bench near the kettles and sets up the lard press. By now contents of the first kettle are nearly all liquid lard. The airy pillows of fat tissue—the cracklings—are the golden brown ghosts of the glistening white cubes. Aunt Hilda fishes a cube out of the kettle, cools it a bit and breaks it open.

"Not ready yet," she announces, showing Kenny that some white fat remains in the center of the cube. In a short time, however, the first kettle is done to her satisfaction: the cracklings are empty cubes, evenly brown inside and out. Nancy is called out of the washhouse to operate the press. Using a saucepan as a ladle, she fishes cracklings from the kettle into the perforated bucket that lines the chamber of the press. When it is full she pivots the lid into place and turns a crank which lowers the bucket into the chamber, squeezing the cracklings and forcing a stream of hot lard out of a spigot at the bottom. The lard is collected in clean five-gallon tins which will be sealed when cool and stored in the cellar for Mrs. Holt's shortening needs.

By the time the lid has been cranked all the way down and the clear stream of lard has become an occasional drip, almost the entire work force has gathered, and Jackie emerges from the house with a salt shaker and a plate covered with paper towels. Nancy opens the press and pulls out the liner, now full of slightly flattened, crisp, hot cracklings. She dumps them on the the plate, salts them, and hands them around.

"They're really not good for you," she says, popping a few into her mouth. The plate is quickly cleaned, and the cracklings are pronounced "very good this year."

"That's because these hogs were killed on the decrease[7] of the moon," Aunt Hilda remarks. "If James had killed on the increase of the moon, the fat would have swelled, and it would have taken forever to brown." She goes on to explain how the phases of the moon affect not only hog killing but crop planting as well. "Plant crops that produce above the ground, like beans and corn, on the increase of the moon, or the flowers will fall off and the fruits won't set, they say. But crops that produce below the ground should be sowed on the decrease of the moon, or they're supposed to rot."

Nancy produces a second batch and this proves enough to satisfy everyone's crackling craving. The rest will be used up in the next week or so in corn cakes (crackling bread), and biscuits. While she waits for the second kettle to fry out, Nancy rejoins the crew in the washhouse.

Nearly two hundred pounds of sausage meat has been seasoned and kneaded to perfection; three kettles full of fat have been cubed for lard, twelve shoulder roasts, twelve butts, twelve loins, and twelve racks of spareribs have been trimmed, inspected for bone splinters and sent to the house where Mrs. Holt, Betty, and Carolyn have wrapped each portion in freezer paper and divided it into shares according to the preferences of each family member. Now the last task of the day is unavoidable: cleaning the chines, or neck bones.

"I hate this," says Nancy, making disgusted noises in the back of her throat. When Aunt Doris earnestly insist that chines make delicious stew, all three sisters pretend to gag. By now the women in the washhouse have been on their feet, bent over the worktable, alternately chilled and over-heated, for more than six hours, but if they are tired, they are still in fine humor. As they work at the somewhat gory task of cleaning the chines, the sisters are overcome by a bout of silliness and make every effort to top each other's stomach-turning suggestions for using the waste they are discarding. Doris remarks that only because they have been spoiled by growing up in time of plenty are they able to regard certain wholesome foods as distaste-ful. The younger women wholeheartedly and mirthfully agree, and before the laughter is done the chines are cleaned, tossed into the last tub, and sent to the packing crew in the house.

All the lard has been pressed, cooled and sealed. The men have cleaned and stored the kettles and the press. The fires are out and the coals raked into the grass, and Rob has gone off to work the night shift on the James

River ferryboat. Across the yard, Holt is working in the smokehouse. He has covered the earth floor with plastic sheeting and laid out a dozen hams, shoulders, and sides of bacon. Two heads have also been preserved for making scrapple; the rest were sold the day before to an elderly black man who also makes scrapple from them, as well as a kind of hash of ground skin, onions and potatoes he calls "hog's head pie." The oblique light of sunset fills the smokehouse as Holt sprinkles the meat with saltpeter. He will wait two or three days, "until the body heat is out of them," to begin curing his meat in a bed of dry salt.

Holt closes the door to the smokehouse, and the sun, about to disappear, turns it golden. Once again the yard bears no witness to all that has transpired. The family loads their cars with tired-looking children and boxes full of wrapped packages. Occasions for visiting each other are discussed before departure, but since everyone lives within fifty miles of the farm, no special farewells are exchanged. The last headlights sweep the field beyond the washhouse and head down the road toward the river. We have been witness here to two days of hard work, some would say old-fashioned work, but work that has been moved by the larger context in the contemporary world further along the continuum from necessary work toward celebratory work, work as a festive affirmation of identity. The community has been recreated through the performance of shared labor connecting it with family traditional life even more surely than it is through such a public display of Surry County's three major industries as the "Pork, Peanut, and Pine Festival" held annually in July at the Chippokes Plantation,[8] a mile down the road from the Holt farm. Here at Jim Holt's place, the performance has been for the community itself and perhaps needs no wider audience.

Notes

1. In the twentieth century the oak forests have been depleted by over-logging, and area hog growers now depend on commercial feeds. Before the advent of expensive harvesting machinery, which their rooting habits would damage, hogs were also allowed to glean peanut fields, but according to hog growers and ham producers in Surry, the belief that Virginia hams come from peanut-fed hogs is a "myth."

2. Charlotte Paige Gutierrez, "Foodways and Cajun Identity," (Ph.D. diss., University of North Carolina at Chapel Hill, 1983). For other reports on hog butchering, see, e.g., "Slaughtering Hogs," "Curing and Smoking Hog," and "Recipes for Hog," *The Foxfire Book,* ed. Eliot Wigginton (Garden City, N.Y.: Anchor Books, 1972): 189–207. Nearly ten years ago, Howard Wight Marshall reported that "custom" butchering had largely replaced home butchering in rural Missouri in "Meat Preservation on the Farm in Missouri's 'Little Dixie'," *Journal of American Folklore* 92 (1979): 407, 413.

3. The term is more apt than poetic if one remembers that choreography is passed from dancer to dancer by demonstration, observation, and repetition; these men work together as they saw their fathers and elders work, year after year, hog after hog.

4. Earl Stewart maintains that his neighbors just *say* he's the best hand at gutting the pig because they don't want to do it. He does, however, perform a crucial task flawlessly.

5. As the men's conversation has clearly established, these Virginia farmers have a solidly middle-class approach to material life. It is not surprising, therefore, to find that they have a distaste for organ meats, which Mary Douglas reports are ranked as lower class, uncivilized cuts. See her discussion of meat as social metaphor in "Standard Social Uses of Food: Introduction," in *Food and the Social Order* (New York: Russell Sage Foundation, 1984), 49.

6. See Erving Goffman's elaboration of "backstage" behavior in *The Presentation of Self in Everyday Life* (Garden City, New York: Doubleday Anchor Books, 1959), 128; also his reference to women's attitudes toward backstage activity, p. 113.

7. Waning. Likewise, the "increase" of the moon is the waxing phase.

8. See Alice M. Geffen and Carole Berglie, *Food Festival: The Ultimate Guidebook to America's Best Regional Food Celebrations* (New York: Pantheon Books, 1986, 96–100). Chippokes is "a model working farm that displays and recreates day-to-day activities of Virginia farm life from the past three centuries." But it does not recreate a hog butchering.

Fieldwork for this article was done as part of an American Folklife Center/Library of Congress Fieldwork project.

8

No Smoke? No Fire:
Contemporary Hamming the Ol' Fashioned Way

Amy E. Skillman

"Tell you what I go by, all right? See that pond up yonder? When there's ice on that pond, I'm ready for hamming." That's what Bud Gardner told me a year ago September when I went to visit him to learn a little about curing hams. So when I drove past the pond near my house one November day and noticed that there was ice around the edges, I hurried home and called Bud to make sure I hadn't missed his hamming. "Oh, no," came his easy response. "We'll be startin' on November 25th. Just get here 'round noon and you won't miss a thing. Should be done by 3:00."

Ham curing in Boone County, Missouri has been part of community life since the mid-1800s. With the exception of Columbia, which is the seat of the University, Boone County is a rural county with an economy based on soybeans, sorghum, corn and hog farming. Situated in central Missouri, Boone County is one of several counties in a vernacular region known as "Little Dixie . . . a section of central Missouri where southern ways are still much in evidence—an island in the lower Midwest settled by migrants mostly from Virginia, Kentucky, Tennessee, and the Carolinas, who transplanted social institutions and cultural expressions to the new landscape."[1] Today, its traditional music, language, religious customs, architecture and foodways reflect those brought to the area by English, Scottish and Irish farmers travelling along the Lewis and Clark Trail from the upland South.

William "Bud" Gardner, 92 years old, has been a farmer in the area all his life raising cattle, corn, and soybeans. His family was one of the early farming families in the Boone County area of Little Dixie, and having grown up on a farm he learned traditional curing as a boy, not as something to do for a living but as part of his traditional life. At the same time, however, the Gardner family has provided civic and social leadersip in the community.

Bud, for example, was instrumental in bringing the rural electric cooperative to the area and has served as a member of its Board of Directors for years. He is on the Administrative Board of his church and a long-time member of the Optimist International Club. He and his family were among the first to cooperate in the Soil Conservation Service's Boone County Soil Conservation District, using their own farm equipment to construct terraces and waterways designed to conserve soil and improve pastures on the farm. Bud told me that when he and his family moved to Missouri, their farm became known as the Model Farm of Missouri. Neighbors have always looked to the Gardner family for help and guidance in farming practices.

Although Bud has been curing hams just about all his life, he'll tell you he has been curing hams for 43 years because it was in 1945 that he won his first Boone County Ham Contest. It was also then that the Boone County Fair had its first ham contest and ham breakfast. The event was initiated by Robert E. Lee Hill, a public relations specialist who was to become the greatest promoter of Boone County hams. Since that first blue ribbon in 1945, Bud has won enough contests, including several at the Missouri State Fair, to fill a display case with trophies. Yet he maintains that the Boone County Fair contest is the most important because Boone County has a reputation for the best ham curing in the world. Some say it is the climate. Mid-Missouri lies in a thin belt across the upland South which has moderate temperatures ideal for ham curing. Others say it is the quality of the corn raised to feed the hogs, and still others say the hogs themselves believe that their transition from pork to ham is a "plunge into gastronomic immortality." Good karma, good ham.

Meat preservation has continued as a tradition in Little Dixie. Families still gather in late autumn for the annual hog killing, and smokehouses dot the rural landscape. Bud and his wife Phala have demonstrated their curing and cooking techniques at Folklife Festivals in Missouri and at the World's Fair in New Orleans. So when I headed out to Bud's house on that November day, I expected to find an old smokehouse and a secret cure that had been passed from father to son for generations. What I found, instead, was a highly regimented curing process in a USDA-approved facility where the floor and tables are spotless, the meat is cooled to a specified temperature before curing, and a pre-mixed commercial cure is slightly modified but kept within federal government regulations—but no smoke. It was then that I began to realize: it is the *event* rather than the technique or cure which has remained traditional in the Gardner family for generations and which serves as an important marker of community identity and values.

When I arrived, I walked into a chilly wooden-framed structure about 30 feet wide and 60 feet long with an open-beamed ceiling. Over 500 wooden pegs, each one about five inches long, studded the beams overhead in an alternating pattern. A few hams from last year's curing hung in the front corner and were displayed for prospective buyers on a table to the right. Two long metal tables, the sort you might find in the kitchen of a restaurant, were positioned in the middle of the southern half of the building.

Bud greeted me in his white overalls and led me to the house where I was introduced to a few of the men and women who had gathered to help Mr. Gardner cure 132 hams. The youngest, Bud's son Virgil, was 63. Except for Virgil, who lived in Kansas City and made the trip annually to help his father, all the men lived nearby and had been helping Bud for many years. While we waited in the warm TV room for the government inspector and the ham truck to appear, the men reminisced about earlier curings. Floyd Martin even remembered curing hams with Bud's father, Thomas W. Gardner. Each time a truck rounded the long curve leading to the Gardner's house, excitement rose and we all peered anxiously to see if it would turn into the driveway. It seemed like hours, but finally around 12:45 p.m. the truck arrived and the action began.

The truck driver pulled up to the entrance of the ham house and slid the back door up. One by one, he handed the hams to an assembly line of men whose outstretched arms were draped with white sacks to ensure cleanliness. The hams were taken into the ham house and placed on the long metal table to the right. Here the government inspector stamped each one with Bud's USDA number, guaranteeing healthy hams. By this time I noticed that all the women had remained in the house. One or two came out to the ham house to see how things were going, but they were not at all involved in the day's activities. Or so I thought at the time.

Once all the hams had been stacked and stamped, the curing began. Bud and Lance Henderson trimmed each ham at the table on the right and handed it to the second man at the table on the left who weighed it and announced its weight to the third man. This man pulled a freshly washed muslin sack out of the old apple basket, wrote the weight of the ham on it and passed the ham and the sack on to the next two men. Here, the ham was placed on a 3-foot square sheet of craft paper. Rolls of cut paper were snugly stored between the beams directly above this section of the table. Using a tin measuring cup, one of the men poured two to three cups of the cure over the ham and packed it into any areas not covered with skin including the hock. The craft paper was neatly folded over the ham, which was passed along to the next team of men who stuffed it into the muslin sack.

The last man in the assembly line reached up over his head to a tangle of twine cut into 20-inch lengths, grabbed a piece of twine, tied a knot to close the bag and carried the ham over to its peg, where it would hang for

Figure 8-1.   William "Bud" Gardner of Boone County, Missouri Helps
His Crew of Nine Unload Fresh Hams from a Local Deliv-
ery Truck
Bud and his helpers will process 132 hams for curing in
less than three hours.
(Photo by the author)

seven months. "The cure takes effect quickly," Bud Gardner told me. "Look over there in 15 minutes and you'll see that it has already begun to drip." He was right. The cure, which reduces the weight of the ham by nearly 25 percent, begins drawing the juices out immediately. In little more than two hours, 132 hams were hanging from the ceiling.

This production-line quality might lead one to ponder the traditionality of Gardner's curing process. Unlike the families living nearby who cure one or two hams from their stock each year, over a two-week period Bud cures nearly 500 hams, which he orders from a slaughter house in Moberly about 30 miles to the north. Bud does not even use smoke or prepare his own cure, although he does alter a commercial cure with brown sugar to achieve a taste that has won him awards throughout the state. He has experimented with enough cures over the years to feel confident that the commercial cure works just fine. In fact, he used the cure for years before becoming a commercial ham curer.

That leap happened as a result of the popularity of his hams. He just couldn't keep up with the requests from friends, friends of friends, church groups, and other organizations who wanted that award-winning ham on their own table. Bud is currently one of the two ham curers in Boone County who are USDA approved to produce cured hams commercially. Yet he is quick to point out that one must come to his home to buy the ham; unlike his competitors', Bud's hams do not appear in local grocery stores. Rather, he prefers to maintain a personal relationship with his customers. To purchase one of Bud Gardner's hams you must visit him in his ham house where he can talk with you and find the ham that is just right for your needs. After choosing your ham with Bud, he wraps it in craft paper and fashions a carrying handle out of heavy string. His label, displaying his USDA number, the contents of the cure, and the weight of the ham, is placed on the ham before it goes out the door. If you are lucky, Phala will be on hand to give you some of her tried and true recipes for cooking the ham.

He has also been known to send hams to the sons and daughters of Boone Countians living in Guam, Germany, Greece, or just about anywhere. Some are in the Armed Forces; others have simply moved away. Most of them grew up on Bud Gardner's hams and their requests, which often come during the holidays, reflect a desire to maintain a family tradition while away from home. Gardner's ham provides the foundation for a meal based on traditional foodways. Thus, those who share the meal become acquainted with the host's "Little Dixie" heritage, thereby reinforcing cultural and geographic identity.

Despite the commercial nature of Bud's curing, I couldn't help feel that this was one of the most traditional events I had attended in a long time. Once the men got used to my presence, they ignored me. They teased

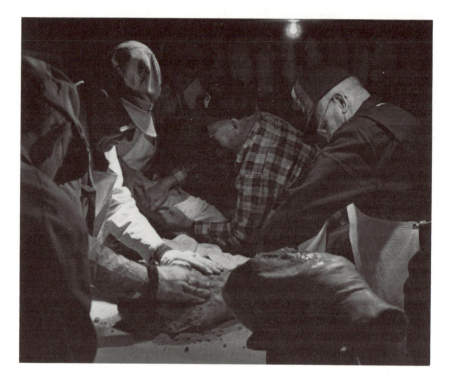

Figure 8-2.   The Assembly Line
The crew of local Boone Countians have developed an
"assembly line" to weigh the ham, label the muslin sack,
pack the cure onto the ham, stuff the wrapped ham into
the muslin sack, and tie it with twine to hang for seven
months.
(Photo by the author)

each other about farming mishaps, shared tricks of the trade, talked about other farmers, recalled past curing feats (like the time they finished 130 hams in less than two hours) and joked about their aging bodies and memories. Bud's son Virgil had driven all the way from Kansas City to be part of the day's activities. Floyd Martin, the oldest at 92, doesn't get out much anymore, but he never misses a curing with Bud Gardner. It became clear that this was an event they looked forward to and cherished as a way of strengthening bonds with each other and reaffirming their position in the community.

After the last ham was hung, we all trooped into the basement of the Gardner's house. It was here that the women's role in the curing process became clear. The basement has a separate kitchen area which is used by the Gardners for larger gatherings. The dining room table was set. A huge percolator of coffee was steaming and the kitchen table offered a choice of four homemade pies. After the men chose their pie and coffee and scuffled back to the dining room to recount the day's successes, the women gathered around the kitchen table to resume their talk. It occurred to me that in earlier times these women might have spent the day baking while the men were in the ham house. Today, however, they brought their pre-baked pies with them, thus affording more time to relax and enjoy each other's company. Our entrance, though greeted warmly, seemed to interrupt their activities. Pie and coffee remain the traditional reward for a day's work well done, but like the men who order freshly prepared hams from the slaughter house in Moberly, the women have reduced the labor element of the event while enhancing its social value.

As I shared in the celebration of the day's work, I realized the growing influence of modern technology on traditionality in the Gardner family. Health regulations prohibit the use of smokehouses, scientifically developed cures often replace the old secret recipe, and microwave ovens enable pies to be made in advance. Some fear these innovations have been the demise of traditional life, but people still gather to cure hams. And in that gathering, they maintain a most traditional aspect of their lives.

But Bud's influence on traditional festive life in the community does not stop when the last ham is hung. Ham curing at the Gardners' is a year-round process. In March, Bud and Phala throw a big ham supper for the men who have helped him in the ham house that year—and the women who have baked the pies and made the coffee. I attended the 1988 Thank You dinner held at a restaurant at Midway, a community just west of Columbia. Fifty people dressed up for this formal gathering. The tables, covered with heavy white table cloths, were arranged in a U, with Bud and his son Virgil seated at the head. The median age was about 70 with people attending whose ages ranged from 35 to 92. Virgil roasted everyone, thanking them for their participation in the hamming. Then Bud spoke more generally about everyone's help that year, thanking the men and women by name for coming and for their help during the last year. He made it clear that helping Phala with the pies and coffee after the hamming was just as important as the men's help with the hamming. It was a celebratory occasion, highly complimentary of Bud. Even though Bud makes some money selling the hams on a cost-plus-expense basis (very carefully figured out), he doesn't pay the men who help except by hosting the celebratory dinner. Yet the men apparently do not feel exploited; they not only respect him and enjoy being around him but they also are proud to be associated with an important Boone County tradition.

But this ham dinner is not only a time to thank the people associated with the hamming but also a time to reaffirm their commitment to help him next year. Then in November, Phala calls all the wives to ask if their husbands will be coming by to help with the hamming. In this way, the women ensure that the ham curing continues as a community event. Their involvement during the curing reinforces this role. Through the preparation and offering of pie and coffee after the work is done, the women provide a relaxed setting for social interaction, reinforcing the sense of community that begins in the work setting. Phala's significant role is that of communicator with the community. In the two years that I have known the Gardners, Phala has been the one to call me on Bud's behalf.

In April or May, Bud and his friends take some of the hams down, wipe off the excess cure to make the ham less salty and rewrap them to hang throughout the summer. Unlike commercial packing house owners who sell their hams after curing them for six weeks, Bud refuses to sell his hams before July. They must hang for at least seven months. Bud says the hot summer months are essential to bring out the full flavor of the ham. In fact, most of Bud's hams are sold in October or November—nearly one year after the curing process began.

In the final step of the curing process, the hams are taken down and unwrapped. Bud explains that the greener the mold, the better the ham. As long as the mold is light in color, the cure has taken well. But if the mold appears dark, a rarity in Bud's ham house, the meat has begun to spoil and the ham is no good. Before the mold is washed off, the excess hock and unsightly protrusions of skin are trimmed. This is actually the second of three trimmings the ham will receive before it acquires the aesthetically acceptable and pleasing shape of a Bud Gardner ham.[2] Next the ham is washed in soapy water and thoroughly dried. It is important to get all the water out of the cracks and crevices so the ham will dry evenly. Each ham is then tested for aroma with an icepick inserted along the hock in two places. The test is largely done to insure that the ham is healthy. However, slight variations in aroma can be detected and a knowledgeable tester can find the tastiest of the bunch by this method. It is also the method used by County and State Fair officials to evaluate aroma in a ham contest.[3]

When the hams are sold individually instead of in large quantities to churches, Bud puts on his final touch to create a visually pleasing ham. Using paprika for color and corn oil for shine, Bud polishes each ham to the reddish brown glow previously acquired by smoking. In fact, most curers will tell you that smoking affects only the appearance of the ham and rarely affects the taste since the ham usually remains in the salt mixture long enough that the skin becomes hardened. This prevents the smoke from penetrating the skin and affecting the flavor. However, months of hanging in a smokehouse do create a rich dark red shade that is the landmark of a well-cured ham and is still considered an important quality.[4] Thus, while Bud's method of achieving the same color may be considered a "newfangled" innovation, as is the sugar curing method itself, the social and aesthetic qualities associated with smoking the ham would appear to be preserved. The action of curing the ham, by whatever means, moves the meat "further away from a natural state as animal to a cultural state as food" (Marshall 408) and acquires the aesthetic qualities important in the community as demonstrated at the Boone County Fair, for instance, where each ham entered in the ham contest is placed on a doily or platter inside a lighted glass case. This museum-like setting supports Marshall's observation that a "well-cured and smoked country ham is considered by the people to be an artistic expression" (414).

The Boone County Fair continues to be an important venue for Bud. Through the popularity of the ham show, the county fair serves as an "agent in the maintenance of ham and bacon curing traditions" in the county (Marshall 414). At the Boone County Fair an entire building is devoted to the ham contest. Adults and members of the 4-H club enter hams. As a frequent winner, Bud's hams often set the standard for excellence. Even the 4-H youth know of Bud Gardner and his award-winning hams. Beyond attesting to Bud's continuing influence, the number of hams submitted each year suggests a continuing preference for ham among Boone Countians. (For example, at Bud's ham dinner for his associates, three men, one of them Bud, started a three-way bantering: one had had some heart trouble and had to eat chicken at the ham dinner; another man began giving him a hard time about his diet since Bud had been eating ham all his life and he was 92 years old.) Leslie Prosterman in a recent study of county fairs points out that the types of foods sold at county fairs reflect not only the economy but also the cultural preferences of the county's residents.[5] She found more dairy products at county fairs in Wisconsin and more beef and corn products in Illinois (82). One can take this idea a step further and find a correlation between the foods available for consumption and those on display for judging. In Missouri, each fair that has a ham contest also has a ham breakfast, which is usually one of the most popular events at the fair. The winner of the ham contest wins the bid for the ham breakfast. Bud's hams have been consistent winners for over 40 years; thus, yet another social and festive venue is regularly created in the community by Bud's hams.

Two other festive events that feature Bud's hams and that provide powerful contexts for *communitas* are the annual ham suppers of the Woodlandville Methodist Church and the Locust Grove Methodist Church, two of Bud's biggest customers who both host their annual ham supper in October. Each year, 32 hams per church are cured, cleaned, trimmed, baked and served to over 600 people who attend the supper. Bud's relationship with these churches is different from that with his other customers and further reinforces the importance of his hamming in the community.

Bud has been attending the Woodlandville Church for 87 years and Phala grew up in the Locust Grove Church. Therefore, rather than selling cured hams to them, Bud loans his ham house to members of the church to cure, store and prepare the hams needed for their suppers. A group of five to nine men from each church becomes the crew under Bud's careful supervision. Like his regular crew, they help cure in November and celebrate in February. These crews also help clean, trim, and test the hams in October two weeks prior to their church suppers. Although these hams will go right to the oven, and are therefore not polished with paprika and oil, each member of the crew has learned this important last step in the hamming process through his association with Bud. Thus, by providing the ham house for these two churches, Bud encourages church members to learn his hamming techniques and the community aesthetics governing the Boone County ham. By passing these skills on to the younger generation in the community, he maintains his own tradition of ham curing and the tradition of the ham supper in his community.

Visiting one of these ham suppers makes clear Bud's stature in the community—and the efficiency with which the church members serve 726 meals. It is also clear that the supper has become a way to honor Bud and the Gardner family. At such a supper that I attended, he and his three sisters were clearly the focus of attention. Nattily dressed in suit and tie, Bud was clearly the patriarch of the gathering. Before sitting, the guests almost invariably sought Bud out for a hello or to discuss the latest issue of importance to the community. Everyone vied to talk with Bud and his sisters (who are 88, 94, and 101 years old, each one just as sharp as Bud). I was invited to the supper by Bud's daughter-in-law (who, like Phala, serves as communicator to the outside). She knew I was documenting the ham curing and wanted to be sure I had a chance to see what she regarded as the culmination of the year-long process. Although the women had prepared 142 pies for the evening, the ham was clearly what brought people to the event. Guests waited patiently in the church pews for an hour or more before being called to their meal in the large community room in the basement. It was a time to chat with friends and share the latest news.

For the most part, the tasks were divided consistently between men and women of the church. The women took money at the door. Once in the door, guests were greeted by Phala who gave them their meal number and invited them to find a seat and shepherded them through the hour-long wait. Other women prepared and served everything but the ham. The men who had worked with Bud in his ham house proudly served the ham, remarking frequently on its great flavor, color, and leanness. Comments such as "well, he did it again" or "no one can cure a ham like Bud" suggested that the supper is Bud's yearly test and the guests are his judges.

Clearly Bud's hams provide a catalyst for community identity and cohesiveness. When a church advertises its supper, the flyer proudly announces that Bud Gardner's hams will be served, a fact that will bring people in. And bring them in it does. Although his Church has only 58 members, 726 people made the trip in 1987 to savor Bud's ham. In this way, Bud's hams provide perhaps the most successful fundraising event for the church, an event which probably keeps the church alive and the community intact.

Bud has adapted his traditional curing techniques to meet contemporary health standards and to provide an added source of income for his family. Some might argue that curing hams in a USDA approved ham house, using a pre-packaged cure that requires no smoking, is far from the traditional method of curing hams. While it is still true as Marshall has argued that "the preservation of pork is at the center of traditional Missouri rural foodways" (404), I suggest that it is not so much the method (salt curing, sugar curing, brine curing, or smoking) which provides the traditionality in the community as it is the communal activity generated by the events associated with it. By involving the community in preserving the meat and in festive events that center on the product of the curing process, Bud Gardner's "hamming" reinforces friendships, strengthens group identity, passes on skills and community aesthetics, creates performances of essential aspects of the community's vision of itself, and maintains traditional community life despite the forces of change that affect the region. Furthermore, the connection of Bud Gardner's "hamming" with the churches of the community helps to maintain the role of the church as an important gathering place by providing both a work-centered event and a festive, fundraising event as venues for social interaction and community performance. While there may indeed be no smoke in the smokehouse at Bud Gardner's, there is surely a strong flame burning of human connection and community at the end of his driveway.

PHALA'S HAM HOCK AND BEANS

Soak beans (navy or great northern—Phala prefers great northern). Also cook ham hock the day before. Let cool and cut meat into bite-sized pieces. Save the liquid from ham hock. Next day cook beans a couple of hours. Add some of the liquid you kept. Add meat and season with salt and pepper. You won't need much salt.

BUD GARDNER'S BAKED HAM

Place ham in container, skin side up. Put about two inches of water in container. Set oven at 275°, not over 300°. Cook 25 minutes per pound of ham (count time when water begins to boil). When ham is done, broth will become clear. Watch for this during the last hour of cooking. Take ham out of broth when cool enough to handle, but not cold. You can remove the bone at this time. At this point, remove skin and glaze the ham to suit taste.

BUD GARDNER'S FRIED HAM

Slice ham 1/4-inch thick. Use low heat. Pour in enough water to cover the bottom of skillet. Place ham in skillet and cover. Cook for 5 minutes on each side. May need to add a minute or so to cooking time to suit taste.

Notes

1. Howard Wight Marshall, "Meat Preservation on the Farm in Missouri's 'Little Dixie,'" *Journal of American Folklore* 92:366 (1979): 400–417.

2. Trim is one of the qualities of a well-cured ham. In fact, in the ham contest, smoothness and trim are worth 15% of the total score.

3. Aroma constitutes 35% of the total score.

4. Color and visual appeal are worth 10% of the total score.

5. Leslie Prosterman, "Food and Alliance at the County Fair," *Western Folklore,* 10 (1981): 81–90.

9

Roast Beef and Pit-Barbecued Lamb: The Role of Food at Two Utah Homecoming Celebrations

Carol Edison

Since the turn of the century, on the sometimes snowy and generally cold, third Saturday of March, the residents of Koosharem, Utah have put on their Sunday best and traveled to the local schoolhouse to meet with neighbors and old friends for a day of feasting, entertainment and dance. On another Saturday in mid-July, folks in a different part of the state don blue jeans and T-shirts, converging on the town of Fountain Green, as they have nearly every year since the early 1930s, to watch a parade and a talent show, and spend the afternoon picnicking and visiting at the city park.[1]

Although they occur in very different settings and were designed to meet very different goals, these two indigenous Utah celebrations—Koosharem's Old Folks Day and Fountain Green's Lamb Day—are both homecoming events and have much in common. They share the festive activities such as musical performance, dancing, socializing, and reminiscing that are typical of homecoming celebrations, often the single most important event on the annual calendar of dozens of small towns in Utah and elsewhere. Such celebrations function in two ways: they provide an opportunity for all residents of a community, both past and present, to join together and renew personal ties with family and friends, and they display and reinforce group-held values and identity. Yet what sets these homecoming celebrations apart is that at the center of both is the preparation and enjoyment of a community-shared meal, with a specific menu of special foods, that reaffirm the origins and affiliations of the community and helps mainstream them for future generations.

Old Folks Day in Koosharem

Between July 1847 when the first company of Mormon pioneers entered the Salt Lake Valley and May of 1869 when the transcontinental railroad was completed, thousands of people walked, rode in wagons, or pushed handcarts across America's prairie lands to join their fellow Mormons in the valley of the Great Salt Lake. In 1875, in recognition of these pre-railroad pioneers and their sacrifices, a day of celebration was initiated in Salt Lake City which was later repeated annually in nearly every Mormon community in Utah, Idaho, Nevada, and Arizona. According to a plaque that still stands at the southeast corner of Temple Square in Salt Lake City, the first celebration was designed to pay respect to those "70 or more years of age," by providing them with "travel, refreshments and entertainment" without charge.

Today, over 100 years later, Koosharem, Utah is one of the few Mormon communities that maintains this traditional day of honor. Settled by English converts in the late 1870s and named for a nineteenth-century Paiute Indian leader, Koosharem is a small ranching community, located at an elevation of 7,000 feet on a sparsely populated plateau in the south central part of the state. With an area population of 200, Koosharem currently boasts a post office, cafe, general store/gas station, a Mormon ward (meeting house) and a two-classroom schoolhouse with a large multipurpose room, stage, and adjacent kitchen.

Both current and former residents of Koosharem and the other small communities in Grass Valley are invited to participate in the annual Old Folks Day activities. It is not unusual for visitors to come from more than 200 miles away to spend the day with friends and relations. Yet unlike most community homecomings, this event is not open to children or teenagers and it is only after marriage or accepting adult responsibilities that one becomes eligible to attend.[2]

The event is organized and produced by a committee comprising twelve to fourteen of the community's younger married couples, those in their 30s, 40s, and 50s. The committee members plan and advertise the event; cook, serve, and clean up throughout the day-long celebration; and often remain on the committee for a number of years until they are old enough to be considered "old folks" themselves.

Despite an historical relationship to the Mormon Church and dependence on school facilities, Koosharem's twentieth-century "Old Folks Day Committee" functions largely through the willingness of local residents to volunteer their time and money. The most expensive component of the celebration, the meat, is purchased with proceeds from the previous year's event, while the rest of the food and all of the labor are donated. As a result, the committee has gradually purchased its own dishes, flatware, and glassware, storing them separately from those used for other special events. In this small community where the leadership and member-

ship of both public and private organizations overlap and community resources are customarily pooled for all activities, the maintenance of separate resources for Old Folks Day suggests its significance for local residents
and their desire that it continue to be celebrated.

Old Folks Day consists of four major components: a midday meal, a
variety show of local entertainment, an evening meal and an old-fashioned
pioneer dance. Guests arrive in time for the midday meal, seating themselves at tables arranged in long rows, each having a beautiful array of baked
goods placed every few inches along the center. The meal, served family
style, customarily includes roast beef, mashed potatoes and gravy, tossed
green salad, green beans, and cooked carrots. Salads, vegetables, bread, and
desserts are provided by local residents who, along with out-of-town guests,
have paid for their own meals. In the spirit of the first celebration, local
residents and visitors over the age of 65 are honored guests who dine free
of charge. After all have had their fill of the main course, the pies and cakes
are passed up and down the table accompanied by speculation about the
cook's identity and discussion about her success.

This menu, including the fine array of sweets, is basically the same
Mormon Sunday dinner that has been popular for several generations and
is still served on a regular basis in many Mormon homes throughout the
Intermountain West. Perhaps this is because a large roast, whether beef,
ham, or pork, that is left in the oven to cook while family members attend
church, is among the easiest and most economical ways to provide a special
meal for typically large Mormon families. Pies, cakes, ice cream and candy
are other regional favorites. (Often called "Mormon vices," the popularity
of desserts throughout the Mormon cultural region is sometimes considered a reaction against doctrinal bans on the consumption of coffee, tea,
or alcohol and the use of tobacco.)

After the meal, residents and visitors alike help rearrange the tables
and chairs in preparation for the afternoon program. The entertainment
takes the form of a variety show, another widespread tradition throughout
Mormon culture, which includes music, dance, and theatrical readings and
features local performers. Selections are taken from both traditional and
popular culture and performances are given by both children and adults.

After the program, some of the local guests customarily take an hour
or two to attend to farm chores while everyone else takes the opportunity
to visit and reminisce. By late afternoon, the committee members have not
only finished cleaning up after the midday meal, but are well under way
with preparations for serving the evening meal.

As guests return and new guests arrive, all are greeted by the smell of
baked ham. The tables are once again put into place, desserts lined up along

the center. The ham, just like the roast beef, is served with potatoes, salads, and vegetables. And once again, the pies and cakes are shuttled up and down the rows, allowing all who wish to have a taste.

After dinner, while the musicians set up on stage, everyone else helps prepare for the dance by collapsing the banquet tables, storing them under the stage, and moving chairs to the room's perimeter. The dance has always featured live music, provided for the last thirty years by the Peterson Brothers String Band from neighboring Wayne County. A variety of old-time round dances, reels, and schottisches are requested by both older and younger couples, as are waltzes danced to contemporary country and western music. Guests call the event an old-fashioned, pioneer dance both because of the type of dancing and because, like the dances of pioneer times, it always lasts at least until midnight.

Although the enjoyment of "refreshments" was an integral part of the earliest Old Folks Days, the relative importance of food to the Koosharem celebration has likely grown, as evidenced by the longtime practice of serving two substantial meals during the day-long event. Perhaps this is because the process of preparing, presenting, and enjoying this special menu provides a unique opportunity for all adult community members to become involved and interact with each other, whether or not they qualify as "old folks." Donating a salad or pie, working on the committee that cooks, serves, and cleans up, or simply attending the event as a former resident or as one of the honored senior guests, makes everyone an important part of the celebration. The result of participation in the group-run event is likely a renewed sense of individual membership in the community and an understanding of one's own role in relationship to the larger community of former and current neighbors.

In addition to reinforcing individual membership in the community, the preparation and presentation of food at this event presents a symbolic display of community-held values that helps define the community's unique identity. While the meat and potatoes menu might be partly attributed to the English heritage of Koosharem's first settlers and the practice of serving large, hot meals at both midday and evening likely reflects the ranching lifestyle of the area, a main course featuring roast ham or beef, followed by homemade pies and cakes, can be considered an expression of Mormon foodways. Moreover, the family-style method of serving is not only typical of sit-down dinners in Mormon congregations, but is culturally appropriate for a religious community that celebrates the family unit.

In terms of menu, quantity and method of service, the meal served at Koosharem's Old Folks Day can be considered both a reflection of the cultural, occupational, and religious heritage of the community as well as a display of the importance that the community places on family, neighbors, and church, both past and present. In effect, the celebration reinforces among both insiders and outsiders Koosharem's identity as one of the region's most traditional, rural Mormon communities.

In addition to the reflective function of this community meal is the prescriptive, reinforcing power it has on the maintenance of local culture and community. Most simply, this ongoing annual celebration, with its prearranged purpose and design, provides an important forum and model from which successive generations of Koosharem's young adults can learn to understand and perpetuate important local values, as well as their community's special identity. By sharing roast beef and homemade pies with the other adult members of the community, each participant is reminded of his or her own place within this community and of the responsibilities which accompany membership in this group. And, as middle-aged members become old enough to be honored and younger members take over the responsibility for the celebration, each new generation also takes on the responsibility for perpetuating and maintaining the cultural values of family, community and church that are symbolically displayed throughout the Old Folks Day Celebration.

Koosharem's Old Folks Day represents a time of homecoming and reunion for the adult population of Grass Valley as well as a time to honor the older members of the group. Yet in this process, participants honor much more than their elderly guests. By continuing to produce a pioneer celebration that features performance traditions and local foodways that originated with nineteenth-century Mormon culture, they honor not only their ancestors and their elders, but they honor and reaffirm their identity with the Mormon cultural heritage which has been at the heart of Koosharem's community life for the last 100 years.

Lamb Day in Fountain Green

With a population of around 600, Fountain Green is one of about a dozen communities of varying size that dot the landscape in central Utah's Sanpete Valley. Settled during the 1850s, this valley became home to large numbers of Mormon converts from Denmark and to smaller numbers of Swedish, Norwegian, English and Yankee immigrants. The valley is cradled between high mountains to the east and the west that provide the rich soil and abundant water that have made the area one of Utah's most important agricultural regions. In addition to hay, alfalfa, and other grains, production of livestock, including sheep, cattle, and more recently turkeys has been a major contributor to the area's economy. Although sheep have always been raised in several Sanpete communities, Fountain Green has long been recognized as the center of the local sheep industry.

Figure 9-1.   Koosharem Old Folks Day

Koosharem's annual celebration of Old Folks Day is a time when adult members of the community, both past and present, come together to share a traditional meal. *(Photo by the author; copyright Folk Arts Program, Utah Arts Council)*

Founded in 1859 by a handful of Danes, Fountain Green is situated at 6000 feet near the foot of the western mountains and adjacent to a canyon which leads to Utah's western desert. This location proved to be an ideal gathering place for Sanpete sheep as they were herded back and forth between the summer mountain pastures and the winter ranges on the west desert.

Andrew Aagard, a nineteenth-century Danish immigrant and sheepman, is credited with developing the area's sheep industry. According to local stories, Aagard brought quantities of much-needed plate glass from the east and traded them to earlier immigrants for sheep. After gathering together an impressive herd, he "sponsored" other Danish immigrants by providing sheep and covering expenses until they could get their own herds started Under Aagard's leadership the sheep industry grew until at one point there were over 100,000 head of locally-owned sheep and the area became nationally recognized for its production of long-fiber wool. In its heyday, when the local population was around 1200, almost everyone in town was involved in the industry either as owner, herder, or shearer.

Today, residents still proudly relate that during the 1920s, the sheep industry made Fountain Green "one of the most wealthy towns, per capita, in the United States." Such notoriety makes it all the more appropriate that over a half-century later this community continues annually to host a homecoming celebration known as Lamb Day. It began in 1932 as an attempt to counteract a slow market for wool that was being aggravated by long-term drought and the Depression. A local organization, the Jerico Wool Growers' Association, specifically designed and initiated the celebration to promote the consumption of lamb. Association members supplied the lambs for a community barbecue, and Hyrum Jacobsen, a local man who had had some experience with pit barbecuing, provided the expertise. Everyone was invited and all of the lamb was given away without charge.

As the event grew in popularity and participation, other activities were added. Boxing and wrestling matches were two early favorites as were dances featuring the local, ten-piece dance band. A charge for the lamb sandwiches was eventually required to help finance the additional activities. During these early days, the celebration succeeded in developing a local taste for lamb, which effectively raised public awareness of the sheep industry's potential for meat production and helped promote its longevity as a vital local industry.

In Fountain Green, as in most small Mormon communities throughout rural Utah, the distinction between business, church, educational and political activities often becomes clouded, simply because the same people are involved in each arena. So it is not surprising that in the mid-1930s when

Fountain Green's Mormon congregation was in need of funds to construct a new facility, Lamb Day emerged as a likely fund-raising tool. For about a dozen years, the church sponsored the celebration, raising funds to match those from LDS (Mormon) headquarters in Salt Lake City for the construction of a new church building.

After the funds had been raised and the church was built, Lamb Day was turned over to the City of Fountain Green which sponsored the event for another ten or twelve years. In 1968, the mayor and city council decided that the city could not continue to commit the same degree of time and resources to the event and called a town meeting to discuss the future of Lamb Day. At that 1968 meeting, town residents who wanted to continue the event appointed a four-person committee to coordinate Lamb Day. As Victor Rasmussen, committee chair, later explained, "There is a little competition between the communities in Sanpete County and we knew that both Ephraim and Mount Pleasant still had sheep and had expressed interest in taking over the celebration. Town pride took over, so when the city quit ... we couldn't let it die. The people wanted it to continue because they were proud of it and because they wanted to pay tribute to those who had started it."

Since that town meeting almost twenty years ago, Lamb Day has developed into an impressive celebration which draws visitors from Sanpete Valley and throughout the state. Beginning on Friday evening and lasting all day Saturday, on a weekend between the 4th of July and the statewide Pioneer Day Celebration on the 24th, Lamb Day features a large number and wide variety of activities. Amid talent shows, a parade, sports competitions and an open-air dance, the central and most important activity, the preparation and consumption of pit-barbecued lamb, takes place.

On Friday evening, while most of the town is at the school enjoying at talent show featuring local performers, a handful of local sheepmen and Lamb Day committee members prepare both the lambs and the pits. Each year local sheepmen supply between 40 and 50 young lambs which they butcher and deliver to an empty store on Main Street. There, a production line of committee members prepare the lambs for the barbecue pit by trimming them, wrapping them in chicken wire, and sliding them onto long, metal poles. As each lamb becomes ready, it is loaded into a waiting pickup truck with the pole straddling the truck bed and the wrapped lamb hanging inside.

Several blocks away, a couple of men prepare two specially built barbecue pits to receive between 20 and 25 lambs each. Located on the same block that houses the elementary school, these pits are the second set of permanent pits that the town has built for this celebration. Approximately four feet wide, four feet deep and twenty feet long, the pits are lined with

Figure 9-2. Lamb Day—Fountain Green

This sign is permanently on display on the state highway at the south end of town.

(Photo by the author; copyright Folk Arts Program, Utah Arts Council)

two rows of sandstone or "sandrock" that is quarried in a nearby canyon. Wood from the canyon is piled high in the pit and then ignited, causing a huge bonfire to light the evening sky. As midnight approaches, the fire burns down, and the sandstone sides glow red with heat, the men remove the remaining coals by lifting out the large sheets of metal that were placed on the pit bottoms before the fires were built. Then, in teams of two, the men quickly transfer the lambs from the trucks, suspending their hanging carcasses from ground level into the depths of the red-hot pits. Just as quickly, the pits are made air-tight by covering them with successive layers of tin, cardboard, canvas, and then dirt. If air were to invade the pit, the lambs would be quickly burned to nothingness, a catastrophe that almost occurred one year. If all goes well, when the covers are removed around noon the next day, the heat from the rocks will have slowly roasted the lamb to a delicious golden brown.

At six a.m. on Saturday, a flag-raising ceremony and chuckwagon breakfast are held in the city park, punctuated by a dynamite blast that awakens any locals who might be missing the festivities. A second talent show follows, presented inside one of the newer church buildings. A variety show composed of music, dance, and comic readings, the event is designed to showcase local talent while featuring quality, out-of-town acts that will inspire continued local achievement. The program provides an opportunity to introduce and honor the Lamb Day Queen and her attendants, Lamb Day committee members and any other residents or guests who deserve special recognition.

The parade is the next event on this very full agenda. Residents and visitors converge on Main Street to sit on car hoods or folding chairs and watch the impressively large parade of floats, marching bands, and horsemen. Waving queens in formal dresses from nearby towns, kids on decorated bicycles, and clowns throwing candy to youngsters from antique vehicles are among the typical entries in the parade. But the importance of the sheep industry to Fountain Green is not forgotten. Lamb Day's own Sheeper Creeper (a tractor pulled "train" for children), vehicles representing local sheep operations as well as the Wool Growers' Association, children dressed as lambs, and live sheep in trucks, are all included in the parade.

By the time the crowd moves toward the city park, committee members have already begun the process of transforming the barbecued lamb into sandwiches. The dirt has been shoveled off the pits and after receiving an okay by walkie-talkie, the canvas, cardboard, and tin are quickly removed. The lambs are then transported by truck to the park where a cadre of volunteers wait to trim and cut up the meat, season it with salt and pepper, and serve it, along with a little mustard, on soft hamburger buns.

Figure 9-3. Lamb Day—Fountain Green

Lamb carcasses in wire cages are carried to the barbecue pit. Notice the rock lining the pit.

(Photo by the author; copyright Folk Arts Program, Utah Arts Council)

Figure 9-4. Lamb Day—Fountain Green
The men who have supervised the barbecue pits for almost twenty years receive the okay from the park and prepare to transport more lambs to the carving area.
(Photo by the author; copyright Folk Arts Program, Utah Arts Council)

Figure 9-5.   Lamb Day—Fountain Green
Sixty local volunteers transform forty-six lambs into about one hundred sandwiches apiece
at the 1984 celebration.
(Photo by the author; copyright Folk Arts Program, Utah Arts Council)

The sandwiches are eagerly purchased and quickly enjoyed by the crowd while a large number are stacked in boxes and packed off to home freezers for later enjoyment.

Hamburgers, hot dogs, soda pop, cotton candy, and ice cream are also available for purchase. A variety of children's games, contests, and rides, a dunking pond, a greased-pig chase, and even a greased pole with a crisp twenty-dollar bill at the top, provide activity for the young people. Adults enjoy the music presented on the outdoor stage, watch the softball games played by local teams, or buy a raffle ticket for the quilt made each year as a fundraiser for the local chapter of the Daughters of Utah Pioneers. But mostly people socialize with each other as friends and families share this day of homecoming. The final Lamb Day activity, a dance, is traditionally held under the stars in the park pavilion. Although everyone is invited, the dance is designed for the town's young people and has recently featured locally popular rock-and-roll bands.

Over the years, Lamb Day has paid for much more than itself. The profit from the sale of lamb sandwiches and the other concessions has not only allowed the committee to purchase grills and other equipment that make the event self-sustaining, but it has provided funds to support a number of local projects and improvements. A new bowery, picnic tables, flagpole, and playground have been built in the park and improvements have been made to the cemetery. Lamb Day funds have helped buy an ambulance for the town as well as EMT training for several residents, and financial support has been given to local ball teams, 4-H clubs, and other small organizations.

Over the last half century, Fountain Green has experienced a significant drop both in population and in the number of area sheepmen. Post-war out-migration to the cities and a shift away from lamb to other agricultural pursuits have combined to change the town's occupational and economic makeup. But even though many current residents are white collar workers, who commute to nearby towns, most townsfolk still claim a connection with the sheep industry through their own family history. Perhaps this is why the time and energy spent cutting and hauling loads of juniper from the canyon or carving and trimming hot lamb creates a special camaraderie among participants. And perhaps these shared experiences, while strengthening ties between generations, serve to solidify and reinforce individual membership within the larger community and create a sense of personal ownership and pride in the town's special occupational legacy.

The fancy homes that were built in the 1920s, the small herds that are still pastured in town lots, and the stock trucks, sheep camps, and other implements of the trade that are noticeable throughout the town and in surrounding fields, all speak to the continued operation and importance of the sheep industry in Fountain Green. The Lamb Day celebration, just like these features of the cultural landscape, provides a public forum to express symbolically this same aspect of community identity. By coming together to share a meal of barbecued lamb, the individual members of the community annually recognize their common occupational heritage and in this process reinforce, for the outside world, this unique community identity. Just like Brigham City's Peach Days, Payson's Onion Days, or Melon Days in Green River, Lamb Day functions for everyone as a way of identifying this particular small town and recognizing its unique historical and economic contribution to Utah.

As the most important event on the town calendar, Lamb Day provides an occasion to crown a queen to represent the town at public functions throughout the coming year and the opportunity to host several games in the county-wide softball tournament. It provides an annual occasion for past residents to return home to visit with family and friends and a way for Fountain Green to raise funds to support community improvements and local organizations. But most importantly, by setting aside a special day to butcher, cook, and serve pit-barbecued lamb, the residents of Fountain Green are teaching everyone, and particularly their children, about their town's unique historical and economic contribution. It is through this process that today's residents of Fountain Green are preserving and perpetuating their community's distinctive identity, making it possible for it to remain a source of pride for generations to come.

All of the elements of a typical homecoming celebration—parades, picnics, contests, performances, and other forms of entertainment—are part of these two Utah celebrations. However, it is the communal meal at both of them that provides a special focal point for the performance of community values and identity. Both Koosharem's roast beef dinner and Fountain Green's barbecued lamb sandwich meal reinforce individual membership within the community and symbolically display community-held values and community identity, thus maintaining those values and that identity for future generations. Perhaps that is why, for nearly a century, Grass Valley residents have gathered in Koosharem on a cold, snowy Saturday in March and why, for over a half century, folks from Sanpete County have returned to Fountain Green on a Saturday each July. Perhaps that is also a reason to predict that the residents of these two Utah towns, and most likely their children after them, will continue to make this annual journey home for a number of years to come.

Notes

1. Field research on these community celebrations was funded by the Utah Arts Council during the spring and summer of 1984. The author wishes to thank Kendall Stapley, 1984 Old Folks Day chairman, and Victor Rasmussen, chairman of the Lamb Day Committee, for their time, insight, and assistance. A special thanks also goes to the residents of Koosharem and Fountain Green for their openness, hospitality, and friendship.

2. See, for example, the essays by Kathy Neustadt, Eleanor Wachs, and Theodore Humphrey in the present volume for discussions of other food-centered homecoming celebrations.

10

"It's a Community Deal Here, You Know": Festive Community Life in Rural Oklahoma

Theodore C. Humphrey

The weather is, as usual, quite hot at 6:00 p.m. at the end of July in Oklahoma, but it is nevertheless a fine time for a community outdoor barbecue at the Calvin Pauley ranch near Morrison.[1] The air lies heavy and moist on the groups of people milling around the kegs of iced beer or the barrels of iced tea and iced water, visiting with each other in the shade of the long pole barn, open on the east side. A work bench along the south wall has been converted to a full bar and is a popular spot. Tables stretch for perhaps 25 feet, covered every foot of the way with butcher paper and Pyrex baking dishes containing vegetables and casseroles, pies and cakes, and containers of salads of every description, all brought by the folks in the tradition of the covered dish dinner. Clouds of dust rising from the section line road a few hundred yards to the west announce the impending arrival of yet more people; their cars pass up and over the turnpike overpass and then loop back into Calvin Pauley's driveway coming to rest finally in neat rows in the bermuda pasture north of the barn. Children play tag among the tables and outbuildings of Mr. Pauley's ranch and race down the slope to the long mound of dirt that marks the site of the barbecue pit. It is about time for Mr. Pauley to crank up the tractor and pull the top off the pit, an exciting ritual that most of the children and many of the adults want to be on hand to observe. The four hundred or so people gathered here, present and former residents of the Morrison community as well as a number of visitors, politicians and ordinary folks, are eager to eat the barbecued beef, pork, goat, turkey, and venison that will soon be lifted from the pit where it has cooked for nearly twenty-four hours, the culmination of days of preparation and planning.

Figure 10-1. Hand-Lettered Sign in the Citizens' State Bank Building in Morrison
Advertising the 1982 Barbecue
(Photo by the author)

Figure 10-2. Calvin Pauley (Second from Right) Greets Visitors to His Ranch
(Photo by the author)

As the meat is unwrapped, sliced, and thrown into large serving containers, the crowd begins to line up and pass along either side of the serving table, helping themselves to as many of the covered dishes and to as much of the barbecued meat as they desire. While people tend to group together in family gatherings, they are open to newcomers joining in to eat in smaller social groups. Lots of hugs, handshakes, slaps on the back, and hands on shoulders and arms among friends and acquaintances suggest acceptance and community. The foods served and consumed will fulfill two kinds of needs: nourishing the physical self and satisfying the physical palate on the one hand and expressing an idea of the community performed by the community's feeding itself together in this festive context. It's an old idea and one that obviously still works well here in Morrison.

For several years I have observed how the festive events of the small, rural Oklahoma community of Morrison, such as the Pauley barbecue, created by particular individuals and groups within the community, have served to bind its members together despite the sort of economic hard times that can tear such communities apart. The celebratory calendar of Morrison is driven by two forces, one natural, the other social, that operate together, overlapping at times to chronicle a set of rich events symbolic of the community—and of dozens like it across the country. The first and perhaps more fundamental force is the seasonal cycle of planting, growth, and harvest. The weather is always interesting and influential in Oklahoma, the seasons strongly marked. Because the community still regards itself as essentially agricultural, the rhythms of this natural year dominate the lives of most residents. But, in late August, when the wheat harvest has been long completed (if the weather has cooperated), and the fields ploughed and prepared for fall planting, the social calendar of the school year gets under way, equally traditional and functional for most residents.

Since the public school is in many ways the chief socializing agency and the focus of much festive activity, one might reasonably locate the beginning of the community's festive year here because of the school's heavy schedule of weekly football games (in the fall), wrestling matches, basketball games, and livestock shows in winter and early spring, and other festive events that involve the community's youth—and most of the rest of the community too—throughout the school year. The high school sporting events begin with eight-man football games played to full stands of enthusiastic spectators, especially since the team has won the state Class B championships several times in recent years. Although food and food behaviors comprise a minor element in these games, they nonetheless contribute to our understanding of the value system of the community and hence of the values displayed in food-centered events. In the football games, for instance, we see heavily symbolic displays of the community's young people ritualis-

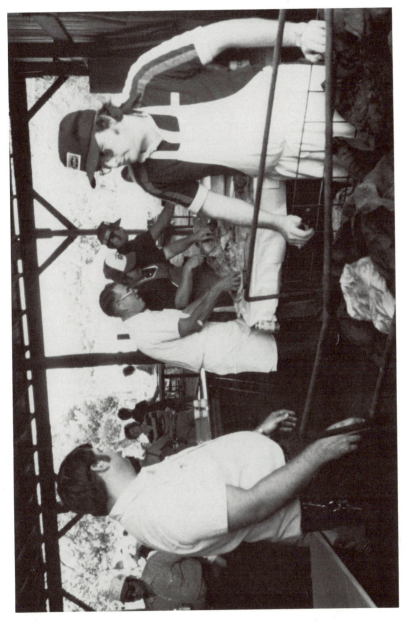

Figure 10-3.   Morrison Community Barbecue
Phil Berkinbile (left) watches Lenard James and other
men slice barbecued meat for serving.
(Photo by the author)

tically enacting the twin values of cooperation and competition in attitudes and conditions of health and fertility. These high school sporting events are seen by the residents as representing and contributing to the continued good fortune of the community at large. On a very fundamental level they are ritual enactments of the community's fear of sterility and a powerful celebration of fecundity. Homecoming games with their oddly archaic yet elevating and triumphal symbols of Queen and King and Homecoming court, celebrate the most important cultural assets of the community, its healthy and triumphant offspring, the community's bid for immortality.

Another important part of the general festive structure of the community is the livestock shows that take place in the fall and early spring; at these shows, the youth of the community emulate the agrestic life values of their elders and role models, and, indeed, of the essential life of the community. Members of the 4-H Club and of the Future Farmers of America compete with each other for place and precedence with their exhibits of sheep, cattle, and swine. In these stock shows, one sees not only direct competition but on a deeper, more symbolic level, a competition with the disintegrative forces of life. Through participation in the county fair in September, the community stock show at the end of February, and the county stock show in March, the young people learn and express the attitudes toward life and values that are fundamental to the community: hard work, craft and competence, competition, the interrelationship of individual effort with outside judgment—exactly the values displayed in the athletic events of the school calendar. In that quintessential rural activity, the stock show, the abilities of the young people to observe and enact these values in full view of their peers and their elders are perhaps more fully realized. In each of these events, the community honors and celebrates its youth for their successful socialization into the symbolic as well as literal life of the community.

But it is on the Morrison Community Barbecue founded by Mr. Calvin Pauley, a kind of harvest festival that ends the Morrison community's public festive year, that this chapter focuses. It occurs in the "slack time" of the year and is a festive event deliberately created by Mr. Pauley with participation by most community residents and continued now since his death in 1986, although it changes in form and location within the community each year. Occurring at the end of the wheat harvest, usually on the last Saturday in July, the event brings together many of the products of ranch and farm. Because Morrison relies heavily on the harvest of red winter wheat for much of its economic life, the barbecue celebrates (or laments) the recently completed harvest. It features barbecued meats, covered dishes and desserts prepared by many of the people attending, and a full bar contributed by the local bank. Before the Great Depression, community-wide picnics had occurred with some regularity on a nearby farm, but when Calvin Pauley and his neighbor, Lenard James, decided in 1976 to hold the first barbecue, the tradition had been dead for over forty years.

It began, according to Mr. Pauley,[2] when a neighbor, Mr. James, who raised goats, decided he wanted to barbecue one. Mr. Pauley suggested that they barbecue the goat at Mr. Pauley's new pole barn. Then, as Mr. Pauley reported, "It just kinda grew." As they talked about their plans with other friends and neighbors, people expressed an interest in participating. By the time it actually took place shortly after the end of harvest in July, the backyard barbecue of two neighbors had become a community-wide festive event, for which they had scrounged grills from half the county to barbecue two hogs, a thousand-pound steer, and a haunch of venison in addition to the original goat. Nearly four hundred people attended including some of the local politicians who "said a few words." As Mr. Pauley said, "Folks had so much fun and I saw people I hadn't seen for years that we decided to do it again the next year." Thus, a tradition was born out of the recognition of the need for "folks to visit," an activity that the improvements and increased mechanization of agriculture in the area had served only to inhibit. While the powerful machinery makes it possible for one farmer to operate hundreds if not thousands of acres, he must work harder to pay for it; consequently, as Mr. Pauley noted, "people just don't visit much anymore," a fact that Mr. Pauley saw as distinct threat to community.

After the first barbecue, which was, he said, a little bigger than he and Mr. James had expected, Mr. Pauley decided to have one the following year, only this time he prepared a narrow pit for barbecue: perhaps 10 feet deep, 20 feet long, and 4 feet wide below his house, redigging it each year until his death in 1986. "I had seen it done somewhere, so I decided I could do it too," he told me. To fuel the barbecue he used his tractor to drag up elm and pecan trees from the creek bottom a few hundred yards to the east until he had "about 6 rick of wood there." Neighbors also contributed wood to the project. (In 1983 I even helped a crew of a dozen volunteers load several trucks with timber from my family's nearby farm to feed the fire.) About four days before the day of the barbecue, he ignited the kindling—boards, pieces of discarded furniture, small branches, whatever would burn—with a portable propane torch until he had a good base fire going. Then having sawed the larger logs into 8–12 foot lengths, he pushed them into the pit one at a time with his Ford tractor. "Once in a while you've got to feed it a little bit more, [a] little wood, you know," he told me. "Got to keep it going."

The food for this event has always been primarily of two sorts: the pit barbecued beef, pork, goat, and occasionally venison, prepared by Mr. Pauley and other men in the community; and covered dishes of various vegetables, casseroles, and desserts, provided mostly by the women in the community, following a long tradition of church suppers and similar community food-centered events.

The animals to be barbecued are always donated by various farmers and ranchers, who usually receive some of the choice cuts of the animals when they are butchered through a male group effort involving Mr. Pauley and four or five others including, usually, at least one professional meat cutter; however, any farmer in the community can butcher a beef or a hog or dress out a deer, a skill one develops while growing up in the community. The meat is hung for a few days in a walk-in cooler (the time of year is, after all, July, among the two or three hottest months of the year in north-central Oklahoma), either one borrowed from a store keeper in Morrison or one owned by another neighbor. When the neighbor died unexpectedly, Mr. Pauley bought the cooler and moved it to his farm, thus concentrating the major technical means of producing the barbecue at the site, a concentration that reflects an analogous concentration of the technical means of farming in the community from group-owned machinery to machinery owned wholly by the individual.

Mr. Pauley's description of how the meat was prepared for the pit is worth quoting at some length. A couple of days before the barbecue, he and some friends (male) would get the carcasses from the cooler, load them in the back of a pickup truck, and move them to his pole barn. Then, "we chunk it up in maybe 20-, 30-pound chunks. And we wrap it, well, we season it [with salt, pepper, garlic, and commercial barbecue sauce] right over here on this table and wrap it up in cheese cloth. About four or five layers of it, you know. And then we wrap it up in that burlap. Then I just throw it in a big water tank. I take this water hose and run a tank full of water and just throw it all in this tank of water.... And I leave it there, oh, 7 or 8 hours.... Then I'll go down there with my tractor and I'll put this [meat] in a big steel cradle and set the whole thing down in this pit, right on those coals.... I've got a three-point [tractor hitch] on there, and I'll let that all down in there, unchain it, and pull that big plate [a sheet of steel a half an inch thick and large enough to cover the pit] back over that hole, and cover it up with dirt, just *like a grave* [emphasis added].... Then at six o'clock [on the evening of the barbecue] I'll go get it out, back in this door [of his pole barn] right here. About 6 or 7 of us hop in there and start unwrapping that. And some of them slice it up. And some of the girls are putting it out there on that long table."

Behind the straightforward account of how the barbecue is prepared, we may see expressed a number of values central to the community's idea of itself. Communal and cooperative activity, for one thing, is enacted that is reminiscent of earlier traditional and historical methods of handling the heavy work of the farms and ranches before the advent of large tractors and other tools of production. Threshing and hay-making crews, organized generally on the basis of work exchange used to be the norm in the community. Cattlemen got together regularly to "work the cattle" (i.e., dehorn, castrate, vaccinate, and perhaps spray for flies and other parasites). Now the opportunities for such male-bonding types of interaction are limited largely to ritual and ceremonial activities.

The preparation of the meat takes place in the barn, traditionally a male domain, and at the fire pit, the preparation, care, and feeding of which is in practice strictly a male concern. Folklorist Thomas A. Adler has suggested that male cookery is festal, socially and gastronomically experimental, dish-specific, temporally marked, and marked by play. He has also noted "the male affinity for outdoor cooking, in which the underlying process is a direct conjunction between the food and the fire. Roasting (whether done indoors or out) is for many people somehow a natural and masculine trait, in contrast to boiling, which is seen as a process of female cookery."[3] The Pauley barbecue bears out this observation. The distinction of sex roles here derives, I think, in part from the symbolic nature of the foods involved and of their traditional domains, and in part from the (still) strongly traditional division of gender roles in the community. These gender-specific roles tend to be strongly reinforced in symbolic and idealized ways in the preparation and presentation of the foods; furthermore, they derive from the community's value system even though the actual social and business reality of the community reflects the general changes that have occurred and continue to occur in our society. Both girls and boys belong to and participate, for example, in the Future Farmers of America at the high school.[4] Women own and operate businesses in the community. While local young women do raise hogs, goats, and cattle as part of 4-H and FFA projects, it is rare (but not unheard of) that a woman will both own and operate a farm or ranch; farming here is still a man's occupation.

Although it has certainly been traditional for farm women to kill and dress chickens (as my mother learned to do as a young bride), men have traditionally handled the slaughter and dressing of larger animals. And in this particular festive context, the men prepared the meat from butchering to "chunking" and seasoning to wrapping, cooking, and slicing. One may find, therefore, in the division of responsibilities for the pit barbecue and for the covered dish portions of the festive event a set of symbolic items and actions that reveals a number of traditional values connected with idealized gender-specific roles in the community rather than those which are operative in the normal workaday world on all levels.

In addition to commenting symbolically on idealized gender-specific roles and values in the community and playing them out as surely as if masking and costuming were an overt part of the barbecue (which they are not), the event also performs and articulates other values in a number of ways, both verbally and kinetically. For one thing, as people arrived, having driven over several miles of dirt roads and down the long driveway, they parked their cars in straight lines, two deep, leaving spaces for passage at the ends of the lines and between the lines in a pasture converted for the occasion into an unattended parking lot. The rectilinear world of rural Oklahoma where the land is laid out at right angles "true to the world" in ranges, townships, and sections, has left its imprint on the behaviors of its inhabitants; drivers cooperated within the psychological framework imposed by the physical layout of their environment.

Another physical arrangement, the serving table, laden with the covered dishes of the attendees, was laid out along a north-south axis at the east side of the large pole barn. To the east of the barn an acre or so of bermuda sod had been closely mowed to prepare for the event. Volunteers had brought tables and chairs from the bank's community room and the high school and arranged them over the grass in orderly rows perpendicular to the serving table. A low-boy trailer was backed into the north end of the barn to serve as a stage for several musicians, including a local high school fiddle player of considerable talent. Everything, in short, was arranged in straight lines, laid out "true to the world" on north-south, east-west axes. It is not too much to say that such behaviors reflect ideal community values of straight dealing, correct behavior, and squareness in many senses of the term. Business relationships here are conducted both by contract and by verbal agreements and a handshake. No lawyer practices in the local community (but attorneys do practice in nearby urban centers).

In addition to idealized patterns of cooperative activity, gender-specific roles, and the values of straight lines and right relationships, another set of idealized values is demonstrated by the event. Competence and skill, the ability to make things work and fix them when they are broken, are highly valued in this community. Every individual is expected to be able to do his or her job efficiently with little fuss or calling attention to oneself. The unearthing of the barbecue pit, an exciting event characterized by a kind of internalized ritual that is perhaps inherent in the activity itself, reveals this set of values especially well. Observed by perhaps a third or so of the people gathered by 6:00 or 6:30 in the evening, Mr. Pauley hooked a tractor to the cable connected to the huge steel plate covering the pit, mounded over with dirt and looking indeed like a huge grave, and pulled it away, clouds of steam and a wonderful aroma arising. He then backed the tractor around to the edge of the pit and lowered the three-point hitch. One of the more daring men leaped into the pit to pick up the cradle's cable and attach it to the three-point. Mr. Pauley then raised the hitch, hauled the laden cradle out of the pit and swung it over to the back of a waiting pickup, which then roared off to the waiting tables at the barn where it was unloaded.

All of this had to be done rapidly and efficiently, Mr. Pauley and others told me, since after a few minutes' exposure to the air the dense bed of glowing coals would blaze up vigorously with such intensity that the meat would be incinerated. At one such unearthing that I witnessed, a hydraulic line broke, showering Mr. James with hot hydraulic fluid and causing the hitch to descend back into the pit. But he and Mr. Pauley were able to fix the problem quickly, rescuing the barbecue from its threatened destruction. The crowd cheered. In all of these actions, Mr. Pauley and his assistants demonstrated their knowledge and competence in the ways expected of them, performing their assumed functions to the discerning judgment and applause of those attending.

When I asked Mr. Pauley to comment on the significance of the barbecue to him and to the rest of the neighborhood, he told me first that "it's a community deal here, you know. All the farmers get together, and all the neighbors that don't see one another for a year." And he was quick to contrast this state of affairs with his recollection of how folks used to visit one another when he was a boy 50 years earlier. "Oh, we don't go see one another like we used to, like when I was a kid and growing up. I know my folks, we'd even get in the wagon. I remember getting in the wagon, you know, a team of horses, and going places, see the neighbors. And likewise, they'd come and see us. And you didn't call them up, go get on that dang telephone and call and say, 'I'm having a card game tonight. Would you like to come over and play some cards?' Or, 'I'm going to come over and see you for the night.' You just went. You didn't have them communications that you've got today. Now ... you [are] just, well, you're busy, you're occupied in everything."

While the recollections of one's childhood may not be objective, the consequences of those memories are what matters. In this case, Mr. Pauley recalled growing up (as one of 11 children) in a time seen as less hurried, more sociable. And he sought a way to regain some of the comforting and sustaining sense of community that he had enjoyed as a child when life was "simpler." Hosting a big community event which featured bountiful food, homemade music, dancing, visiting, and neighboring fulfilled an important need not only for Mr. Pauley but for the community as well. It continues in a somewhat altered form as the community barbecue, a successful means of sustaining and performing the ideas and images that are central to this community's sense of its identity and purpose.

That individuals within a community may revive or initiate a tradition specifically to create and maintain community in the face of disintegrative

Figure 10-4. Morrison Community Barbecue
As Calvin Pauley backs his tractor to the pit and lowers the boom, a worker hooks up the
cage containing eight hundred pounds of barbecued beef, pork, venison, and goat.
(Photo by the author)

forces, has been noted by several recent scholars. Lin Humphrey in her analysis of small group festive gatherings,[5] for instance, surveys expressions of this idea in a variety of American community settings. In *All Silver and No Brass* Henry Glassie argues that the two men who revived mumming for a time in a portion of Northern Ireland, James Owens and Peter Cassidy, "intelligently diagnosed their community's ills and prescribed a cure. They recognized mumming's functional potential . . . harnessing an old tradition to a new task . . . helped in making the period between the world wars one that everyone [there] remembers as a relaxed, peaceful time."[6]

It is perhaps in this functional and psychological particular that this festive gathering and the others discussed in this volume differ most significantly from the sorts of festivals analyzed by Robert Smith, Alan Dundes, and Alessandro Falassi.[7] While the figures of the aproned men, preparing to retrieve and serve the barbecued meat from pit and barn may bear closer examination since, as Adler has suggested, "any regular pattern of male cooking probably contains some elements of symbolic inversion,"[8] this community barbecue does not appear to involve overt masking, inversions, or visible licentious behavior. Accentuating a tribal sense of remembered closeness, of homecoming, of plentiful food, of unthreatened and unthreatening exchange, of welcoming to the community, the behaviors here are restrained and "mellow." It is, therefore, in the multileveled meanings of homecoming that we find the most essential values of this event, in the visions of idealized family and community that form for many of the participants a refuge from the realities of the harsher outside world. As Henry Glassie has so wisely pointed out in *All Silver and No Brass,* "Events in the past, held in the memory, can be as influential upon people's actions as events in their immediate lives" (57).

The history of community picnics, festivals, carnivals, and a host of other sorts of communal events in Morrison suggests that even though the barbecue is a relatively recent tradition, it does occur in a traditional context. In June of 1894, just 9 months or so after the area had been settled, a large barbecue and community festival took place near the future townsite of Morrison; attended by 2,000 people, the event featured politicians speaking, games, contests, and, of course, plenty of visiting. In the 1920s, community Fourth of July picnics, sponsored by the local Farmer's Trading Association, were held on another farm near Morrison. A covered dish communal picnic with barrels of iced water and possibly even early watermelons provided material sustenance while horse and food races and traditional political and patriotic orations provided complementary themes. Later, these picnics died out, replaced for a while with a Farmer's Trading Association sponsored summer carnival, which featured food and contests, including a hog-calling contest. But during the time I was growing up in the community from 1940 to 1956, no such events took place.

The Pauley barbecue differs in a number of externals from these earlier community festive events: it is essentially the creation of one man with others "helping out," although its continuation has been taken over since his death by ad hoc committees within the community; it does not feature contests (although there was a drawing one year for a door prize to be awarded to one of the ladies present) and only rarely political speeches (although local and state politicians often are invited and do attend); it features a "theme food," pit barbecue, done in a traditionally learned manner ("I had seen it done"). But its function has clearly been the same: to bring the neighbors together for food and fun in an environment where the communal nature of the human being can be explored, developed, and maintained, and the essential values of the community symbolically represented and celebrated in the forms and behaviors of the event.

Whereas in the earlier years of the community, the requirements of farm life often dictated sharing labor—in threshing, in putting up hay, or in working cattle—thus providing another context for *communitas,* today's labor-saving machinery makes it possible for one man to do the work of very many, thus obviating the need for sharing labor—and thus destroying one route toward satisfying the urge for community. But this is a most powerful urge in the social animal and he will find a way to satisfy it. The barbecue begun by Calvin Pauley and Lenard James was born out of that urge; its forms and the forms of the other festive events in the community express the values of the community and nowhere more clearly than in the foods themselves.

Notes

I am grateful to the National Endowment for the Humanities for a Faculty Fellowship and to California State Polytechnic University, Pomona for a sabbatical leave that together made possible the fieldwork on which this paper is based. I also wish to thank Lin T. Humphrey for her wise counsel—and her forbearance and support while I was dong the fieldwork. I am also indebted to Roger Abrahams, Robert Georges, Michael Owen Jones, Elliott Oring, Simon Bronner, and Alessandro Falassi for their helpful comments and encouragement on this and other papers dealing with my Oklahoma Project. They are, of course, in no way responsible for shortcomings in any of the reports of that project. My greatest debt, however, is to the late Calvin Pauley, and his wife, Lorraine "Lort" Pauley; my parents, Jewel Humphrey and the late Carl M. Humphrey, whose forty years in the community opened not a few doors; and the people of Morrison, Oklahoma, who tolerated my visits, my questions, and my tape recorder with grace, good humor, interest, and support, and more than anything else made me the recipient of their continuing friendship. Thank you.

1. Morrison, Oklahoma is a farming community in the eastern end of Noble County, which is part of the so-called "Cherokee Strip," an area settled by land run on September 16,

1893. The village itself was incorporated in 1903 partly as the result of the St. Louis–San Francisco railroad's efforts to promote development along their right-of-way from Tulsa to Enid. It enjoyed a modest boom in the mid-1920s when an intense burst of oil activity a few miles north had everyone excited. But the agricultural and more general depression of the late 1920s and 1930s followed, and the town began to wither until 1961 when it had fewer than 300 people, a school that many thought would be consolidated into nearby larger, more urban districts, and a farm economy laconically recalled as "tough" by the men and women who lived through those times. An energetic banker, a risk-taking builder, and a general improvement and diversification of Oklahoma's economy combined to bring the village back from the dead to a population of around 670 in 1980. (The economy declined again, however, with the collapse of the oil boom in 1981 and hard times in agriculture throughout the 1980s.)

2. Interview 1982 with Mr. Calvin Pauley. All quotations from Mr. Pauley are from this interview unless otherwise noted.

3. "The Male Cook in Family Tradition," *Western Folklore,* 40 (January 1981): 51, 53.

4. This change took place in the 1970s. When the FFA was established in 1953 in Morrison, it was a male-only organization. The Future Homemakers of America was established several years later but was disbanded because of a lack of interest in the early 1980s.

5. "Small Group Festive Gatherings," *Journal of the Folklore Institute* 16: 190–201.

6. Bloomington: Indiana University Press, 1975: 136–37.

7. See for instance: Robert J. Smith, *The Art of the Festival As Exemplified by the Fiesta to the Patroness of Otuzco: La Virgen de la Puerta* (Lawrence, Kansas: University of Kansas Press, 1975); Alessandro Falassi, ed. *Time Out of Time: Essays on the Festival* (Albuquerque: University of New Mexico Press, 1987).

8. Adler, ibid.

11

"It's All from One Big Pot":
Booya as an Expression of Community

Anne R. Kaplan

Libeled as "the goulash of the working class" and lauded as "the most nutritious life-sustaining stew around these parts,"[1] booya is both the name of a food and the boisterous community event at which it is consumed. Churches, clubs, volunteer fire companies, and neighborhood associations host annual booyas as fundraisers.[2] Making booya is always an undertaking of gargantuan proportions. A typical recipe for about 300 gallons, for example, calls for 300 pounds of beef bones, 150 pounds of chicken, 100 pounds of garlic, 3 pounds of pickling spice, 10 pounds of salt, 17 gallons canned tomatoes, 9 gallons each of canned peas, green beans, creamed corn, and whole-kernel corn, 100 pounds of oxtails, 300 pounds of potatoes, 100 pounds of celery, 75 pounds of carrots, 2 pounds of parsley, 3–4 pounds of allspice, 80 ounces of Worcestershire sauce, and 10 pounds of pepper. This does not include the secret seasonings, which are a major component of every booya recipe. "Exotic" tastes, however, are frowned upon, and no single flavor should dominate the finished product. Making booya that everyone will like is the goal.[3]

On the surface booya (the food and the event) bears some resemblance to a number of other traditional foodways. People familiar with Kentucky burgoo point out at least superficial similarities in the recipes and note that both booya and burgoo are made in large quantity, are usually consumed in public, and are the subject of familiar jokes about the disappearance of neighborhood pets, galoshes, bowling pins, and the like.[4] The setting, attendance patterns, and accompanying entertainments at most booyas are similar to those of midwestern fundraising food events such as corn feeds and church bazaars. Yet booya stands in a class by itself, distinguished not only by the food but also by certain traditions: the way the basic recipe is handed down, the secrecy of the vital seasonings, methods of preparation, and specialized gender and age roles. Not all booyas, of course, are the same; as with any living tradition, there is ample latitude for variation. Although the tradition is limited to particular neighborhoods of a few cities or small towns, mostly in Minnesota, specific booyas clearly bear the marks of their makers. In fact, making, selling, and eating booya can be a powerful expression of community on several levels. One could say that the pattern for a booya exists in the public domain as a generic tradition.[5] But as a group brews the food and hosts the event over years—often decades—the tradition is interpreted and elaborated; it is personalized. The group comes to view booya as its own tradition, a food and an event that helps focus and express those salient values and facets of identity, such as ethnicity, occupation, or neighborhood, that the group uses to define itself. In the end, booya (the food) becomes a badge of identity while the process of making it models or recreates community structure.

Two intrinsic aspects of the tradition help explain this symbolic process: the nature of fundraisers in general and the distribution of the booya tradition in particular. Both of these factors operate as givens; they are the backdrop before which every booya is enacted. Their interaction creates a complex sense of community that is both inclusive and exclusive.

Booya is unquestionably meant to be a social event, where the focus is on eating, drinking, playing games, and talking. Viewed from the top down, all who attend are participating in a community event and sharing the experience. But the underlying purpose is to raise money, and a fundraiser, by nature, creates insider-outsider distinctions among participants. Some people gather early and donate their time to prepare food for a specific cause; others come later to buy the food, thereby supporting the cause. Not only does booya comprise hosts and paying guests, then, but some customers will benefit from the sales, while others will get only a bowl of booya and perhaps a feeling of satisfaction in return. Yet the monetary success of the event depends on the smooth interaction of the sellers and buyers who are, on a social level, almost always friends and neighbors. Thus, the principle at work is one of inclusion-exclusion; "group-within-a-group" and insider-outsider distinctions are both created and integrated at a booya.

Likewise, the push-pull of inclusion-exclusion is at work in defining an ever more specific sense of community among people who participate in the entire booya tradition. All those who belong to the generic universe of booya feel a sense of camaraderie that comes from sharing specialized knowledge and experience. It is difficult for a total outsider to gain access to the tradition: one almost has to know about booya to learn more about it. Unlike more descriptive titles for fundraisers such as "corn feed," "bean

feed," or "cake walk," the name itself tells one nothing.[6] Booyas are traditionally advertised by way of posters in neighborhood businesses and a
banner at the park where the event is held. Poster text, however, is sparse,
but this fact in itself is revealing. Often the cook's name appears along with
the sponsoring organization's, the date, and park name—but no time or
specific place. While this information might not get a stranger to the right
place at the right time, it does imply a tight sense of community where one
man's name—one cook's reputation—means enough to be advertised. Actually, the posters serve mostly as a memory jog. Most insiders learn of
upcoming booyas because they belong to the sponsoring group, or by word
of mouth from friends.

But within the unity of cognoscenti are many rival factions, for booya
has been adapted and then further refined by regional, occupational, religious, ethnic, and neighborhood groups. Thus, while St. Paul booya makers
as a community might compare themselves favorably to those from northern Minnesota, within St. Paul there is competition among firemen and
church and neighborhood groups as to whose booya is best.

The nature of the food would seem to limit its consumption to members of an in-group who know and trust the cook. In her study of American
food habits, Margaret Mead hypothesized that Americans' fear of strange
foodways accounted for the tasteless foods found in most public eating
places. She concluded that the safest preparation for a "mixed group"
would be single foods cooked separately with a minimum of seasoning,
served individually with condiments on the side.[7] Booya, on the other hand,
is a hodgepodge of meats, vegetables, and seasonings cooked to an unrecog-
nizable paste. In fact, its hallmark is this mysterious quality: "Good booya
is just mush. You can—maybe [see] a few kernels of corn or a piece of bean.
But no potatoes, no chunks of meat."[8] Traditional jokes about pets missing
from the neighborhood on booya day and wild-animal tracks stopping right
outside the cookshack door acknowledge and play on the anomalous quality of the food. These and more straightforward accounts of undesirable
substances supposedly found in the booyas of rival groups—chicken bones,
gizzards, or skin—point out that booya flirts with the line that divides order
from chaos, purity from danger, edible from inedible. It is therefore not
surprising that booya is a highly localized, community-based tradition con-
trolled by well-known and respected members of a given group.

It is difficult to pinpoint the origins of booya. Ephemeral advertisements are rarely archived, and few organizations seem to maintain records
of this sort of event. Evidence collected to date shows a cluster of booyas
beginning in the 1930s. The North St. Paul Volunteer Firemen's booya,
however, dates to 1922, and informants remember that in northern Minnesota the Vermillion Old Settlers Association hosted booyas at least as early

as the Great Depression. In fact, booya figures prominently in the Depression-era memories of many informants, as well as in the writings from that era of populist-feminist author Meridel LeSueur and in the printings of her brother Mac. The Silver Fox Club, an all-male social group from West 7th Street, a blue-collar neighborhood in St. Paul, began its booya in 1936; the West 7th St. Pleasure Bowling League followed in 1938. That same year the Allied Czech Societies of St. Paul held a booya, but it is unclear whether this was a regular event.[9]

Most people trace booya to the French-Canadian fur traders who supposedly sustained themselves by stewing up vats of whatever wild game and vegetables were on hand. By dubious etymology they claim that the name "booya" is an Anglicized version of the French "bouillir" (to boil).[10] Such speculation aside, living memory dates booya to the late 19th century, when bars along West 7th St. began brewing booya to lure in customers. In fact, a minority of informants, pointing out the food's similarity to goulash, think "booya" is a corruption of an unknown Bohemian word.[11] After the turn of the century the food was appropriated by churches, clubs, and other organizations. Today booya is almost always used to raise funds, although occasionally a group of neighbors or a large family will host one, typically for a Fourth of July gathering or family reunion.[12]

The vast majority of booyas are held on summer Sunday afternoons in public parks; a few take place in VFW, church, or fire halls. In St. Paul, for example, the busiest facility is Highland Park, known as "the pavilion that booya built"; six gas-fired kettles are permanently installed in a cookshack adjacent to a covered area complete with serving counters, concrete floor, and picnic tables. From May through August the pavilion is booked every Sunday for booyas. In North St. Paul the volunteer firemen built and donated to the city a booya building that holds 12 gas-fired vats.[13]

All booyas have the same basic structure, follow the same general rules for preparation, and depend on the same kinds of gender and age divisions of labor. Numerous levels of participation are available to potential booya makers. Men, and to some extent women and children, choose a role depending on their degree of commitment to the endeavor. People assigned to different tasks thus form the substrata of the group of insiders directly responsible for the food. As an event, booya has two distinct components: the preparation and the serving. For the insiders who make the booya, the preparation is the festive social occasion, much more so than the next day when the booya is sold and consumed.

The most apparent and widely shared facet of identity among booya makers is gender: booyas are held and managed by groups of men. The groups may exist for male-only recreation with some community service functions, for family-based recreation, to benefit various church functions,

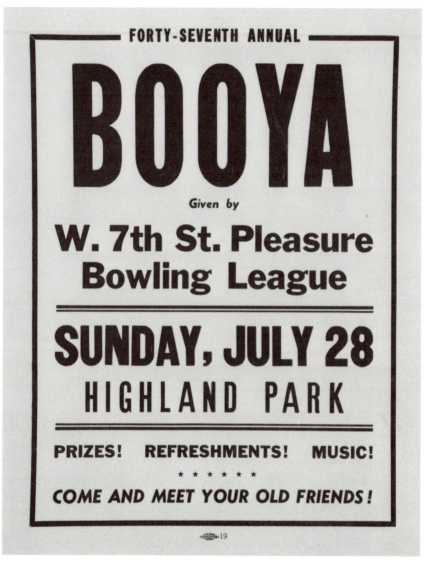

Figure 11-1   Poster, 1985, Taped Inside (Facing Out) a Booya
Maker's Car Window
Telephone poles and store windows are more common
posting places for such advertisement.
*(Collections of the Minnesota Historical Society, St.
Paul)*

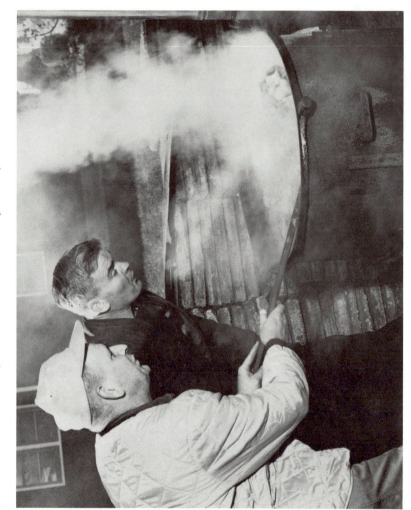

Figure 11-2 Nicholas D. Coleman (Rear) and Charles Korlath Check the Brew, ca. 1962 Coleman, a state senator for eighteen years, used this powerful image in some of his early campaign literature. Booyas were an important fund-raising tool for Minnesota's Democratic-Farmer Labor Party through the 1970s.
(*Collections of the Minnesota Historical Society, St. Paul*)

or purely for community service. When members of these male groups gather to make booya, various status rankings become apparent. "Old timers" are revered. They have their pick of the tasks or have the right to show up after the work is in progress simply to socialize. Middle-aged men are expected to carry the full weight of responsibility. The booya chef—the one man nominally in charge, who orders and inspects ingredients, who alone knows the secret recipe for spices, who supervises the process, and who tastes the concoction and pronounces it ready before it is served—this man usually comes from the ranks of the middle-aged. But he has apprenticed with the holder of the recipe, typically his father, father-in-law, or uncle, before the older man became too decrepit to pass it on. Thus he has close ties to the older generation and deep roots in the booya tradition. Young men are welcomed and they work hard at many of the same tasks as the older and middle-aged men, but they are clearly treated as beginners; their work is supervised. Teenaged boys are on the periphery. They may perform a few tasks such as sawing the bones for stock, but mostly they are onlookers. A boy who is 14 or 15 and has a father in the middle ranks may be allowed to spend the night at the pavilion with the booya crew. This rite of passage entitles him to join the ranks of the young men.

Single women do not help out with booya. When women are in attendance, they are the wives of the middle-aged male contingent and, occasionally, their pre-teen daughters. And their tasks as well as their socializing are clearly limited. To the women of St. Francis parish, for example, falls the task of peeling ten pounds of garlic. These women, gathered by the wife of the booya chef, meet at her house two nights before the booya is held. There they share food and wine or beer—and peel garlic. The next day they resume work at the booya pavilion where they peel potatoes while the men chop vegetables. Although they share in the beer and cigarettes, they do not mingle. The women work at a separate picnic table, several tables removed from the men's work.

This separation of the sexes is a prime example of the way in which making booya is a model of community structure. The preparation tasks are by no means assigned according to physical ability or dexterity; rather, the duties are culturally determined. Booya fits the American system wherein men are allowed to cook at outdoor, "roughing it" events—barbecues, picnics, pig roasts—whereas women cook in the home. More specifically, making booya is considered recreation and, among families interviewed for this study, men and women generally socialize in same-sex groups. It comes as no surprise, then, that for an event sponsored by all-male groups, the duties and responsibilities of women are both segregated and circumscribed.

Making booya is a time-consuming task. Starting at about 9:00 a.m. on

Saturday, the day before the event, the vegetables must be cleaned and cut. All are chopped separately and stored, on ice, in metal trash cans lined with plastic garbage bags. Around six o'clock at night water is heated in the 30-gallon kettles. All of the meats are added and cooked at this point. At about midnight, with two men to a kettle, the meat is removed, boned, and returned to the pot. From here on, periodic checks are made for bones. The secret spices, in bags, are added in the night. Around dawn the vegetables and other flavorings go in. From this point on, the booya must be stirred constantly to prevent the potatoes from sticking to the bottom and burning. Around 10:00 a.m. on Sunday the chef begins tasting the booya and adjusting seasonings. Most booyas open to the public at noon, about 24 hours after the men's work began. And most like to claim that they are sold out by 2:00 p.m.

Different organizations handle the nighttime vigil differently. At some, work is done in four-hour shifts by different crews of men. At others, one crew cooks through the night and is relieved at dawn. At very few booyas are women present through the night;[14] night is the time for women to be home supervising the domestic scene. Among those at all familiar with booya, the social side of the nighttime work is well known. In this typically all-male event, beer and stories flow freely, often starting early in the afternoon and continuing at least until dawn. In the words of one fireman, "This is the one occasion that brings us all together. We used to bowl, drink a few beers, play cards. Now people don't have time, or the wives don't like it, or whatever. For this [booya] the retired come back. It's our biggest social function."[15]

The booya itself is an entirely different social occasion that emphasizes integration, not separation, of the sexes and ages. Unlike preparing booya, the public part of the event *is* family-oriented, and it is not unusual to see three generations lounging around a picnic table, or families pitching horseshoes, or teenagers gathered around a large radio.

Most people who attend a booya are part of the social network of the hosts. Thus, any given booya is overwhelmingly a neighborhood event, a parish event, or an organizational event. But as such social networks have long tentacles—friends who have moved away maintain neighborhood ties, families bring relatives and friends from the outside, and so forth—it is also a time for broadening and reintegrating community ties.

At the booya, attenders, of course, eat booya. They also have the opportunity to buy beer or soda, candy bars, hot dogs, potato chips; to play carnival-type games like show-down poker; to participate in a raffle; and, occasionally, to dance to a one- or two-piece band. While many people buy gallons of booya to take home and freeze for later consumption, insiders consider it boorish simply to purchase carry-out food. Booyas are meant for socializing, for mingling and lingering over beers, for spending money on hot dogs and games of chance after the booya is gone.

At the public event, thus, the inclusive side of booya is reasserted for reasons both economic and social. Booya sells for $1 per bowl, and most people estimate that it costs volunteers 80¢ a bowl to make it. Organizations make most of their profit from beer, candy, and soda sales in addition to the income from games of chance. Therefore, it is better for the host group if people make a day of the event, talking, eating, drinking, and playing games for the entire afternoon.

In addition, booyas are a place and time for entire families to relax and visit with one another. People complain that their pace of life and leisure-time activities make it difficult to assemble the whole family around the dinner table, much less have time to see friends and neighbors with *their* extended families.[16] Booya is a time set aside for such socializing, for putting into practice the value of family and community that informants say they strongly believe but can rarely achieve. People demonstrate their commitment to community by choosing to devote a Sunday afternoon to booya rather than to fishing or watching television, gardening or painting the house. Merely purchasing a few quarts of food at the carry-out line would demonstrate a degree of financial support, but would also imply that other affairs are more important than community. In the words of one man who grew up in the West 7th neighborhood, "Booya is not just a bowlful of stew; it's a celebration that brings together the people.... You can't just eat booya. You go to a booya."[17]

While booya is all about community, however, it belongs to no one group in particular. Most observers of the tradition, including many who make booya, believe it expresses ethnicity. However, not only is it impossible to prove its French-Canadian origins, but also in St. Paul the "Bohunks on West 7th," "the Krauts on Rice St.,"[18] and the Czechs in South St. Paul all proudly claim booya as their own. And even this ethnic characterization is a gross overstatement, as the so-called West 7th Bohunks, for example, include Irish, Germans, and French Canadians within their ranks. The Finns and Slavs in northern Minnesota also participate in the rivalry over whose booya is best. And, furthermore, the suburban volunteer fire companies have members from a variety of backgrounds. Ethnicity is not even a salient factor in their group identity.

Nor can booya be tied to any single locale. Enthusiasts stoutly argue that theirs is a purely Minnesotan food. In fact, a South St. Paul florist, formerly a rodeo director, has undertaken a one-man crusade to add booya to the roster of state symbols. In 1985, for the third consecutive year, he organized an Annual World Booya Championship Contest, hoping, actually, to spread the gospel of booya statewide![19] In the process of promoting these events, it came to light that the Belgians and French Canadians of Green Bay, Wisconsin, also make something they call "booyah." There followed a nasty exchange of brags and name-calling in the hometown newspapers, in which loyalists sought to impugn the authenticity and quality of their rival's products, that ended abruptly when Wisconsin backed out of bringing its booya to the contest.[20] The fact that booyas also exist in Canada also confounds Minnesota's claim to the foodway, although the tradition is clearly confined to a fairly limited region of North America.

But even in Minnesota booya exists only in isolated pockets, in particular neighborhoods of particular cities in particular regions of the state. At first glance it appears to be an urban tradition, and even so, as far as research can show, booyas are only held in the metropolitan Minneapolis-St. Paul area and several hundred miles north, in the small towns in Minnesota's iron-mining district. In fact, class, more than anything else, seems to be the common denominator of booya, which flourishes in blue-collar neighborhoods and working-class Catholic parishes. Iron Range towns in northern Minnesota exhibit many urban characteristics precisely because they were established to house the workers of heavy industry; they are unlike Minnesota's rural small towns where booya is an unknown phenomenon.[21] Yet it is important to note that class is not stated as a salient factor for participants in the tradition. Rather, as mentioned above, communities that host booyas define themselves in terms of ethnicity, neighborhood, interest group, and so forth.

In any case, the shared traits of being workers in Minnesota do not work to forge much sense of community among members of these two regional groups. Instead, booya becomes a focus for rivalries between these two, re-expressing longstanding regional prides and hostilities wherein Twin Citians refer to the rest of the state as "out-state" with all the implications of being backward, unsophisticated, and quaint, while Iron Rangers hold Twin Citians in contempt for their supposedly soft and favored existence, skimming the cream off of state programs. For example, when a native St. Paul newspaperman ventured to say in print that "Folks on the Iron Range occasionally sup of something called 'booyeh' that may be similar"[22] [to St. Paul's], an angry Iron Range resident replied:

> The St. Paul variety is surely a far cry from the original. The voyageurs couldn't lay hands on those exotic ingredients such as pickling spices, parsley, garlic, etc. I don't know where they got that recipe, but unlike their recipe, which many dislike, I don't know anyone who has tasted the Iron Range Booyah who doesn't say it is utterly delicious. And the cost of our booyah is a great deal less than St. Paul's.[23]

Within the Twin Cities, St. Paul, which has the reputation of being the more ethnic, neighborhood-oriented of the two, hosts numerous booyas. Across the river in Minneapolis, the city that bills itself as "the Minneapple" and projects a cosmopolitan, cultured image, residents are largely ignorant of booya.[24] Yet even in St. Paul booyas exist only in isolated pockets, mostly in solid working-class neighborhoods of varying ethnicities. Catholicism is the predominant religion in these areas, but it is not correct to say that booya is a Catholic epiphenomenon, because booyas held outside of these neighborhoods show no such affiliation. Although the working-class link does not figure in community self-definition, it is important from an analytical standpoint, especially when considering that residents of the middle-class Macalester neighborhood, less than two miles from West 7th, hardly know of booya. And residents of the equally middle-class Highland area, which coincidentally houses the park pavilion where most of St. Paul's booyas occur, rarely if ever attend these events that are in, but definitely not of, their neighborhood and community.

The foregoing discussion briefly outlines the basic contours of the booya tradition. Examples of the annual booyas held by the parish of St. Francis de Sales and by the North St. Paul Volunteer Fire Department clearly demonstrate how specific communities use and adapt the generic tradition, making it a powerful medium for enacting and expressing a sense of community. The settings for these two booyas differ; the church is located in the heart of the booya belt in the West 7th St. neighborhood, while the fire company is in a late nineteenth-century town that has become a suburb of St. Paul. Likewise, the nature of the groups or premises for joining them are very different. The church has built a family-based community grounded in shared spiritual beliefs and strengthened through the continuity of generations of the same families from the same neighborhood regularly interacting at sacred and secular functions. The fire company, on the other hand, is composed only of men who volunteer a portion of their time for a specialized kind of community service. Membership is based on individual commitment to an ideal. The community they serve is a political entity, much broader than the social or cultural groups to which individual firemen belong. These men may not know the people they will help, nor, in that case, do they expect to establish relationships with their "clients."

St. Francis de Sales

The West 7th St. neighborhood in which the church is located is best characterized as a solid, stable, blue-collar enclave. "You have your upward mobility, but not here. Here people stay. Generations . . . families live in the same house or block. People might move away, but they come back."[25]

Cross-cut by railroad tracks and a freeway, bounded by downtown St. Paul to the east, the Mississippi River more or less to the south, the site of the Schmidt brewery, oil-storage tanks, a power plant, and numerous auto repair garages, second-hand stores, and small businesses, the neighborhood is one of St. Paul's oldest. Many men grew up there to work on street construction crews, for the railroad, meat-packing houses, or in trade unions as machinists, welders, assemblers, electricians, and the like. As in many traditional communities, women did not work outside of the home until fairly recently. In addition to churches of several Protestant denominations, the neighborhood houses three Catholic churches: St. Francis, originally the German parish; St. James, originally Irish; and St. Stanislaus, originally Bohemian (mostly Czech). Today church membership is mixed; people have been known to transfer allegiances among the three, but generally they stay with the family parish, a choice originally based on ethnicity and proximity to the church building. All three of the churches have held booyas; of them, St. Francis's is the most visible.[26]

The men and women of St. Francis make about 300 gallons of booya for their church picnic; theirs is the recipe quoted earlier in this article. Parish members can not date when the church began holding booyas; they speculate that the tradition goes back about 60 years. Since the late 1940s or early 1950s when Highland Park Pavilion was built, they have always used that facility.

The preparation process follows the age and gender rules listed above: the women gather in a home to peel garlic on Friday night and execute different tasks from the men's on Saturday at the Highland Pavilion. Youth has a special role at this booya; the son of one participant saws beef bones with a hacksaw under the supervision of an "old-timer." His is perhaps the most physically demanding job. Joe McDonough, the chef, oversees the work and takes "a lot of guff," both serious complaints from choppers about the quality of the vegetables, and light-hearted (the usual: "Hey Joe, someone's wondering where his cat is"). McDonough inherited the recipe from his father, who got it from Jim Kane, a janitor at St. James Church. While the amounts and kinds of vegetables and meats are a matter of public record, no one, not even his wife, knows the ingredients that flavor the mix. St. Francis booya makers credit him, aided of course by the recipe, for their superior booya. McDonough cooks the chicken in separate pots, "lets it settle, degreases the broth, and then just puts in stock. That way you're not picking out skin and bone."[27] This and the preparation of beef stock from bones is all accomplished before 6:00 p.m. mass. Thereafter, crews of men begin taking four-hour shifts, cooking the meats together, and adding the vegetables in proper sequence. Around 3:30 a.m. McDonough returns with the secret spices all mixed in a cloth bag.

The nighttime vigil is a social occasion that the men enjoy despite its grueling aspects. Crowding into a small outbuilding with six large, hot kettles of booya, constantly stirring massive amounts of thick, heavy food on a humid August night has strenuous moments. The old-timers tend to step back and let the middle-aged or younger men handle the toughest physical labor. But the work draws them together, and the vast amount of not-yet-finished booya, the reason for their gathering, is put to good use. The men float cobs of corn or polish sausage in the vats, and these snacks absorb some of the flavor and aroma of the brew. Thus, on this special occasion, the men share not only the beer, jokes, and stories that might be part of their everyday social interactions, but also ordinary food made special for, and because of, their participation in making booya.

The nature of the longstanding and intertwined family-neighborhood ties and traditional age and gender roles that characterize the church community make joining the inner circle of booya makers a slow and difficult, almost organic, process. The church, of course, welcomes new members. And the booya makers nominally encourage participation: many hands make light work. But newcomers get no closer than the Saturday-afternoon vegetable chopping for many years. In 1985, for example, one man, aged about 30, attended the afternoon session, but when the vegetables were all chopped and the workers pushed back from the tables, lit up cigarettes, and poured themselves more beer, he got up to leave. After his departure the old-timers and women spent considerable time trying to remember his name, place his face, and relate him to a known family.

At the booya on Sunday the principle of inclusion, or the larger community spirit, ascends. Booya makers mingle with the crowd. The men who stand behind the sale counters or circulate throughout the park retrieving trays and discarding empty bowls and plasticware wear no identifying clothing or buttons. The occasion is a parish picnic, attended also by close friends and neighbors of churchgoers. Outside of the church, word of the upcoming booya travels informally. Posters are not widely distributed or conspicuously displayed. As with most booyas, "People *know* when the booya is on. Word gets out—'The men are working at the booya. It's gonna be this weekend.'"[28]

In fact, the event highlights a larger-than-parish sense of community, owing to the fact that West 7th recognizes and presents itself as a solid booya enclave. Yet within it, the booya tradition is decentralized. Various groups hold booyas to raise funds for sundry, specialized purposes: church and ethnic fraternal organizations, recreational equipment, club operating funds, and so on. Many of the men of St. Francis belong to other social and recreational groups in the neighborhood. Thus, while rivalry exists about whose booya is best, membership in different organizations does not suggest a conflict. Members of the Silver Fox Club or West 7th St. Pleasure Bowling League, for example, come to the St. Francis booya because they like the food and because they or their friends also belong to the church.

These same people who may go to three different booyas in the span of eight weeks, however, do not attend those held outside of the neighborhood. People are well aware of other booya traditions; they volunteer information that Rice St. booya is greasy or the booya in North St. Paul is made in such quantity that it is thin (it is not), but this talk has the quality of legend. No one will admit to attending these other events; they simply have heard all the facts about the inferiority of the product outside the borders of their neighborhood community.

Thus, the annual St. Francis parish booya is a clear expression of both personal and group identity, of community on several levels that, like an inverted pyramid, grow ever broader or more inclusive. The unstated rules and roles for making booya model traditional family structure and values. The actual process of making booya enacts and reinforces these divisions, but it also draws participants together, forging a sense of group identity based on shared traditions and activity, family, neighborhood, and church membership. And attending the booya is, most of all, a powerful expression of community built on family, religion, friendship, and neighborhood allegiance: "You can't make a little of it. You can't make it yourself. It's all from one big pot. Everyone shares."[29]

North St. Paul

In North St. Paul the picture is somewhat different. Although the area today has become a suburb of St. Paul, it was founded in the late 1880s as a separate entity. "The town rose virtually overnight ... to a bustling town containing more than a dozen factories."[30] Several decades later twenty-seven factories graced the area, ranging from several iron works and a brick company to furniture, piano, and casket manufacturers. A fire in 1933 destroyed much of the town.[31] The suburban appearance and aspects of North St. Paul are more prominent today than in 1922 when the volunteer fire company began holding booyas.

Change and mobility are themes that run through conversations with the volunteer firemen, whether they are discussing the community or their booya. Currently, people who live in the town may not work there. Likewise, people who now live there did not necessarily grow up in that area. Members of the fire department include men originally from Minneapolis, northern Minnesota, and even Chicago. These men—tradesmen and professionals—come from a variety of ethnic and religious cultures.

Volunteer firemen, of necessity, are derived from the immediate community, and their desire to join is motivated by several ideals: "It's the social function . . . and the chance to help with no commitment, no responsibility. If I get a fire call or an ambulance call, I go out, do my thing, and walk away from it. That's all. I don't need thanks. I've got the satisfaction, and that's it. It's over."[32] The larger community that the group serves is, in some ways, abstract. There need be no personal ties. Yet the group itself, formed for community service, does fulfill social needs for its members, some of whom join specifically as a means of establishing a sense of community in a new place.

This booya, like St. Francis's, follows the general pattern of age and gender role separation. The booya, however, is twice as big, filling thirteen kettles and totaling about 700 gallons. The nighttime stirring is handled by one crew—the same men who clean the permanently installed kettles. As in the West 7th neighborhood, nighttime is the prime social time: "A lot of the old-timers come back, sit around, drink a beer, and bull. It's real nice."[33] In North St. Paul, however, the old-timers and even middle-aged men ruminate frequently on changes in their tradition, rather than continuity. Before the department built and donated to the city its current pavilion in a park in 1981, the booya had been held in at least three different parks. The men cooked over wood fires in canvas tents, and, although all involved are pleased at the relative ease of using stationary kettles and gas flames, several people maintain that the booya flavor suffers without the wood smoke.

Over the years, booya ingredients have become more divorced from the community. Firewood used to be donated; vegetables at one time were all locally grown garden produce, except for the potatoes which were grown by the treasurer's relative about forty miles north of town. Currently the treasurer purchases all ingredients from a produce wholesaler and a meat market.

Perhaps the most discussed change, however, is the nature of female participation in the event. On Saturday afternoon, in the North St. Paul firehouse, a handful of women and young girls sit in a circle spatially segregated from the men's work just as at the St. Francis booya. Their sole task is to string and snap green beans. In 1985, there were too few women to complete the task in time; a young boy began cutting beans, but did so on the tables where the men were working. Asked about this discontinuity, one fireman replied: "Yeah. Used to be about a dozen women would be sitting around cutting beans, talking about whatever women talk about. And the men were real chauvinistic. Wouldn't cut 'em [the beans]. 'That's women's work!' Well, now the women would just say 'Sh—[doesn't complete the word].' You can read lips, can't you? . . ."[34]

Other commentary reveals the firemen's booya to be a microcosm of social change. "Used to be the backbone, the Ladies' Auxiliary. Now things

Figure 11-3.   Booya Advertisement Posted Near the Entrance to
Casey Lake Park.
*(Collections of the Minnesota Historical Society, St.
Paul)*

are different."[35] According to department members, the wives of the younger firemen who have replaced the retired older generation of volunteers either work outside the home or have other commitments that preclude participation in the booya. In addition to preparing beans, women used to make pies and cakes; their auxiliary ran a bake sale at the booya. "Now we hardly have any, and it looks bad ... I think it's better to have nothing than just a little."[36] The cookies and bars which women currently donate are easier to prepare than pies and cakes and possibly bespeak less time for commitment.

The social changes affecting the lives of the firemen as well as the nature and composition of the department makes the annual booya an especially significant event for members. As in other organizations that host booyas, the recipe is a secret part of the tradition that binds this group. In North St. Paul the lineage of recipe holders encompasses two families: William Weber, who started the booya, retired in the late 1950s or early 1960s and passed the secret spice combination on to his son-in-law. That man died young, and the recipe went to Weber's son, who is currently on the verge of retirement. "Who he's passing it on to, we don't know."[37] It is interesting to note that the department members cherish and respect the secrecy of the spice ingredients. The formula, for safekeeping, is locked in a bank safe-deposit box. "We could go look, but we choose not to. It's kind of a little tradition. Everyone needs traditions, you know."[38]

Advertising for the North St. Paul booya is a broader-spectrum affair than in the West 7th St. neighborhood. Rather than relying on posters in the windows of community businesses, in recent years the event has been announced over local radio, and, in 1985, on cable television. People are said to come from many of St. Paul's northern suburbs, but never from the city's well-known booya neighborhoods. The fact that all 700 gallons are usually sold within three hours attests to the success of the advertising.

At the booya, the firemen are clearly identified by their uniforms, including name tags. This garb is probably necessary to mark them as hosts, since people who attend the booya are not necessarily friends and neighbors who will recognize those in charge. In fact, in contrast to the St. Francis booya, this one, although it is a longstanding North St. Paul tradition, no longer serves as a community social event. "We try to make it a family day. People used to sit around and socialize more. People of today—I guess we're just in too fast a world—they just buy it and go. A few do stay, but not like they used to."[39]

Department members cite various reasons for this state of affairs. Some say that the booya sells out so fast that there is nothing to stay for. Others claim that since there are few or no games (these are a costly risk to rent if little participation is expected) and not much of a bake sale, there is nothing to tempt people to stay.[40] Still others claim that people prefer to buy vast quantities of booya and freeze it for use in cooler weather.[41] Whatever the reasons may be, the booya sells rapidly, but the attractive picnic grounds facing the lake are sparsely populated.

The nature and mission of the sponsoring group perhaps explains why this booya succeeds better as a fundraiser than as a social event. The community that the firemen serve is the entire city of North St. Paul, an abstract political entity rather than a personalized group of friends. The funds they raise go to the firemen's relief association general fund, to fire prevention posters, prizes for the city's Junior Fire Marshal program, to support civic doings like the Lions Club fishing contest and the local American Legion, to host regional firemen's meetings, to supply the fire station with beer and soda, to make donations to the city's athletic association, send flowers to funerals of past members, condolence and get-well cards, presents, and the like. The department spent $22,000 alone on the booya shelter which residents of the city may use throughout the year as a park building. "Everything has basically gone back into the city one way or another."[42]

The booya makers themselves, on the other hand, derive and reinforce a sense of community through their participation in the tradition. Membership in the department is a way for men to foster and share a sense of community in what they perceive as a highly mobile society where traditional values are in flux. Participating in the company booya intensifies their commitment to the group and their ties to its past. The North St. Paul Volunteer Firemen's booya is a totally different kind of social occasion set in a very different community context than the St. Francis parish event. Each group has shaped the generic booya tradition into a clear expression of its contemporary sense of self.

Notes

1. *Minneapolis Tribune,* September 6, 1981, p. 1B; *Minneapolis Star and Tribune,* December 8, 1984, p. 1B.

2. For a discussion of the social role of such organizations in promoting the consumption of foods not on grocery shelves, see Simon Bronner, *Grasping Things* (Lexington: University of Kentucky Press, 1986), Chapter 4 *passim.*

3. What constitutes "exotic," of course, is a matter of opinion. To members of other booya traditions, both the garlic and pickling spices mentioned above are offensive and too esoteric, respectively; Betty Wiljamaa to Editor, *Minneapolis Tribune,* September 27, 1984, p. 12A; interview of Howard Anderson, North St. Paul, August 8, 1985; interview of Ron Ritchie, North St. Paul, September 8, 1985.

4. Interviews of Arnie Leitner, Joe McDonough, and Joe Reichert (St. Francis de Sales Church), St. Paul, August 10, 1985; Frank Lewis, North St. Paul, September 8, 1985; *St. Paul Dispatch,* September 25, 1984, p. B1; Cathy Barton, "'It's Nothing But a Big Bowl

of Soup!': Kentucky Burgoo and the Burgoo Supper," *Kentucky Folklore Record* 24 (July–December, 1978): 110.

5. In fact, new communities begin to hold booyas from time to time. The Apple Valley Volunteer fire company's event is only in its ninth year, and the tiny town of Finland, located about six miles west of Lake Superior in northern Minnesota, attempted its first "Harvest Booya and Finn Fest" in 1985. Booya came to Finland through a former resident of St. Paul, who decided the food would be a welcome addition to the annual harvest party. The recipe was obtained from a man in South St. Paul who has been cooking booya for forty years.

6. Insiders tell jokes about how outsiders are puzzled by or sadly misconstrue the meaning of the name, thinking, for example, that the posters advertise a new dance craze, a terrorist group, or point to a taxidermist's: Body A (a misreading of a hand-lettered sign); *Minneapolis Star and Tribune,* December 8, 1984, p. 1B; *St. Paul Pioneer Press,* February 22, 1973, p. 19.

7. Margaret Mead, "The Problem of Changing Food Habits," in Committee on Food Habits, *The Problem of Changing Food Habits* (Washington, D.C.: National Research Council Bulletin No. 108, Oct., 1943).

8. Here to end of paragraph interview of Arnie Leitner, St. Paul, August 10, 1985; interview of Patrick Coleman, St. Paul, July 3, 1985; Mary Douglas, *Purity and Danger: An Analysis of the Concepts of Pollution and Taboo* (London: Routledge and Kegan Paul, 1966); Roger Abrahams, "Equal Opportunity Eating: A Structural Excursus on Things of the Mouth," in *Ethnic and Regional Foodways in the United States: The Performances of Group Identity,* Linda Keller Brown and Kay Mussell, eds. (Knoxville: University of Tennessee Press, 1984): 19–36.

9. Meridel Le Sueur, *The Girl,* reprint ed. (Minneapolis: West End Press and MEP Publications, 1982); Mac Le Sueur, "Untitled," painting ca. 1934–41; Allied Czech Societies of St. Paul, poster, Joseph Pavlicek Papers, Immigration History Research Center, St. Paul; West 7th St. Pleasure Bowling League, poster, collections of the Minnesota Historical Society, St. Paul; *The Community Reporter* (St. Paul), July, 1984, p. 3.

10. In fact, booyas are held in Canada's Ottawa Valley. The food and form of the event are different, but the communal base is consistent. Neighbors donate chickens to be raffled, and at the end of the raffle all fowl is stewed in a common pot and shared. I am indebted to I. Sheldon Posen for this information.

11. This theory appears to be the weaker of the two. Mrs. B. A. Ebert of LeCenter, Minnesota contributed a family recipe to a cookbook with the information that "a top favorite would be the Booya, or *'Vomachka' as we Bohemians call it* [my emphasis] made from the gizzards and hearts of ducks"; Virginia Huck and Ann H. Andersen, *100 Years of Good Cooking* (St. Paul: Minnesota Historical Society, 1958): 92.

12. Interview of Gene Gagner, St. Paul, July 28, 1985; Patrick Coleman, St. Paul, July 3, 1985.

13. Interview of Howard Anderson, North St. Paul, August 8, 1985; St. Paul Park System Record Books for 1985; *Minneapolis Tribune,* September 6, 1981, p. 1B.

14. Women do participate in the night vigil at the West 7th St. Pleasure Bowling League's and the Sokol Minnesota's (a Czech organization) booyas. Both of these groups stress that they are family oriented, clearly cognizant of their anomalous status within the

tradition. Interviews of Gene Gagner and Brenda S., St. Paul, July 28, 1985; John Carl Hancock, Minneapolis, January 15, 1986.

15. Interview of Frank Lewis, North St. Paul, September 7, 1985.

16. See, for example, interviews of Gene Gagner, July 28, 1985; Nicholas J. Coleman, September 26, 1985; Dominic Cincotta, September 8, 1985.

17. Nicholas J. Coleman, in *Minneapolis Tribune,* September 6, 1981, p. 1B.

18. Interview of Robert Hess, St. Paul, August 2, 1985.

19. *Minneapolis Star and Tribune,* August 26, 1984, p. 4B.

20. *St. Paul Pioneer Press,* September 25, 1984, p. B1.

21. In this vein, however, it is curious that booya is also unknown in the city of Duluth, which perfectly fits the profile of a locale for the event. It will be interesting to discover whether the Finland booya takes root.

22. *Minneapolis Tribune,* September 6, 1981, p. 5B.

23. Betty Wiljamaa to Editor, *Minneapolis Tribune,* September 27, 1981, p. 12A.

24. Like most popular generalizations on booya, this one is not entirely correct. In the Minneapolis suburb of St. Anthony Village, the parish of St. Charles Boromel held booyas in the 1940s, and in nearby suburban New Brighton, St. John the Baptist Church has a vigorous booya tradition. Both parishes are composed of an ethnically mixed population which migrated out of the city's northeast, largely working-class, neighborhoods. I am indebted to Mark Haidet of the Minnesota Historical Society for this information.

25. Interview of Gene Gagner, St. Paul, July 28, 1985.

26. Connie X., for example, recently joined St. Stanislaus but continues to help cook for the St. Francis booya, as she has for twenty-five years; interview, August 10, 1985. St. Francis actually hosts two booyas per season, one as its parish picnic and the other, held by the Casinos, a men's club in the church, to benefit the church's athletic fund. This paper focuses on the parish event, which is more broadly representative of the community.

27. Connie X., August 10, 1985. She is contrasting St. Francis booya with others that do not use a stock but put all meats directly into the booya pot.

28. Interview of Nicholas J. Coleman, September 26, 1985.

29. Ibid.

30. North St. Paul Coordinating Committee, *Bicentennial Celebration, Souvenir Edition* (North St. Paul: The Committee, 1976): 2.

31. Linda Olson, *An Abbreviated History of the Community of North St. Paul,* n.p., n.d.

32. Interview of Frank Lewis, September 7, 1985.

33. Interview of Ron Ritchie, September 7, 1985.

34. Interview of Ray Z., September 7, 1985.

35. Interview of Frank Lewis, September 7, 1985.

36. Interview of Dominic Cincotta, September 7, 1985.

37. Interview of Frank Lewis, September 7, 1985.

38. Here and the quote below, interview of Howard Anderson, fire chief, August 8, 1985.

39. Interview of Ron Ritchie, September 8, 1985. Ritchie has ties to West 7th through marriage and claims that although he has been to city booyas, none of the West 7th folk will ever come to his.

40. Interview of Howard Anderson, August 8, 1985.

41. Interview of Dominic Cincotta, September 8, 1985.

42. In fact, booya is so popular among deer hunters that the firemen hold a smaller booya in October strictly so hunters can stock up. At this latter event booya is sold only to carry out. Interview of Howard Anderson, August 8, 1985.

Part III

"Boosterism," Food, and Festive Performance

Introduction to Part III

As a characteristic of American culture, "boosterism" finds its expression in food-centered or food-augmented festive gatherings as it does in other aspects of American life. Promoters of business interests, individuals catering to special interests, and even professional folklorists ("applied folklorists") who, through their understanding of how traditional cultures work, meet the needs of newer communities, have created another class of festive performances, one with which the next three papers are concerned.

Thomas Adler finds at the intersection of commercial and private food preparation at bluegrass music festivals a richly symbolic texture of values congruent with those performed in the music itself: a vision of "down home" and an idealized past shared by a community set apart from their ordinary lives in the festive context. Food in Adler's analysis performs both the pragmatic function of feeding musicians and audience while away from home and the symbolic one of creating a community of shared values, heightened by music and fellowship, a "re-creation of social indentity through complex and cooperative foodways patterns." Payday may be a long way away but fried chicken, festival beans, fish fries, and country breakfasts distract the mind.

Not all community festive events are enduring. Anthony Rauche chronicles the demise of one community's attempt to celebrate its ethnic heritage. Rauche details how the scale of the event and a conflict between the clichéd ethnic expectations of "outsiders" on the one hand and memories of what a "real" *festa* was in the old country combined to destroy the *Festa Italiana* in Hartford, Connecticut. The fragility of efforts to create community exemplified here is a sobering reminder that human performances in any genre are subject to the variabilities of human emotions and expectations, not to mention the pressures of commercial exploitation.

In contrast to the experience described by Rauche, the final essay in this section affirms the power of food-centered constructed festivals to create a degree of understanding among diverse ethnic groups thrown together in a modern city. James Griffith describes the success of festival organizers in creating a forum in which ethnic groups can develop a sense of community among themselves while at the same time displaying that sense to the rest of the citizens of Tucson. Not surprisingly, food is a powerful and effective device for expressing (along with music and dance) key elements in the identity of these groups precisely because they can be performed, displayed, and consumed.

12

Bluegrass Music and Meal-Fried Potatoes: Food, Festival, Community

Thomas A. Adler

In the nearly twenty-five years since the advent of weekend bluegrass music festivals in the United States, the annual number of such festivals has grown to over 500. Festival audiences have ranged from mere dozens to many thousands, but since most fans "camp" at the festival in tents and motorized campers, and since almost all take active part in the musical performances (on stage or off), even a small weekend festival constitutes a temporary settlement that—at least at times and in part—is connected closely enough to call forth a sense of community created at bluegrass music festivals. Because, as one analyst of festival folklore succinctly put it, "Festival rarely, if ever, occurred without music and food,"[1] bluegrass music festivals provide a further example of how food and behaviors associated with foods in the context of bluegrass music festivals help create community out of specialized but shared interests.[2] Every bluegrass festival has elements in common—the musical experience at the core, of course, but also the campground experience, both physical and metaphysical.[3] Food, as usual, is intertwined with both and contributes in several significant ways to the creation of a sense of community among bluegrass festival fans.

This sense of community has numerous immediate sources. For one, bluegrass is music overtly made in the name of tradition, and it constantly invokes (in song texts) both romantic and realistic images of family and community life. For another, the bluegrass band links individuals together in an uplifting creative flow of musical energy. The linkage is realized in sound, but is metaphorically a surrogate for close kinship, a kind of idealized brotherhood that always recalls the "brother acts" and family bands of early commercial hillbilly music. Yet bluegrass, unlike most pre-bluegrass string band music, is immediately playable by strangers. Just as the regular bluegrass band can be looked at as a surrogate family, so the whole week-end bluegrass festival is a scene in which the kinship of music is discovered repeatedly by strangers, and the settlement becomes a community with a sense of itself. The weekend bluegrass festival community even has a gov-ernment of sorts: the promoter and his festival staff act in concert with local police or sheriff's offices to keep order, but many bluegrass festivals exhibit a more important moral order imposed by the participants' own expecta-tions. People at a festival interact in many ways—from enduring bad weather together to enjoying the license of the setting—that resonate with an idealized image of community life. Finally, each bluegrass festival creates a context in which festive foodways contribute significantly to the forma-tion and performance of ideas and images of community.

Consider bluegrass festival food first in the commercial sense. Since the early years of bluegrass festivals, festival advertisements in *Bluegrass Unlimited* have cited an ever-growing number of festival features, activities, facilities, and concessions, many of them having little or no direct connec-tions with bluegrass music but reflecting the importance accorded food concessions by festival promoters.

As bluegrass festivals have grown into profitable venues for portable concessions, festival advertising has become more descriptive; the bare terms "concessions" or "refreshments," often used in ads run during the first decade or so after bluegrass festivals originated, began to give way in advertising to modified and qualified phrases like "concessions by Lion's Club," "24-hour concession stand," "good food concessions," "dining room," and even "cocktails available," all implying that the number and quality of festival food concessions have increasingly been seen and pro-moted as a selling point.

Although commercial providers of food at bluegrass festivals are obvi-ously there to make a profit, some of them are also concerned with promot-ing a sense of community: local concessions run by local "nonprofit" groups are supposed to generate financial rewards. But the profits are "for the group," and usually such groups (a square dance society, a church auxiliary, or a volunteer fire department) also attend in hopes of gaining new kinds of group support or new members for the organization. As concessionaires, these local volunteer groups typically rely on traditional foods of two kinds: elemental generic dishes which are well-established in rural repertoires, and (if this isn't a contradiction) traditionally widespread "modern" foods like hot dogs, french fries, and hamburgers on buns. (See the essays by Griffith and Kaplan in the present volume for additional discussions of foods and fund raising at community food events.) Additionally, fundraising groups tend to emphasize foods they see as emblematic of local "country cooking": in Kentucky and southern Indiana and Ohio, that means fried fish, fried chicken, barbecued pork or beef, homemade pie and cobbler, or cornbread and beans. Concessionaires offer them up without pretense to benefit a worthy cause and in a straightforward way that validates local perceptions of one's friends, neighbors, and fellow bluegrass fans as "regular folks."

Concessions at a very small festival may be offered by the promoter himself, for his own complete profit. A promoter may capitalize on a single traditional food's symbolic value in advertising or staging the festival. At the Watermelon Park Festival in 1968 in Berryville, Virginia, for example, promoter Carlton Haney included in the printed festival program the announcement:

> BLUEGRASS FRIED CHICKEN will be served at meals along with hot dogs, hamburgers, ice cream and drinks. Mr. John Miller, owner of Watermelon Park, requests that NO ALCOHOLIC BEVERAGES be brought into the park area.[4]

"Bluegrass Fried Chicken" was just fried chicken, of course; but by so naming the dish and so phrasing the announcement, Haney affirmed the bluegrass fans' basic sense of being a community—a community with a cuisine that is at once unique and familiar. But promoters' concessions (and advertisements) usually seem more pragmatic than symbolic; since soft drinks and candy are easy and profitable, they are the staples of the promoter/concessionaire. Sometimes the festival promoter runs a variety of concessions, as Bill Monroe does at his Bean Blossom (Indiana) Festival, held each June since 1967. Monroe's outdoor concession facilities consist of several roughly built but permanent wood-framed stands at the top of the gentle hill behind the audience. They dispense a slightly wider range of foodstuffs than the volunteer organizations, and lean towards the universal essentials of modern fast food: one can usually purchase cheeseburgers and hamburgers, hot dogs, polish sausages, french fries, soda pop, potato chips, candy, and ice cream at Monroe's stands. Such foods are well known to most Americans, of course, but as a collective offering in the context of the festival, they more strongly suggest a festive orientation than an ordinary one. Many people think of such foods—which can almost all be held and eaten conveniently without utensils or dishes—as regular "fair food," which suggests both familiarity and festivity. So while most of the foods offered at festival promoters' concessions are conservative in a mass-cultural sense, they are not as symbolically evocative of conservative "old-time" or "rural" foodways as the foods served by the volunteer organizations.

Since a good many people eat while watching the show, commercial food concessions are oriented towards the stage; when the festival is being set up, the mobile dealers will typically arrange themselves in a location fixed by custom and convenient to the stage area, so that fans and vendors alike may continue to hear the show as they buy and sell food. The mobility of modern concession operations permits the greatest flexibility in running the festival, so fewer and fewer of the concessions, even promoter-run concessions, are established in permanent buildings. James Monroe, for example, updated his father's range of concessions for a time by maintaining a concession van to make and sell pizzas and simultaneously advertise the Monroe festivals.

Concessions run by independent tradesmen, however, dominate the commercial public foodways scene at large festivals. Their offerings usually incorporate the regular generic dishes already mentioned, but also capitalize on novelty and exoticism, e.g., a stand labelled "Uncle Junior's Downhome Kentucky Barbecue" features bratwurst. The foods offered by nomadic summer festival concessionaires include the old familiar dishes, but they also include new temptations, foods that signal festivity by their absence from the daily repertoires of most bluegrass fans. In southern Indiana and central Kentucky, bratwurst is hardly the ordinary item it is in Milwaukee; and in any event, the festive context is reinforced by the *simultaneous* offering of bratwurst, barbecue, and a variety of other recognizable but festive foods, like corn dogs and elephant ears. Many foods hawked by festival concessionaires succeed commercially, in part, because they lie outside most fans' repertoires of daily dishes or are familiar foods given a new or exotic name, e.g., boneless strips of chicken sell very well from a concession stand at which they are garishly billed as "Chicken Lips!" Most bluegrass fans, indeed, most American festival-goers of any kind, understand from childhood the festive nature of concession foods like cotton candy, caramel corn, curlicue french fries, nachos, tacos and burritos, cheese taste-ohs, corn dogs, funnel cakes, and "gourmet" popcorn in such various flavors as watermelon, chocolate, green apple, cinnamon apple, blueberry muffin, cherry, and maple. The flavored popcorns exemplify the rapid impact of new commercial food technologies; the process permitting the complex flavoring and coloring of popcorn was developed only three or four years ago, yet now there are both franchised and independent concessionaires pushing the new product anywhere they think they can sell it. Finally, we should certainly note the borrowings of some concession foods from traditional cuisines—"Mexican" or Tex-Mex nachos, on the one hand, and Pennsylvania Dutch funnel cakes on the other.

There are occasionally other public sources of food at festivals too. "Free" bean suppers, fish fries, or barbecues are sometimes put on by the management of bluegrass festivals, ostensibly to encourage the sales of weekend or combination tickets and of daily tickets for the slowest days of the festival. Though free dinners or suppers are probably more typical of small festivals than large ones, they have been featured at various times at even the largest festivals. Bill Monroe's Bluegrass Festival in Bean Blossom, Indiana, traditionally designates the festival's first weekday as "Bar-B-Que Bean Day." In the years of the late 1970s, when the festival spanned two weekends and the week between, Barbecue Bean Day was typically held on Monday or Tuesday, often on the same day as the "Little Miss Bluegrass Contest," when the crowd would be at its smallest, and would consist mainly of diehard bluegrass fans taking their vacation time to attend the festival. In the early years at Bean Blossom, the cooking of the beans was overseen annually by Tex Logan, a well-known bluegrass fiddler and professional mathematician. The meal generally centered on Tex's beans and cornbread, always prepared in the small building reserved for this use on Barbecue Bean Day. In the past few years, Barbecue Bean Day seems to have declined somewhat; Tex is not always there to cook the beans, and there may even be a substitution of purchased white bread for the cornbread. Still, this event and others like it go on, and though comments about the quality of such "free" suppers put on by festival promoters are often critical, the practice generally continues and the diners continue to line up. Given the trouble and expense such offerings cause for promoters, and the apparent consensus that the food is not always so great, the general continuation of the promoter's free festival supper likely reflects not only the promoter's hopes for better weekend ticket sales, but also a generalized desire to invoke or increase the sense of community felt by everyone at the festival. Concomitantly, the promoter who includes a "free" meal in his festival plans may feel that he is fulfilling the powerful Southern mandate to be hospitable, or at least to be seen as hospitable. Of course, "hospitality" is not extended by all Southerners to all clients in all commercial settings, but bluegrass festivals have easily incorporated and retraditionalized those customs that are seen, rightly or wrongly, as folk cultural, or as old and traditional. So the practice goes on: a 1984 Georgia festival advertisement tells fans to "avoid the rush on Friday afternoon by coming early and enjoying our Southern hospitality. We are going to have a good old-fashioned fish fry for our weekend guests."[5]

A more complex blend of hospitality and group participation underlies another 1984 ad, for the 10th Annual Dahlonega Bluegrass Festival, which notes a prefestival "Free Bar-B-Q & Covered Dish Supper" held the night before the festival's first day of stage shows for everyone buying a four-day ticket, and to which guests were requested to bring a covered dish. With the sharing of responsibility for such meals more evenly divided between the promoter and the participants, the "free" festival meal becomes an event signifying the ultimate oneness of all the participants, just like church-based potluck suppers and dinners-on-the-grounds.

Many bluegrass festival foodways center on the campground area, or parking lot, that liminal territory where private and public interests coincide. It is an essential part of bluegrass festivals that household privacy is knowingly foregone to a modest degree: strangers can be expected to walk all around one's camp and/or car at close quarters, but no one objects. Each camp is both private and public, in that it visually reveals a cooking-living area which no stranger is expected to enter but which all can see. The closed interiors of privately owned cars, buses, and recreational vehicles are the most private spaces available, and naturally a good deal of cooking and eating takes place inside.

At the Festival of the Bluegrass, for example, Ruby Whitaker often makes full festival breakfasts of fried ham, eggs, biscuits and gravy, sliced tomatos, doughnuts, and coffee on a tiny RV stove. Although Ruby says she plans for a bluegrass festival by buying foods that all the members of her family can make for themselves—sandwich fixings, potato chips, and so on—in fact she prepares or oversees most of the meals eaten by her family and the band she is part of, The Next of Kin. Though the larger RVs provide all the comforts of home, many fans eat outdoors whenever they can, and most actually create an outdoor cooking area which constitutes the social hearth of their camp. Outside, while the other members of her family and band relax, Ruby may cook up some meal-fried potatoes, an old-time dish which Ruby considers a "bit out of the ordinary." Ruby and her husband Ira identify most of the dishes they eat at festivals as "ordinary" fare, yet they don't normally eat large country meals including all these ordinary dishes for breakfasts and suppers any more; it might be more accurate to note that at festivals Ruby cooks meals that recapitulate in both quantity and repertoire the bygone patterns she and Ira recall from their childhood days. So, when suppertime comes along, Ira and the other band members take some small responsibility for feeding themselves, yet count on and look forward to Ruby's corn-cakes and other old-time delights.

The general taxonomy of main meals at bluegrass festivals is based on that widespread old rural American pattern once common everywhere and still typical of the rural South: the meals are called breakfast, dinner, and supper. The newer triad of breakfast, lunch(eon), and dinner, however, is so commonly known that its use occasions no comment whatsoever. Everyone knows the equivalence of dinner and lunch(eon) and of supper and dinner, at least as time references. Still, at bluegrass festivals, emcees and fans alike refer to the late-afternoon intermission in the show as the "supper break." Though many festivals begin their formal programming after noon, and hence have no midday "dinner time" or "dinner break" to announce, even that term is heard frequently enough to confirm the predominance of the old breakfast, dinner, supper terminology.

Food consumption outside the named meals is called "snacking," "having a bite to eat," "feeding one's face," "having," or "getting" a certain food, or just "eating" again. Eating at times other than named mealtimes is so commonplace at festivals that it is accepted as a matter of course. This is not to say that no rules or limitations on eating continue to operate during the festival—certainly parents, especially mothers, go on trying to direct their children's consumption, as always—but a primary consequence of the basic conception of a bluegrass festival as a *festival* is license—a relaxation of the normal rules and constraints on eating behavior; on all consumption behavior, as a matter of fact, which is why the festival ads also increasingly prohibit alcoholic drinks, or suggest that they not be consumed in the public stage area. But people may be seen eating and drinking at any hour and in any place at bluegrass festivals. For individuals who choose to eat alone, especially, the festival setting licenses any kind of eating outside the normal temporal and spatial settings allotted to meals. Whether sitting alone in the back of a pickup truck, watching the show, or walking across a field, the lone eater is answerable to no one, and may almost completely disregard the rules and conventions that normally govern social eating. It might be noted that the principal mode of eating while watching the show is essentially solitary; given the arrangements of seats and the focus of attention, eating at the show means eating alongside, but not "with," one's friends, family, and the surrounding crowd of strangers. Such eating may involve some sharing of food, but it hardly conforms to our usual conceptions of socially-grounded eating. Eating together while watching is an essentially asocial act. Though asocial eating takes place away from the show too, social eating is the norm in the campgrounds.

The most remarkable thing about the whole vernacular foodways pattern seen in bluegrass festival campgrounds is that it entails two opposite responses to the festival situation. The first response is in the direction of a pattern emphasizing diversity ("whatever you like"), pragmatism, and asocial eating; the second response leads towards traditional, familiar, and social eating in a special festive mode. The crowded and chaotic conditions of bluegrass festivals frequently lead diners to rely heavily on concession food and simple, self-prepared picnic foods. Apparently as often, however, the festival encourages the re-creation of social identity through complex and cooperative foodways patterns. That is, while some fans buy hamburgers or make baloney sandwiches for themselves in the camper and then hurry back to hear another stage show, others go through elaborate preparations in the camping area to put on one or more special festal meals during the festival.

In many cases, the impulse to eat and share old-time foods during a bluegrass festival leads to the planning of one very special meal, social and celebratory in nature, sometime during the weekend. The Meal is typically large and abundant, though not fancy, and whether it is called a dinner or a supper, it is usually served during the supper break to an extended family or band, their friends, and their network of picking acquaintances. Within a particular network, a given family or couple often bears the annual responsibility for putting on the feast within the festival, either because they are a kind of social focus for their friends anyway, or because they can provide the essential components of The Meal: foodstuffs, labor, skill, and special utensils or tools for preparing the food. Many regular bluegrass festival fans build or buy unique cookers for fish-frying, barbecuing, turtle-frying, and bean-simmering. The labor of the family assuming main responsibility for The Meal is augmented by that of a small additional group of provider/preparers. These friends, who know of The Meal as a planned event before it happens, bring additional foodstuffs; in general, this means only that the women of the family and women representing other households of friends and their kin will each bring a dish of some kind: potato salad, macaroni salad, coleslaw, a sheet apple cake, a watermelon, or any kind of casserole that can be prepared ahead and brought to the festival. When The Meal is actually ready, a good many more people participate as diners, including not only the central extended family and the families of the other provider/preparers, but also musicians and passers-by who are part of the musical network of the musicians among the central group. In all, a really good-sized festival dinner may involve twenty or thirty people.

While The Meal can be based on any food, from hot dogs and hamburgers to barbecued chicken to steak, it is frequently focused on indigenous foodstuffs that can be harvested free by the providers of The Meal; that is, with only the investment of the providers' time and skill at procuring the fish, the turtle, the squirrel, the doves, or the frogs legs that make up the central dish of the event. Sometimes the skill itself is a matter of tradition; in Bluegrass Kentucky, men take considerable pride in their ability to go out squirrel-shooting, fish-tickling, turtle-noodling, or frog-gigging.

Harvey Durrum, for instance, is a dedicated fisherman who, with his wife Rose, has hosted fish fries at the Lexington Festival of the Bluegrass since its beginnings about twelve years ago. Each year the Durrums tell their bluegrass-picking friends which day the special meal will be held on during the festival. The invitation is low-key; Harvey will ask, as if reminding the person of something he already knows, "Hey, you gonna eat some fish with us? We're gonna have fish Saturday night." Early on the appointed afternoon people start to gather, and Harvey and Rose begin to make ready.

Harvey's participation is critical; in fact, it seems likely that one of the distinguishing features of The Meal is the involvement of men, not only in procuring the wild foodstuffs, but in actually preparing them. Harvey catches and cooks the fish, just as other men who put on festal festival meals locally catch and cook the turtle- or frog-legs, or barbecue the venison. As the afternoon draws to a close, the eaters assemble. Some, like Ira and Ruby and the rest of The Next of Kin have planned on participating, while others passing by are hailed and invited to have a beer and stay for some fish. The diners serve themselves, and no one counts the helpings; as with all festive foodways, one of the signifiers of festivity is superabundance, and there is always plenty for those who have arrived on time as well as those who wander by later on. Harvey and his friends enjoy the camaraderie even more than the food; as Harvey says of such a meal, "You just got to have it to get everyone together." People linger over the table and stay around afterwards for a long time, talking about whether the bream was better than the mullet or the perch.

Taken as a whole, The Meal stands in approximately the same relation to general patterns of bluegrass festival eating as the remembered Sunday dinners of the Whitakers, Hensleys, and Durrums do to their bygone patterns of traditional ordinary foodways: the meal reflects greater quantities and choices, and it embodies a feeling of shared experience and the hospitality of the meal's hosts. In considering the hidden functions of this nominally secular event, one immediately sees the aptness of Robert Cantewell's assertion that "Bluegrass music, particularly the summertime outdoor bluegrass festival, with its potluck supper, jam session, gospel sings and the like, has swept into the social and psychic space occupied a century ago by religion and by religious revivals and camp meetings."[6]

Notes

1. Beverly J. Stoeltje, "Festival in America," in Richard M. Dorson, ed., *Handbook of American Folklore* (Bloomington: Indiana University Press, 1983): 242.

2. Some of my conclusions in this regard are based on a study of advertisements from *Bluegrass Unlimited* magazine; I also relied on interviews and, happily, participant observation conducted at Indiana and Kentucky bluegrass festivals between 1984 and 1986. In Kentucky, the Festival of the Bluegrass (held near Lexington) and the McLain Family Band Festival (near Berea) are each attended by thousands or tens of thousands annually, while smaller festivals held repeatedly near Clay City, Irvine, and Richmond may draw from a few dozen to a few hundred fans who camp for the weekend.

3. Robert Cantewell's *Bluegrass Breakdown* presents the most thoroughgoing consideration of the intertwined meanings of religion, philosophy, and worldview that are embodied in bluegrass music and the social contexts in which it thrives.

4. Berryville, Virginia Festival Program, in *Bluegrass Unlimited* 3:3 (September, 1968): 27–30.

5. Advertisement for Maggie's Lake Bluegrass Festival, near Glenville, Georgia. *Bluegrass Unlimited,* April 1984.

6. Robert Cantwell, *Bluegrass Breakdown: The Making of the Old Southern Sound* (Urbana: University of Illinois Press, 1984): 38.

13

Festa Italiana in Hartford, Connecticut: The Pastries, the Pizza, and the People Who "Parla Italiano"

Anthony T. Rauche

From 1978 to 1985 *Festa Italiana* was held during the second weekend of September in Hartford, Connecticut. From a modest beginning the festival grew to become one of the largest ethnic festivals held in New England, attracting close to a quarter million people, and it became the primary ethnic celebration for the Italian and Italian-American community in the city of Hartford. The original idea behind this three-day festival was to rekindle the traditional *festa* and present Italian culture to the greater Hartford area. The *Festa* provided a glimpse into Italian music, crafts, tradition, costumes, and food. Although the main logo for *Festa Italiana* was a singer portrayed in the Italian tricolor of red, white, and green, the underlying cultural and ethnic message of the festival was the abundance of food and its importance in Italian life. Indeed, food very quickly and easily became one of the most important elements at the *Festa Italiana*, and its dominance was amplified by the inclusion of vendors whose foods were clearly non-Italian. While the prominence of food did create and reflect a unified symbolic "Italian" image, it also sent conflicting signals to non-Italians about the identity of the Italian community. In fact, the role of food in this festival context was a major part of the conflict between what the Italian tradition of *festa* was for community members, and how *festa* was being projected to the greater Hartford non-Italian community, a conflict that ultimately led to the discontinuation of *Festa Italiana* in 1985.

Italians first arrived in Hartford in the late nineteenth century, between 1870–1880.[1] The earliest immigrants came from Potenza, Calabria, Salerno, and Abruzzi, but by 1925 the largest group of immigrants was from Sicily.

In general, they were attracted to Hartford by employment opportunities on the railroad, large construction projects, and farming in the Connecticut River valley. They lived primarily on the east side of the city, along the Connecticut River, although a substantial Italian population also developed in the north end. Their neighborhoods were characterized by a close-knit spirit and pride in their traditional culture and family lives. The festival life of these Italians and Italian-Americans centered in their own parish, Saint Anthony's, with religious festivals an important part of community life. But, when urban renewal and redevelopment forced the breakup of the eastside neighborhood in the 1950s, these communities were dissolved. Businesses and families moved to the "South End," along Franklin Avenue. This area of about fifteen to twenty blocks became the new reorganized Italian neighborhood, now in a larger physical area, but more centrally organized, with most of the businesses on Franklin Avenue.

The spirit of *festa* and festival occasions, both important in traditional community life, ended with the merger of St. Anthony's Italian parish and St. Patrick's Irish parish, a direct result of the relocation of the east side Italian neighborhood. Chief among the characteristics of the traditional *festa* is its association with a particular saint. In Italy, devotion to a patron, or a particular intercessor, was traditionally celebrated by the entire village. The *festa* began with a religious procession, usually followed by the celebration of the Mass. There might also be special devotional activities, including the re-enactment of the life of the saint, noting his or her special powers, and the events which caused the saint to become associated with that village. These were the core elements of a traditional Italian *festa.* Food-related events occurred only after the core celebration had been completed.

The festivals observed in America followed that pattern of celebration for many years and were known by their particular association with a patron saint, such as St. Anthony or St. Joseph. The most important festa for the Hartford Italian community was the Santa Lucia festival. (The celebration of San Gennaro, the patron saint of Naples, although very popular in New York, Boston, and other cities, was never very prominent in Hartford because there was not a substantial Neapolitan immigrant group.) The first immigrants shared common beliefs and practices, and generally congregated with members of their own village or region. To the extent possible, they maintained traditional celebrations, but successive generations of these immigrant groups reacted to the influences of festivals, fairs, carnivals, and other urban celebrations.

Changes in the Italian *festa* in America were not unusual and were perhaps inevitable in a multilayered urban society. In an urban context *festa* gradually moved away from the traditional focus and began to accom-

modate these new influences. Traditional religious devotions were culti-
vated primarily by the older community members and receded into the
background of the *festa*. As the first immigrants became fewer in number,
the original associations of *festa* continued to weaken, in particular, the
association with a saint and the overall religious orientation of *festa*. Coupled with this change was the incorporation of nontraditional activities that
were a part of American urban life, or which had been part of traditional
American rural celebrations. Carnival rides, vendors selling trinkets and
novelties, and sporting events became prominent features for the general
public. Both of these changes contributed to the growing secular nature of
the Italian *festa* in America. Changing attitudes about food may also have
contributed to the shift from a religiously oriented *festa* to an urban celebration of eating and drinking. Finally, the growing number of non-Italian
participants also contributed to this evolution, the "urbanized" *festa* appeal-
ing then to a broad spectrum of urban dwellers with diverse experiences
and interests.

For Italian immigrants, moderation in food consumption, as with almost everything else, was a celebrated virtue. These immigrants came
armed with traditional sayings such as: *Poco magnà, poco dolore* [Little
food, little pain]; *Lo poco abbasta e lu troppe faci murì* [A little is enough
and a lot makes you die]; *Chi magna assai scatte e chi fatâ mitte a parte*
[If you stuff yourself, you'll burst; if you work, you'll get rich].[2]

The Italian immigrants had to make several adjustments once in America. Certain vegetables and fruits were not readily available to them. The
growing season in New England and along the East coast was shorter and
not as hot as that in Southern Italy, the home region of most Italian immigrants. Meats and fish were different, and familiar staples were not available
in American grocery stores. Furthermore, as the Italian-American began to
earn more money, the humble diet of the old country began to give way
to a richer and more "Italian" one. Phyllis Williams has noted that the
traditional Italian meal usually consisted of one main dish, salad or fruit, and
bread, with the ordinary menu including cheese, beans, potatoes, greens,
and only rarely meat or eggs.[3] The change brought about by increased
prosperity prompted Humbert Nelli to write:

> Their traditional kitchen withstood Americanization . . . and the production of or import
> from Italy of olive oil, spaghetti, artichokes, salami, and other foodstuffs provided an
> important part of the neighborhood economy. The immigrants craved their Old World
> dishes in part because it was only in the New World that they could begin to afford
> them. . . . In America, poor immigrants began to enjoy an Italian diet that was abundant,
> varied, and rich.[4]

Traditional foods could be "improved" by adding more and new ingredients. These adjustments provided tangible proof of the immigrants' achievements while still offering familiarity and continuity.[5] More importantly, these new Italian foods proved to be very popular with Americans, and the growth and development of Italian restaurants proved to be very profitable economic ventures.

It would certainly be incorrect to suggest that food is not important in Italian and American-Italian life. Indeed, festive meals, special holiday foods, and traditional food activities (such as the making of wine, cheese, and sausage) are integral to the Italian way of life. The symbolic power of food is celebrated in the expression, *A tavola mai s'invecchia* [At the table no one ever grows old]. Food has power to stop time and the normal passing of life. To the extent that food is able to do that, its role in *festa* is important, because the *festa* also interrupts the normal day-to-day activities; it is a leap out of ordinary time into "festival time," which is reckoned only by the immediate experience of the present moment. One does not grow old during *festa*, just as one cannot grow old while celebrating and enjoying an important meal.

As revived in Hartford, Connecticut, the *Festa Italiana* was organized by a group of business persons, a clear indication of its detachment, at least in its initial focus, from the traditional religious context of *festa*. The Franklin Avenue Festa Association (FAFA) in 1978 saw the first *Festa Italiana* as a threefold venture. First, it was a way to provoke concentrated business activity during a short period of time, namely, three days. Second, it was thought of as a revival of the old neighborhood festival that had been a part of earlier community life. Third, it was planned as a way of promoting business renewal and community growth in the South End. Through the 1960s businesses in the inner city and in older ethnic neighborhoods were threatened by shopping malls and the growth of the suburbs. For FAFA, a community celebration was a very practical solution to impending financial problems. More importantly, it would also reach back into the ethnic cultural tradition and memory and reaffirm the Italian identity of that neighborhood.

What makes a ten-block section of Franklin Avenue a likely "core" site for an Italian festival? The concentration of Italian restaurants (eleven), bakeries and pizza shops (eight), espresso cafes (five), Italian grocery stores (six), and "Italian spoken here" businesses (well over twenty-five) makes this area the Italian part of town, reflected by the nickname "Santa Lucia Boulevard" given it by some Hartford residents.[6] Here, the FAFA committee had its organizational headquarters centrally located during the year-long preparation of the *Festa*. Here, a small section of Hartford became a large slice of Italian festival life.

The transformation from a city avenue to a carnival ground began Thursday afternoon before the official start of the *Festa* Friday evening. Banners, streamers, and posters announced the celebration. The traffic line down the middle of Franklin Avenue was painted with the Italian tricolor, which appeared on everything from welcome signs for Geraldine Ferraro in 1984, to sport hats and clowns. If it was not green, white, and red, it was not Italian, and not part of the *Festa*. This was emphasized in 1982 when FAFA adopted a tricolor singer (a red and green singing male figure with an outstretched hand on a white background) as the logo of the *Festa*. (The singer is an important ethnic symbol for the community, whether thought of as a singer of Neapolitan songs or opera, because in the mind of the Italians, music and festivals go hand in hand.) At each end of the ten-block festival area there was a stage, also decorated with flags and banners, where the main entertainment and official announcements took place. Local radio stations would broadcast from various spots along the avenue, and one station translated one of its slogans, *Nessuno vi offre più musica di noi* [No one offers you more music than we do]. An important attraction for the Italian community were the broadcasts of Radio Italia with Lucio, a well-known local Italian radio personality. Some of the most popular performers at the *Festa* were Gianpaolo DiGrazia and Premier, a local rock group, known for their performances of Italian as well as English songs. DiGrazia was billed in the neighborhood newspaper as the "Julio Igelsias of Connecticut." In 1984 Paola Semprini, a popular singer from Parma, appeared along with Les Sortilegese International Folk Dance ensemble from Montreal, which performed a variety of folk dances, including a staged version of an Italian tarantella. FAFA regularly invited an Italian choral group from Boston, Folkloristico Orsognese. In their colorful costumes they performed representative Italian folk music, incorporating the singing styles of both northern and southern Italy. By far, the spotlighted performers were well-known American-Italian singers: Enzo Stuarti, Al Martino, and Julius LaRosa, among others. Their performances were always scheduled during the second and third evenings of the *Festa*, and often attracted the largest crowds. In particular, their prominent place in the *Festa* reflected the musical logo adopted by FAFA, and in general, the appreciation and love of music by the Italian community.

An important component of the Saturday morning activities was the parade, which began at the north end of the stage area and headed down to the south stage. FAFA had its members ride or walk, and everyone emphasized the tricolor of Italy in their clothing. The Italian Information Center sponsored a small local tarantella group every year, mostly female with only a few male members. Community organizations also sponsored floats. The Sons of Syracuse marched with its banner and float. The Italian-Ameri-

Figure 13-1. Les Sortilegese International Dance Company of Montreal Performing a Tarantella on the South Stage of *Festa Italiana,* 1985 *(Photo by the author)*

can fire fighters St. Florian organization and Christopher Columbus—who in 1984 rode on a truck but in 1985 was able to ride in a boat!—all had a place in the parade. Some of the musical groups and performers, bands from the greater Hartford area, political officials, community leaders, and other notable citizens marched along Franklin Avenue.

If there was any time during the *Festa* when the community addressed only its own members, it was Sunday morning. There was a procession up Franklin Avenue to the north stage for an Italian-language Catholic Mass. In 1983 the procession was rather substantial, with at least two religious societies represented in the procession. Mass followed, and by noon, the quiet, religious part of the festival was finished, and most of the other activities were just beginning to resume. This aspect of *Festa Italiana* diminished from 1983 to 1985. By 1985 the procession was much smaller. While they may be important links with religious festivals of the past, the religious procession and the Italian-language Mass appealed only to a small percentage of the community, especially the older generation. The religious customs that did survive were quietly maintained and observed, again, by the older generation. The practice of pinning money on statues of favorite saints, like Saint Anthony of Padua, was one of the most notable, and was always observed during the eight years of *Festa Italiana*.

What did the non-Italian community associate with *Festa Italiana*? Food! In its first year, 1978, the *Festa* attracted only local merchants who set up booths along the avenue. Italian food was the biggest attraction for most people. By 1982, when I first started observing *Festa Italiana*, it had reached full capacity with almost all available booth spaces taken by local and nonlocal vendors. Most booths at the festival were food concessions, and most of these featured some Italian specialty. Italian ices, meatballs from the "meatball factory," sausage and peppers, fried dough with sugar or tomato sauce, and a variety of pizza filled the minds and stomachs of most *Festa* visitors, and this was in addition to all the bakeries and restaurants which catered to the large festival crowd.

Other booths along the avenue sold typical carnival and fair trinkets. There were carnival rides for children, and a variety of fanciful drinks and beer, not at all unique to this particular festival. There were a few specialty stores which set up booths for the festival, like Nostalgia Italiana. It has had a rapid growth over the last several years, and has a varied clientele interested in Italian records, magazines, newspapers, and literature, as well as posters of Italian and American rock stars and movie stars.

How did non-Italians view *Festa Italiana*? At *Festa* time most non-Italians immediately thought of Italian food, an association emphasized in all the pre-*Festa* publicity in neighborhood and city newspapers. The *Festa* organization itself promoted the festival as an Italian three-day feast. This emphasis also resulted in FAFA increasing the number of food booths each year. Apart from the festival, the South End had long suggested good Italian food because of the concentration of Italian restaurants in the area. In this respect, the *Festa* only intensified what was already an ongoing association. Some non-Italians might have enjoyed the entertainment, others a few beers, while still others came to the festival only to walk down the street in an unfamiliar part of town. For most of them, *Festa Italiana* was an Italian-flavored carnival which occurred every fall for eight years.

Members of the South End Italian community had a much more complex participation in, and reaction to, the *Festa*. In its first years, the neighborhood residents enjoyed the revival of this street festival and the attention it brought to their community. What was to be included in the *Festa*, then, appears not to have been in question. This suggests that a mutual trust and understanding existed between the FAFA committee and members of the community about what was Italian and what was not, and a view of what should constitute a traditional Italian *festa*. It also suggests that a concept of traditional Italian celebrations had been maintained even through a period when there were no large-scale public *feste*. But more and more vendors were anonymous personalities who made an annual appearance in Hartford. While a certain number were tolerated, the large percentage of such vendors eventually changed the character of the *Festa*. Italian foods competed with Japanese tempura, Southern style ribs, Greek, Argentine, and Jamaican foods. Increasing numbers of street performers, although sanctioned by FAFA, competed with the entertainment at the north and south stages. Among the residents of Franklin Avenue, dissatisfaction grew with the *Festa* vendors, who were increasingly messy and created too much garbage; with the serious problems caused by the larger crowds, especially at night; and with losing the Italian origins of the *Festa* because so much of the *Festa* had become non-Italian. Criticism in 1985 was so strong that the future of the *Festa* was finally put to a vote in the community and thus stopped that year. One of the strongest editorial reactions to the *Festa* was entitled: "*Ascoltate bene* [listen well]: Give the *Festa* back to the Italians." My next door neighbor at that time, a Sicilian woman who had lived there for approximately seventeen years, was upset that Lucio with his Radio Italia program was not broadcasting from the south stage. She commented, "After all, this is the *Italian* fest."

The problems of the *Festa* may all have been based on the desire for more profits, and in that respect, critics say that the FAFA organization was no longer representing Italian culture for the community. As non-Italian as the *Festa* grew to appear, there were still elements—apart from the food—which were distinctly Italian: staged tarantellas, Italian choral music, Italian operatic performances, and Italian and Italian-American popular performers. And within the community it has always been important to maintain direct contact with Italian expressive culture and products. As the owner of *Nostalgia Italiana* said about some memorabilia: "These are right from Italy."

What appeared to be in conflict when *Festa Italiana* was discontinued was how the concept of "Italian-ness" was both formulated in the minds of community members and realized within the *Festa* context. This conflict resulted from the changing associations that individuals had about the *Festa*. Some remembered and identified with the religious *feste* of the past in this country; others recalled the regional and religious *feste* they had attended in Italy; others identified with contemporary Italian culture; and still others identified with an Italian-American culture which is certainly more urban-American than it is Italian. For this community Italian ethnic identity was much more than the surface activities of *Festa Italiana*. It was a cultural framework of traditional values and concepts which generated those activities. The framework on one hand was maintained, but on the other, was challenged to adapt to a contemporary urban-American festival environment.

The conflict which caused the discontinuation of *Festa Italiana* in Hartford occurred when the older, traditional meaning of *festa* for Italians and Italian-Americans was overshadowed by the assumed importance of food by non-Italians. In 1978 a brief newspaper article announced "Italian Festival To Be Revived."[7] As presented in the article, this was to be a revival of an Italian street festival. The older community members remembered what a traditional Italian *festa* was like. The association of religious customs and beliefs was central to this remembrance. Although the survival of religious activities in *Festa Italiana* was minimal, initially it was enough to satisfy those traditional expectations. Italians eventually perceived that *festa* as they had understood it was being smothered by the increasing emphasis on food with a decrease in emphasis on religious devotion. The introduction of non-Italian food and activities, the increasing number of people at the *Festa* each year threatening the neighborhood spirit of the celebration, and the ultimate conflict, the feeling that all the "outside" vendors who travelled from city to city were not showing any regard and respect for personal property, aggravated the situation. It was not so much that the *Festa* was growing non-Italian, but that the community's tolerance was being pushed to the limit. The eruption of some incidental crowd violence in 1985 and the growing sense that their neighborhood was being violated contributed to the move to discontinue the *Festa*, at least as it had been for eight years. For many community members, a street festival was a good general event, but a *festa* was a particular event with its specific associations.

The Hartford Italian community projected food in much the same way its members had done in their homes and in restaurants for many years. Italians could provide good food and lots of it. The *Festa* became a concentrated expression of that role to which non-Italians had grown accustomed. They grew to expect the three-day *Festa* to be a walking Italian food feast. And while no one in the Italian community could argue with that assumption, they understood it to be fundamentally incorrect. Food and *festa* were a happy pair, but *festa* came first.

As the roles of *festa* and food began to cause friction, there did not seem to be any appreciation of how the traditional *festa* had been transferred from Italian villages to American cities, and how it had been transformed from a public religious event to a public secular event. All expressive cultural events undergo change to some extent, and the stress of opposing factors eventually is balanced and the old gives way to the new, or at least there is some adaptation. One of the most striking adaptations observed in *Festa Italiana* was its economic genesis, a congenital adaptation. FAFA members had built the *Festa* on the basis of what they understood a *festa* to be, and as younger members of the business community they were particularly sensitive to what economic renewal could do for their neighborhood. Reviving the street festival meant more business for neighborhood merchants, with the money filtering back into the community. In the first several years of the *Festa* this was not a problem. Only after the number of outside vendors increased did community residents react strongly to the threat that the money being made at the *Festa* was not returning to the community. Although not a part of any traditional concept of *festa*, this economic adjunct is not uncommon in American ethnic festivals. The money raised is usually offered to some charity or used to run the sponsor's special charitable activities. In its last four years there was increased questioning about what happened to the *Festa Italiana* monies raised. This economic spark added to the friction already evident.

Three threads intertwined in this *Festa:* first, the traditional concept of *festa;* second, the projection of food within the context of the *festa;* and third, the economic viability associated with the *festa*. Whether conscious of it or not, the Italian community projected the first two together in order to generate the third. The non-Italian community misinterpreted the first and second as being synonymous, and therein the conflict grew. For them, the third thread was irrelevant, unless they were vendors at the *Festa*.

Festa Italiana did celebrate pastries and pizza, not in themselves, but as symbols of the affections and attitudes toward eating that Italians have long maintained. "Pizza" and "Italian" are synonymous in American thinking, and the transformation of pizza from a peasant, village food into a virtual gourmet staple of American diets is in itself an incredible projection of Italianness into American life. When the local Italian pizza vendors would talk to me, they were quick to point out that they were Italian, making an Italian food in an Italian manner. Their identity was directly linked to being an Italian in American society and to their maintenance of traditional food preparation. They were not the average carnival vendors, with fancy booths labelled "meatball factory." They were the owners of shops along Franklin Avenue, or from greater Hartford Italian communities. They were intimately connected with the community identity because it was their own identity, and the preservation of Italian culture in America, accompanied by great pride for a musical, poetic, and culinary heritage, was preeminent in their minds. Selling pizza and pastries was not just selling food; it was selling a little part of themselves. They were speaking to the non-Italians through these foods; they were "speaking pizza" and "speaking pastries"— using the language of food to communicate. "I make this just like my grandmother," one man told me; or another, "You know, you can't find pizza like this everywhere; here it is the best." Both statements are clearly indicative of one's "connectedness" to family, community, and country.

But food was not the only language of the *Festa*. Speaking Italian was the obvious "other language" which one would hear along Franklin Avenue during *Festa*, or at any other time of the year. In contrast to the use of food as a language with which to address non-Italians, speaking Italian was a way to address the community within itself. This is not to say that it was a way to talk about people behind their backs, or that it was necessarily a way to talk about non-Italians while they were present, although both circumstances might be possible. There was really no explicit concern for the use of Italian in that regard. Rather, community members used Italian because it was the conversational mode of choice. Perhaps the language itself is only one aspect of the entire exchange of ideas and words. The conversational exchange includes the gestures, the presentation of ideas, and the references, as well as the words. The experience centers on contact with essentially familiar shared conversational and linguistic components. While all this might be considered the casual exchange of neighbors and friends, or the necessary exchange of merchants and customers, there are examples of how this phenomenon was projected within the *Festa*. Who understood Paola Semprini when she offered a little patter between songs? Who understood the Italian dialect texts of the songs sung by Julius LaRosa? Who understood the prayers and sermon offered at the Sunday morning Mass? And who listened to Gianpaolo DiGrazia sing rock songs only because they were in Italian? The answer is clear that the community members reinforced their identity and their sense of community in these moments: speaking Italian was a public act which reflected inward toward the speakers themselves and their community.

One might be surprised that the community voted to stop *Festa Italiana* in 1985. It had been successful, raised money for the community, and managed to attract more and more people each of its eight years. In 1986, the first year after the *Festa* was cancelled, a local newspaper food editor wrote: "So there won't be the sound of Italian music along the avenue or the aroma of fried peppers and sausage permeating the air. You can't go to the Festa this year, but you can bring a flavor of the ethnic festival to your home."[8] Yes, the non-Italian community was remembering all the pastry and the pizza that the *Festa* provided, and it was possible to make some of these delights at home, or to purchase them at the shops which lined Franklin Avenue.

But no one really could create a *festa* at home because the foods were not *festa*. Although they were the most visible element for non-Italians, the foods were in reality only marginal *festa* elements which somehow overtook the entire celebration. When the Italian community realized what had happened to their *festa*, they stopped it. *Festa* and food were a wonderful combination, and each was respected for its own value in community life. Combined in this particular *festa*, they quickly started cancelling out each other. For the Italians of Hartford's South End, there was too little emphasis on *festa*, and too much emphasis on food. The saying, *Lo poco abbasta e lu troppe faci murì* [A little is enough and a lot makes you die] rang all too true.

Notes

The original version of this paper was presented at the 1985 meeting of the American Folklore Society in Cincinnati for the panel, "Ethnic Identification and Ascription of Ethnicity," chaired by Doris J. Dyen and Philip V. Bohlman. I am grateful for their invitation to participate on that panel, and for sharing some of their ideas about ethnicity in an urban context.

1. Robert E. Pawlowski, *How the Other Half Lived: An Ethnic History of the Old East Side and South End of Hartford* (Hartford, Connecticut: Robert E. Pawlowski, 1973): 42.

2. Carla Bianco, *The Two Rosetos* (Bloomington and London: Indiana University Press, 1974): 134.

3. Phyllis H. Williams, *South Italian Folkways in Europe and America: A Handbook for Social Workers, Visiting Nurses, School Teachers and Physicians* (New Haven, Connecticut: Yale University Press, 1938): 58.

4. Humbert S. Nelli, "Italians," in the *Harvard Encyclopedia of American Ethnic Groups,* Stephan Thernstrom, ed. (Cambridge, Massachusetts: Harvard University Press, 1980): 556.

5. Bianco, 1974: 134.

6. The former mayor of Hartford, Dominic DeLucco, was successful in having Market Street in downtown Hartford renamed "Columbus Boulevard," to reflect the heritage and contri-

butions of the Italian community in the city. However, his proposal that Franklin Avenue be officially renamed "Santa Lucia Boulevard" was not approved.

7. Bill Grava, "Italian Festival To Be Revived," *The Hartford Courant*, August 19, 1978: 21 col. 3.

8. Linda Giuca, "This Year, You Can Celebrate with a festa at home," *The Hartford Courant*, September 3, 1986, E1, col. 1.

14

"We Always Call It 'Tucson Eat Yourself'": The Role of Food at a Constructed Festival

James Griffith

Tucson Meet Yourself is an annual festival, now in its 14th year, that takes place on the second weekend of October in this rapidly growing Sunbelt city of well over half a million in Southern Arizona. Officially described in its publicity as "a celebration of the richness and diversity of the living traditional arts of Southern Arizona's folk and ethnic communities," the festival is sponsored by the Cultural Exchange Council of Tucson, Inc.; Pima Community College; the Southwest Folklore Center of the University of Arizona; and the City of Tucson. Starting as a small experiment in 1974, it has grown to be a large and successful event on the city's cultural calendar, attracting an audience estimated at 35,000 people over the course of the weekend. It was begun in the early 1970's when a few Tucsonans, concerned by the extreme fragmentation they perceived in their community, became intrigued by the possibilities of a local folk festival that would draw upon the various ethnic and occupational communities of the region. After they visited the First Annual Border Folk Festival at El Chamizal National Monument, El Paso, Texas, in 1973, enthusiasm crystallized into intention, and the first edition of Tucson Meet Yourself was held in October, 1974. Although the festival has grown tremendously over the years, it has remained constant in its general shape and its purpose—to provide a dignified forum for the area's regional and immigrant cultures—as well as its function: to create community.[1]

Briefly put, the shape of the festival is as follows: It takes place in a small park located between the county and city buildings in downtown Tucson. Scattered over the park are booths selling traditional ethnic foods. In the 1985 festival there were 40 such booths, each operated by a non-profit organization identified with a specific cultural heritage. At one end of the park is a main stage where formal presentations of traditional music and dance take place during formal festival hours. These are from 7–10 p.m. Friday; from 11 a.m.–10 p.m. Saturday; and from 1–6 p.m. on Sunday. (Booths usually open a bit earlier and close a bit later than this.) At the opposite side of the park, in the shaded courtyard arcades of the Old County Courthouse, specially invited folk artists and craftspeople demonstrate their skill during the daylight hours. A final area is designated the workshop stage. Here one finds informal discussions by various tradition bearers—a *corrido* competition, a *piñata* party, traditional games, demonstrations, lessons, and similar activities requiring a greater degree of interaction between tradition bearers and audience than is possible on the main stage.

Although the festival is carefully organized and presented to provide a sense of informality and even spontaneity, it is in fact the result of careful planning, fieldwork, and consultation and has been so from the beginning.[2] The goals of its founders as set forth in press releases and other printed material were—and remain—to provide a setting in which the traditional arts of as wide a cross section as possible of Tucson's cultural makeup could be presented accurately and respectfully to a wide segment of Tucson's population.[3] A second goal was to strengthen organizations which maintain those traditions by allowing them an opportunity for respectfully organized public exposure combined with a chance to make some money. From the first, it was considered vital to try for as broad a cultural spectrum in the audience as on the stage, and to concentrate on presenting "traditional" rather than "revivalist" performers. In actual fact, it appears that there are basically three kinds of performing groups at the festival. One, which could be called "traditional," does on stage pretty much what it does or has done in the context of their own culture. A second, which might be labelled "folklorico" or "revitalization" groups, presents versions of traditional performances, arranged and choreographed for export beyond its own culture. The final group, which could be called "revivalist," consists of people demonstrating skills associated with cultural traditions not their own, which they have consciously learned as performance skills. Although this latter group is always present in some form at Tucson Meet Yourself, it is deliberately deemphasised in favor of the two others. The festival staff frequently explains this by statements on the order of: "Tucson Meet Yourself is a celebration of the fact that many individuals and communities in the area have managed to hang on to their own aesthetic heritages."[4]

Originally established in 1775 as a Spanish *presidio* or military installation next to a village of Piman speaking Indians, Tucson has always been at least a bicultural community. During the nineteenth century this cultural complexity increased as immigrants moved into the area from several directions, especially after the Gadsden purchase had added Southern Arizona to the United States. Considering the fact that nineteenth century immigrants included Jewish merchants, Black soldiers and cowboys, Chinese laborers and merchants, Irish soldiers and cowboys, and French priests, it is a bit misleading to refer to new arrivals by the commonly used term, "Anglos." To this heady cultural mixture was added in the late nineteenth sentury a large number of Yaqui Indian immigrants from Sonora who were fleeing the genocidal policies of the Diaz regime. Their descendants still live in cultural enclaves in the Tucson area, and have preserved to a great extent their traditional, native, Catholic ceremonialism.

The present century has seen the development of several large institutions in Southern Arizona which have added to the cultural complexity of the region. The University of Arizona, established in 1885, has long maintained a specialty in arid lands studies and has attracted scholars from the Middle East and South Asia. Fort Huachuca, sixty miles to the Southeast, was manned by Black regiments until after World War II and now serves to attract potential immigrants from all over the United States, as does Davis-Mothan Air Force Base on Tucson's east side. Retirement communities in and near Tucson attract their share of new arrivals as well. The city's location sixty miles from the international border ensures a constant stream of temporary and permanent residents from all parts of the Mexican Republic.

Tucson's greatest growth, however, has occurred in the past 40 years, following the development of efficient and practical cooling and air conditioning systems, which appreciably lessen the discomfort of Southern Arizona summers. From 45,454 people in 1945 the city's population has grown to 354,533 in 1985. One result of this continuing growth is an extremely fragmented community, both geographically and culturally. There is no longer any meaningful nucleus that one can call "Tucson," other than a group of offices and government buildings in the old commercial district. Partly because of post-war growth patterns that produced a seemingly endless spread of residential developments interspersed with shopping centers and malls, and partly because the flood of immigrants arrived in nuclear families that were often isolated from others of similar cultural background, local and regional culture has been swamped. Aside from Mexican-American barrios and three predominantly Black districts, Tucson has nothing equivalent to the ethnic neighborhoods, complete with businesses and religious institutions, which have been a feature of so many older cities. About the only way to establish and maintain contact with others of one's region or ethnic group is by way of social organizations. Such groups as the Italian American Club, the Czechoslovakian American Social Club, and the German

American Social Club have long played an important role in the lives of immigrant Tucsonans who wish to maintain cultural ties with their communities of origin.

Such social organizations seldom have their own clubhouses, and many do not have regular, formal membership meetings. They do, however, have regularly scheduled dinner-dances at different times during the year. These are occasions when members can get together, perhaps converse in the "old" language, eat traditional festive foods, and dance to the music they were accustomed to in their original communities. Such groups play an important role in the annual Tucson Meet Yourself festival.

All four of the different festival activities outlined above are important to the festival. Although the staff views the main stage, crafts demonstration and workshop areas as important settings for the educational activities so critical to the festival's aims, the entire event can be said to hinge on the preparation and sale of the traditional ethnic foods that provide the central public image of Tucson Meet Yourself. It is mentioned on the festival poster and in all the written and verbal publicity produced by the festival staff. Staff and the media often indulge in images expressive of the total impact of the festival. These invariably include food, as in "a man dressed in the garb of a German folk dancer admiring a young Hispanic's low rider car while munching on a Vietnamese delicacy"[5] or, "It's the only occasion in Tucson where you can eat a Lao egg roll and watch a Ukrainian woman decorate Easter eggs while listening to a Papago Indian polka band."[6] Every article in the local press that deals with the festival seems to emphasize food preparation and sales. One paper even had a reporter review the festival for its regular restaurant review column.[7] A final hint as to the importance of food to the event lies in the joke that staff members hear dozens of times over the course of each year: "I don't know about anyone else, but WE call it 'Tucson EAT Yourself'!"[8]

Because the festival is presented free of charge in a park with several entrances, there is no accurate way to gather statistics regarding attendance, length of stay, or what people do once they get there. But it appears to most of the people involved in putting on Tucson Meet Yourself that food is the event's major attraction. Once in the park, visitors will watch main stage performances, visit the crafts demonstration area, or perhaps take in a workshop. Fans of one particular genre or performing group or people with a specific ethnic heritage will turn out for specific parts of the program, of course. But sampling ethnic food is a major, if not the major, drawing card of the festival.

Much of the success of Tucson Meet Yourself depends on ethnic food sales. This is not entirely accidental. In the initial planning for the festival in 1974, it was decided that traditional ethnic food sales would be a major part of the event for several reasons. We live in a consumer-oriented society, and one way to present ethnicity (or anything else) in such a society is to provide the public with an opportunity to purchase things. Americans in the seventies seemed to enjoy sampling each others' foods. (This was long before the current "foodie" boom became apparent to observers of popular culture.) Many ethnic organizations in the Tucson area already had experience preparing and selling their traditional foods at church bazaars, annual dinner dances, and other public occasions. Even if a specific ethnic community in Tucson did not include traditional musicians or craftspeople, it was thought likely that it would have some good cooks. Thus, the festival organizers decided that the sale of ethnic food could be an effective basic activity in an event dedicated to the sharing of a wide range of cultural traditions with the general public. It was.

Food booths, elaborately decorated in ways intended to reflect and symbolize the identity of the groups who are operating them, first demand the visitor's attention at the festival. Mexican-American organizations embellish their booths with bright colors and paper flowers. Germans, Ukrainians and others have built permanent, architectural facades for their booths which are used year after year. Traditional crafts objects, both locally produced and brought from the "old country," add to the decor and make symbolic statements of identity. (Some groups sell crafts from their booths as well as food. Festival regulations require that these be locally made and within the cultural tradition of the group operating the booth.) Booth operators are often dressed in traditional costumes. Some booths feature additional kinds of traditional statements. Musicians frequently play outside Irish, Spanish, Scots, and Thai booths. Other groups play native music on tape recorders. Spaniards and Germans do informal dances near their booths, Lebanese show slides of Lebanon, and Armenians tell fortunes by reading coffee grounds. All this activity helps create a festive and exciting atmosphere at Tucson Meet Yourself.

This atmosphere carries over to traditional food, and the policy of the Tucson Meet Yourself staff towards food sales is relatively simple. Participation is by invitation only and is restricted to nonprofit organizations having as a significant part of their agenda the maintenance of their own traditional culture. Organizations with purely political, charitable, or religious agendas are less likely to be invited to participate. No charge is made for participation, although a donation is suggested for groups wishing to occupy a double ($8' \times 16'$) rather than a single ($8' \times 8'$) booth. (Further opportunity is given to donate to the festival's operating budget after the event is over. It must be emphasized that these donations are voluntary, and, in fact, some groups which regularly do not make a donation are invited to participate with equal regularity.)

Groups are requested to serve foods and non-alcoholic beverages traditional to their own cultures. (Soda pop is sold at the festival, but is the monopoly of the Cultural Exchange Council, which raises funds for the festival. Alcoholic beverages are neither sold nor served at the festival.)[9] Although groups choose their own food and set their own prices, the staff is always ready to assist with general advice, particularly to new groups, regarding what sorts of foods have seemed to "go well" in the past. Staff will also urge groups to prepare their own foods, and to present food as a cultural statement as well as a fund-raising device.[10] (The festival staff, which started off as two people in 1974, now consists of approximately 15, itself multicultural and meeting on a year-round basis. Although there is a food booth committee, nonroutine decisions concerning food sales and other matters are at least discussed by the full staff. Staff decisions are by consensus.) In addition, groups selling food are urged to decorate their booths and are required to abide by Pima County health regulations, which are explained at a prefestival meeting.

In 1985, food at Tucson Meet Yourself was provided by 45 organizations representing 37 cultural culinary traditions. There was Mexican, Papago, Yaqui, Afro-American, Cuban, Chilean, Colombian, Irish, Scots, German, Norwegian, Danish, Finnish, Swedish, Italian, Spanish, Hungarian, Polish, Ukrainian, Greek, Yugoslav, Armenian, Persian, Turkish, Israeli, Lebanese, Arab, Indian, Sri Lankan, Cambodian, Thai, Vietnamese, Lao, Japanese, Chinese, Filipino, and Angolan food, all prepared and sold by people raised in those culinary traditions. By far the greatest number of organizations presenting food were social/cultural maintenance groups on the order of the Ukrainian American Society of Tucson. Some of these were admittedly rather ad hoc groups of families formed mainly for the purpose of selling food at the festival. There were a few religious organizations (two Black churches, for instance, and a Lao Buddhist group) and a scattering of such neighborhood and support groups as the San Ignacio Yaqui Council and the Amphi Indian Education Parents' Committee. Workers in the booths were for the most part older adults; a few student organizations participated, but by and large it was the parents and grandparents who made and sold food at the festival.

While there is a sense in which all the food served at Tucson Meet Yourself is "traditional," in fact a number of criteria seem to be used in choosing the food to be served by any particular group. Examining the foods served at the 1985 festival by three different organizations—the Ukrainian American Society of Tucson, COMWOLEI (a Mexican-American social club), and the Desert Indian Dancers group—suggests the range of cultural expression. While all the foods are in some sense "traditional" to the cultures selling them, this traditionality takes on a range of shapes and depths of meaning.

Thus, Eastern European groups tend to select sausages, potato dumplings, and cabbage for their Tucson Meet Yourself sales. Much of the food served at these booths is similar to what one finds at their regularly scheduled public celebrations. The Ukrainian American Social Club, for instance, served stuffed cabbage, *vereneky* (potato dumplings), Ukrainian sausage, poppy seed cakes, *kolachkis* (braided bread), and other pastries—almost exactly what the same organization prepares for its semi-annual dinner dances. These foods—holiday foods all—seem to have become, for Tucson Ukrainians, symbols of their Ukrainian heritage and identity, and as such are served on occasions when that identity is being celebrated.

COMWOLEI (the acronym stands for COMmunity, Work, and LEIsure) is a group of older Mexican-American couples who occasionally get together for social, cultural, and fund-raising purposes. Their 1985 menu consisted of freshly made flour tortillas with butter, *machaca burros,* bean *burros,* tacos, *nachos,* and *empanadas*. A *burro* is simply a large flour tortilla wrapped around some sort of filler. (Similar objects are called *burritos*—little *burros*—in California. According to some Arizonans, this reflects the fact that no one in California can make the true *tortilla grande de harina,* and must therefore settle for a smaller version. The size of the tortilla, of course, determines the size of the *burro* or *burrito*.) *Machaca* is a regional specialty consisting of shredded beef cooked with onion, tomatoes and green chile; *nachos* are fried tortilla chips covered with melted cheese; and *empanadas* are turnovers—in this case with a sweet squash filling. The *empanadas* are a regional variation on a food known all over Latin America. Tacos are a universal Mexican and Mexican-American food, while *nachos* are rapidly approaching hot dogs and popcorn in mainstream popularity as a snack.

This is an interesting menu. Large flour tortillas are a local specialty; in fact, they are only made in a small area of South Central Arizona and North Central Sonora. Within that area they are the cultural property of Papagos, Yaquis, and Mexicans. The COMWOLEI members brought a small, wood-burning stove to the park and the women made their tortillas on the spot. They also happily gave lessons when they had free time, as the making of large flour tortillas by hand is seen as an important but disappearing aspect of local culture. Thus, the COMWOLEI cooks cater to several degrees of sophistication in their choice of Mexican food. But it should be noted that their tour de force, and the activity which has given them a good deal of fame (including frequent newspaper coverage), is the making of flour tortillas, a staple food which is also a symbol of regional identity.

Figure 14-1. Costumed Ukrainian Dancers Outside the Booth of the Ukrainian American Social Club of Tucson

The menu on the booth lists the following foods: holubtsi (stuffed cabbage), vareniky, mlintzi (blintzes), kasak plate (a combination plate), cold raspberry tea, and coffee. A separate card marked "Desserts" lists the following: pampusky (donuts), rosettes, poppyseed cake, halachi, and coffee.

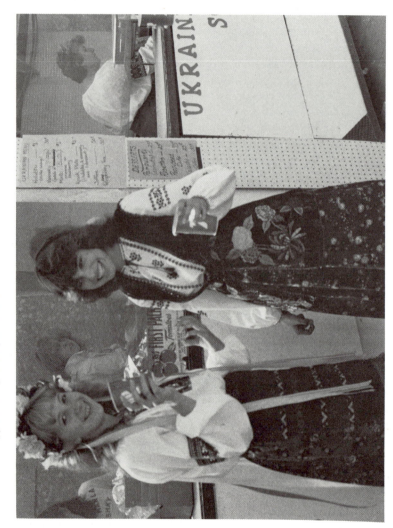

The Desert Indians, a Tucson area Papago Indian dance group[11] in which Papago children learn a repertoire of traditional Papago dances and songs taught by older adults, makes several public presentations each month within the Tucson area. It has participated in Tucson Meet Yourself since the festival's inception. Each year the Desert Indians operate one of the most popular booths at the festival, selling a local variety of pan-Southwestern Indian fried bread called Papago popovers. Popovers can be eaten plain, with honey, or as a sort of taco filled with beans or a red chile and beef stew. (Papago red chile stew is usually quite "hot"; a specially mild variety is made for sale to outsiders.) They are inexpensive to produce and are made on the spot. There are always long lines outside the popover booths at Tucson Meet Yourself and other local festivals. Popovers have been an important Papago culinary export for at least 20 years and are popular, not only with non-Indians but with members of other tribes. Popovers are sold to the general public at local street arts and crafts fairs and pow wows, and on Sundays outside the historic mission church of San Xavier del Bac, located in the San Xavier district of the Tohono O'odham Nation (formerly the Papago Reservation), approximately 12 miles south of Tucson.[12]

Interestingly enough, popovers do not seem to be a particularly important part of Papago cuisine in other contexts. One friend told me that in his house they would not be served to a guest because they are considered "hard times" food. Another man mentioned that when he was growing up in the reservation village of Gu Oidak,[13] they would have popovers once or twice every couple of weeks, mostly at the request of the children of the family. I have never encountered them at formal Papago meals, either those aimed at expressing Papago culture to non-Papagos or those attended mostly by Papagos. At the former meals, adaptations of desert plant foods (such as cholla bud salad or ice cream with saguaro syrup) are usually featured, while at the latter one finds acculturative foods such as flour tortillas, oven-baked whole wheat rolls, red chile stew, menudo (a Mexican dish made of tripe and hominy), potato salad, fruit punch and coffee. (I should mention in passing that fiery red chile stew and potato salad are among the real Papago contributions to the regional cuisine. The two sets of flavors combine magnificently.) So Papago popovers are something a little different from the Ukrainian symbolic identity statement, or the local Mexican-American presentation of regional and other foods. They appear to be simply an item of the traditional Papago culinary repertoire that has proved to be a successful and popular export. For non-Papagos the popover may be turning into a Papago identity symbol; it does not appear to be so for most Papagos. These three examples should give a notion of the range

Figure 14-2. Members of COMWOLEI Making Large Flour Tortillas on a Wood-Burning Stove

The woman on the right is removing the finished tortilla from her arm, where the final forming took place, and spreading it on the stove top to cook.

(Photo by Bill Doyle)

of cultural expression embodied in the foods that are sold at Tucson Meet Yourself.

Regardless of the traditionality embodied in the foods sold at the festival, it seems to be the opportunity to sell food that entices many ethnic organizations to participate. Occasional references in ethnic organization newsletters to the "Tucson Meet Yourself fundraiser" suggest that many of the cultural aims of the festival are not always as apparent to some of the participants as they are to the staff. Some groups, in fact, treat the festival as just that—an occasion for raising funds. However, all groups are urged by festival staff members to use food sales as an opportunity for making some sort of statement concerning their cultural identity. It has also been the staff's experience that groups that approach the festival purely as a fundraising occasion frequently get discouraged by the intense, hard work required for relatively small financial returns. The secret of success seems to be a combination of fund raising, social occasion, and ethnic self-advertisement. Occasionally ethnic organizations do not wish to participate in the festival with food sales. Some groups would prefer to operate information booths instead. This is discouraged on the grounds that Tucson Meet Yourself is an arts festival, rather than a celebration of cultural and national diversity. The feeling of the staff is that this is the easiest line to draw in order to avoid political confrontation at a public event that includes, for instance, Israeli, Arab, Armenian and Turkish participants.

No matter what the profits at the festival may be (and they seem to run from a few hundred to as much as two thousand dollars), one thing that happens at Tucson Meet Yourself is that Tucson's ethnic organizations make some money. Answers to a questionnaire sent out to food sales groups in the past have revealed that funds so raised are spent on a wide range of materials and activities. Many of these are involved in one way or another with the maintenance of cultural identity. Funds raised at Tucson Meet Yourself have sent musicians to Piper's College and Sweden to study fiddling. They have been spent on dance costumes and church choir robes. They have gone to local charities and been set aside for church, temple and clubhouse construction. They have helped recently arrived immigrant families. They have helped finance scholarships, a Yaqui religious fiesta, and a Hindu celebration. Thus one of the results of food sales at Tucson Meet Yourself is to provide some of the organizations most concerned with maintaining the identity of Tucson's ethnic components with some extra funds. This, as I suggested earlier, was one of the hopes of the organizers of the event.

Of course raising money is not the only important function of Tucson Meet Yourself. A lot of participants look at it as fun—hard work, to be sure, but fun all the same. Members of several organizations have told me that

Figure 14-3.   Members of the Desert Indians Dance Group Making
                Papago Popovers Behind Their Booth
                The woman in the center is forming a raw popover; the
                woman on the right is removing popovers from the hot
                cooking fat.
                (Photo by Denny Carr)

annual participation in Tucson Meet Yourself provides much of the "glue" that keeps those organizations together. There is a great deal of planning and preparation, followed by several days of intense cooperative activity at the park. All this tends to bring the group together working towards a common goal. In addition, the festival is a time to meet old friends and make new ones. And the making of new friends is very important in several different ways.

Many organizations recruit at the festival. Due to Tucson's size and fragmented nature, it is not always easy for newly arrived members of an ethnic group to make contact with others of similar background. Tucson Meet Yourself, with its attendant publicity, is an excellent setting for learning "who else is in town." Making a public statement of identity to the public at large is also very important to some organizations. I quite often hear phrases like "We just want people to know we exist." One Colombian explained that the Club Colombia was participating in the festival "to let Tucsonans know that Colombia has a culture aside from drugs." However, while political, social and religious agendas may well figure in this eagerness to become known, festival policy absolutely discourages the overt expression of these agendas at Tucson Meet Yourself. The staff considers it vital to the continued success of the festival that it be limited to a celebration of cultural diversity through the traditional arts, as free as possible of the tensions and conflicts that are an inevitable byproduct of that diversity.

A main part of this celebration is food sales. The prospect of selling food draws many members of ethnic organizations to participate in the festival. The booths, many of them specially decorated and operated by people in national or regional traditional costumes (and sometimes featuring music as well), provide a good deal of the festive ambiance of the occasion. And the prospect of sampling exciting ethnic food brings many of the visitors to the festival. Once at Tucson Meet Yourself, members of ethnic groups do more than sell food and raise money (some of which goes back into the operation of the festival). They participate in main stage presentations of music and dance, give workshops, and demonstrate traditional crafts. And the visitors attend those workshops, craft demonstrations and main stage presentations. But in a very real sense, it is the food that sticks the festival together. This should come as no surprise to the observer of cultural dynamics. Once again, as happens over and over, a social occasion is given meaning and cohesion by the preparation and sharing of traditional foods. The label "Tucson Eat Yourself," with its suggestion of self-celebration through communion, is entirely appropriate.

Notes

1. Tucson Meet Yourself is described at greater length in the following: James S. Griffith, "Tucson Meet Yourself: A Festival as Community Building," *Southwest Folklore* 1:1 (Winter 1977): 1–10. Jim Griffith, "Tucson Meet Yourself" in *Folk Festivals, A Handbook for Organization and Management*, ed. Joe Wilson and Lee Udall (Knoxville: The University of Tennessee Press, 1982): 131–43. I was one of the founders of the festival and am still heavily involved in its production. Data not otherwise referenced are from personal experience. Additional information, programs, clippings and other documentation concerning the festival are in the Tucson Meet Yourself files at the University of Arizona's Southwest Folklore Center. This is not the appropriate setting for an extended discussion of the decisions of inclusion and exclusion involved in the production of a festival such as Tucson Meet Yourself, or of any of the issues raised by the existence and shape of what one might call the "folk festival movement." Readers interested in these issues are directed to Charles Camp and Timothy Lloyd, "Six Reasons Not to Produce Folklife Festivals," *Kentucky Folklore Record* 26 (January–June, 1980): 1–2, and David E. Whisnant, "Folk Festival Issues," *JEMF Special Series*, No. 12 (1979).

2. Fieldwork has continued off and on since the festival's inception in 1974. It has been carried on by myself and other staff members, and is usually casual and sporadic in nature. Frequently it consists of following up references to performing groups previously unknown to us. These references come through personal contact and the local media. Over the years staff members have done considerable consulting with local tradition bearers as to what should be presented from their traditions and the best ways in which the various arts should be presented. Considerable discussion inevitably proceeds any innovation to the festival. For a more detailed discussion of these topics, see Griffith (1982).

3. This or a similar phrase frequently appears on press releases and other printed material describing the festival, all of which are on file in the Southwest Folklore Center of the University of Arizona.

4. I and others on the festival staff frequently use this or a similar statement in explaining the festival in interviews or while attempting to explain our criteria for inclusion and exclusion of performers to would be participants.

5. Robert S. Cauthorne, "Don't Eat Until You Meet Self. El Presidio Event Has Food, Music," *The Arizona Daily Star*, October 12, 1985, B1. The article is illustrated with a photograph of Mary Carrillo of COMWOLEI making a flour tortilla.

6. This is a phrase frequently used by staff members in interviews and oral presentations concerning the festival.

7. John Jennings, "Tucson Meet Yourself," in "Elbows Off The Table," *Tucson Citizen*, October 7, 1982 Calendar Section, p. 13.

8. This phrase has recently started appearing in print. An example is in the "Best in Tucson" survey published in *The Tucson Weekly*, July, 1987.

9. This ban on alcohol exists for several reasons. High among them is the notion that we are attempting to present traditional music and dance as art forms worthy of respect—a concept which is never easy to get across, even to a sober audience. Many performers at the festival disapprove of drinking alcohol, and might well be reluctant to participate were beer or other intoxicating drinks served. Finally, interethnic tensions at the festival can run high and would only be exacerbated by the availability of alcohol. This does not

mean that the park is totally "dry." A number of gurgling paper bags are always present, and discrete drinking does take place. But by not officially sponsoring alcoholic consumption we feel that we avoid a number of problems and preserve the "family outing" atmosphere of the event.

10. These suggestions are invariably just that—suggestions—but they are based on the staff's sense of the purpose of the festival as being a sharing of traditional art forms rather than a fundraiser or a food fair. Suggestions are sometimes couched in terms such as "Are there kinds of foods that you all have that other folks don't have—foods that are special to your cultural tradition?" Staff members also occasionally reassure members of groups newly arrived to the festival, the community, or both, of the willingness of festival-goers to sample unfamiliar foods.

11. Since the earlier drafts of this paper, the people who were formerly called Papagos formally changed their tribal name to Tohono O'odham. This phrase, which translates into English as "The Desert People," is what they traditionally called themselves, Papago being a Hispanicized version of the epithet "Bean Eaters," bestowed on them by a neighboring tribe. For the purposes of this paper, however, I will continue to use the more familiar "Papago."

12. The San Xavier District of the Tohono O'odham Nation is a small tract of land 12 miles south of Tucson. It contains San Xavier Village, and is not contiguous with the main body of the reservation.

13. Gu Oidak (also known by its English name "Big Fields") is a village in the center of the main Tohono O'odham Nation. This reservation lies west of Tucson and is the second largest Indian reservation in the United States, covering over 2,700,000 acres of desert land. It stretches to the Baboquiveri Mountains to just east of the mining town of Ajo, and from the International Border to just south of Interstate 8.

Afterword: Discovering the Symbolism of Food Customs and Events

Michael Owen Jones

Eating is unique. No other activity in which human beings engage involves so many senses and sensations. We experience hunger pangs as well as the fullness of satiety and the painful aftereffects of gluttony. We smell food and are capable of differentiating hundreds of odors. We can taste that which is sweet or salty, bitter or sour. We see colors and imagine textures. We discern temperature. We feel the texture of foods directly or through the use of utensils. We hear the fire sizzling, the meat frying, the pot boiling; the clatter of pot, pans, and platters as food is dished up to be served; and the clink and scrape of utensil against plate as we eat. Having such impressions, and remembering them, it is no wonder that sometimes we crave something moist and tart, crisp and salty, chewy and sweet, warm and doughy, or thick and filling; that we cherish some earlier experiences with food; or that we long to reproduce an event that was memorable. "Just thinking about having soup and sandwiches on a cold, rainy day makes me feel good," remarked one person. "Then, already having that pleasing image in my mind, actually having soup and sandwiches on a cold, rainy day is like a dream come true." "Tuna sandwiches have always been fun for me," said one person, "because they remind me of carefree summer vacation days, picnics, and parties at the beach." Since she associates the food with pleasant, even festive occasions in the past, she enjoys it now. Even the sight or aroma of a tuna sandwich might trigger warm memories and evoke positive feelings.

Even though eating is always an individual act, the social dimension tends to dominate—to the extent that when dining alone we are apt to turn on the radio or sit in front of the television set for companionship or recall snatches of conversation with others. "Friends are worth Smirnoff" reminds us of the social realm of food and drink. A type of food, the presence of food, or the preparation of food by someone may symbolize care, concern, and contentment. "Homemade with Love" reads the headline to an ad for Libby's pumpkin pie filling and Carnation condensed milk; a slice of pumpkin pie topped with a dollop of whipped, white sweetness and balanced on a pie server is suspended over a dessert plate, and superimposed on the right of the picture is a recipe the following of which will be a performance enacting and communicating a set of concepts and feelings: "You can taste all the love you bake into a Libby's Pumpkin Pie," we are told.

A frequent physical activity, eating is also largely repetitive. But we know from personal experience that there are ways in which eating-related activities nourish and sustain us intellectually, emotionally, socially, and spiritually. Given our propensity for the symbolic and festive—in combination with the sensual and social nature of eating—we are likely to generate habits, customs, and rituals by assigning meanings to recurrent, repetitious, and seemingly patterned behavior. Traditions develop, many of which become cherished. An ad for Welch's frozen cranberry juice cocktails invites us to "start a delicious holiday tradition." We are also encouraged to "bring Knudsen home for the holidays," told that Bird's Eye "creates delicious holiday memories," and informed about Jones Dairy Farm where, "for 150 years, there's been a great Jones holiday tradition," namely, "sharing" (the ad focuses on a worn, much handled, handwritten card with a recipe for Aunt Sally's sausage stuffing).

These three sets of ideas inform this book: (1) Much of human communication and interaction is symbolic. We assign meanings to virtually anything and everything, unable to avoid attributing significance to sounds, movements, and objects, or associating phenomena that happen to be coincident in time or space, or hypothesizing relationships. We use metaphorical language, tell stories, and ritualize. (2) Human beings tend toward celebration and joyousness. Sometimes, especially at work, a festive spirit results from accomplishing something; or it is invoked as antidote—a means of coping, escaping, or projecting hopes and desires rather than reflecting the reality of the situation. (3) Eating is a unique sensory and intellectual experience, one that is intensely personal while also often social. It is a physiological requirement as well; by being met frequently and repetitively, it results in the formation of habit and custom, of "performances," that in turn may become symbolic.

Food marketing and food-centered celebrations illustrate all of these points. For the food to appeal, advertisements and commercials must dwell upon aroma, taste, texture, and appearance. To attract and hold attention, marketers depend on the use of familiar sayings and situations in ads. To precipitate action, advertisers need to invoke pleasant associations, feelings, and memories of food experiences that can be transferred to the product advertised. Reference to symbols, traditions, and the sensual-festive nature of eating dominates. Consider this example of symbolism in regard to food. "I have a sense of well-being when I eat any kind of meal on a special occasion. The well-being is generated by enjoyment of the people I am with," said one person. "I have a sense of well-being when I eat oatmeal," she continued. "I am sure this feeling is associated with TV commercials about Quaker oats in which oatmeal is synonymous with motherhood." Recently Quaker coined "Mother's" as a brand name for grain products. "We Love Our Mother's" shouts the headline above a photo of four burly but friendly sailors holding a box of Mother's oat bran, a pitcher, and bowls of this "tasty water-soluble fiber source." Concludes the ad: "Mother's knows what's good for you."

Just as we rarely think about how an ad is constructed, we tend to take for granted, too, the food customs and symbolism in our everyday lives. A book on food and the festive performance of community brings to attention one of the most pervasive, interesting, and significant aspects of social life and human behavior. Although the subject has not been studied in such detail previously, there is precedent for considering it.

A few humanists and social scientists have examined the role of food in social life and spiritual affairs. A particularly influential study is Audrey Richards's *Hunger and Work in a Savage Tribe,* first published in England in 1932 and printed again in the United States in 1948. Her mentor, Bronislaw Malinowski, waxed enthusiastic about the book, writing in the preface, "After reading it, my conviction deepened that society is not animated by one obsessive force, that of sex."[1] His statement is noteworthy if for no other reason than that he had recently published four books dealing largely with sexual behavior in savage society. He was to contend, however, in the preface to Richards's book on the cultural aspects of food and eating: "Among the Melanesians whom I studied, the most important motive in the life of the community and in the interests of the individual is food, not sex."[2] He notes further regarding Richards's book: "In having written the first scientific memoir on the subject of the sociology and psychology of nutrition, she reaps the reward of pioneering achievement. No serious anthropologist can afford to neglect the present study, which opens new prospects and dictates new questions in fieldwork."[3]

Richards intended her study to complement and supplement Malinowski's research, not to supplant it. She set forth her pronouncements within a conceptual framework taught her by Malinowski and others, and still subscribed to by many. Her position differed from her mentor's mainly in her focus on food-getting rather than reproduction as a—or perhaps *the*—primary biological need of human beings, serving as a locus of culture perpetuating society, at least among savages.

Like Malinowski, she began by assuming a fundamental unity in social life. While she believed that shared sentiments bound together members of a group, she puzzled over what those attitudes concerned: reproduction, food, shelter? Malinowski had emphasized procreation; Richards concluded food-getting. Why food? Because it is both a "more primary and recurrent physical want," for the impulse to seek food recurs regularly and cannot be long inhibited or repressed. As a constant necessity, food-getting—not some other biological need—determined the nature of social groupings and their activities.[4]

Having decided that nutrition was primary in shaping the social institutions which presumably were unified into a whole, Richards sought to illustrate her thesis. "I want to examine the human relationships of a primitive society as determined by nutritional needs," she writes, "showing how hunger shapes the sentiments which bind together the members of each social group."[5] Her study, then, became a functional analysis of how food is used to symbolize certain relationships in a primitive tribe, maintaining cohesion and thus perpetuating that society.

Richards's study is also grounded on her notions of a "nutritional system" and how it must have developed initially in man's earliest existence. The individual is driven to hunger, she contends, which renders food-getting a compelling urge, investing it with a meaning and value unique among human activities. The most basic social relationship is that of mother and child, which is also physiological, based on food supply. Hence, the family is held together by the object of procuring food. Within the family structure and its food-centered activities, the child learns who will provide sustenance and with whom and how it must be shared. Families are linked together in "ties of reciprocity" to form a larger social system, facilitating the food quest and regulating the ownership and distribution of food sources. Once this system has been established, the individual's behavior, through the family initially, is determined in regard to diet and manner of eating by social customs and group sentiments.[6] In primitive conditions, therefore, writes Richards, "Food itself becomes symbolic of the human relationships which it brings into being."[7] Indeed, "Food as a Symbol" is the title of the concluding chapter of Richards's book.

Other researchers after Richards have been concerned with the apparent emotional and social significance of food as well as the extranutritional meanings sometimes attributed to food, its preparation, distribution, and consumption. Many have been intrigued particularly by the meanings and social functions of food sharing, contending that communal eating is a cohesive act uniting participants as members of a group, differentiating the group from all others, and maintaining solidarity.

For example, at a recent birthday party honoring a department manager, pots, bowls, and trays of food covered the table. Many celebrants had brought their favorites from home, preparing the dishes themselves rather than simply purchasing something impersonal at a supermarket. They sang "Happy Birthday" with gusto. The manager became teary-eyed as he described the occasion. This party differed significantly from the one the year before which few had attended. The small number of food items—snack food, really, not warm, filling casseroles or unusual delicacies to delight the palate—came from a store. Singing lacked enthusiasm. The "best wishes" were perfunctory.

During the interim, the manager had mounted an all-out effort to recognize and reward employees and to change the climate or ambience of the unit. He began with introspection, probing to uncover personality traits and to assess his managerial style. Discovering inconsistencies between what he professed to believe and how he actually behaved, he brought values and their expression into greater alignment. He sensitized himself to needs and concerns of organizational members. Instead of criticizing people, he complimented them. He instituted rituals in which individuals' contributions were publicly proclaimed and honored. In recent interviews, employees remarked on the dramatic changes of preceding months. It is not surprising, therefore, that the birthday party this year had a festive air, that many department members invested themselves in the preparation of the food, or that the occasion and the manager's memory of it were emotion-laden.[8]

It is important to be aware that members of the unit do not constitute a single body with one set of values and ways of doing things. Many interactional networks have formed, each with its own notion of how things should be done; every individual expresses her or his own sentiments and aspirations as well. Moreover, no one seems to feel that the manager has been entirely successful in changing his style, in recognizing others' contributions to the organization, or in changing the ambience. Celebrating the manager's birthday may have been less a reflection of group unity and more a projection of the kinds of feelings and commitment to common goals that members would like to have—sometimes. The human need to feel joyous might have led to a festive event, itself a symbol of a host of unarticulated and otherwise unexpressed ideas and feelings. If we have learned anything from half a century of research on food customs and symbolism, perhaps it is that some of the models and assumptions from the past are not borne out in the complex social worlds of contemporary Americans.

Like its predecessors, the present book on food and festivity explores situations in which food is the nexus of social relations. It isolates symbolic communication and interaction from the continuum of human experience, scrutinizing them for the messages conveyed or inferences made by participants in events. It assumes that there is more to food-related behavior than simply the satisfaction of a biological need.[9]

When exploring some of the emotional, intellectual, and spiritual aspects of food and festivity in the everyday lives of their family and friends and in the social sphere of neighborhoods and towns, the authors depart from some of the predilections of the past. An obvious bias in earlier years, of course, was to focus on savage societies or folk groups, the latter defined either as the lower stratum of society or as an integrated, homogeneous, and like-minded community (typically ethnic, occupational, or age-defined, if not regional or rural); people were labelled a group on the basis of external, arbitrary, and inconsistently applied criteria.[10] Now, however, more attention is paid to the concept of interactional networks;[11] and rather than assuming that food unifies participants in an event, achieving some mysterious *communitas*, the researchers here examine particular situations to understand the variety of meanings that obtain and the complexity of the process by which symbols are created and used. There is an implicit challenge to long-standing assumptions about geographical, technological, and cultural determinism and an increasing awareness of the role of individuals in the generation and perpetuation of traditions.

As evident in these essays, research is growing away from the study of foodways as an index to historical and sociocultural processes to an interest in food-related activities as behavioral phenomena, inquiry into which can tell us much about how people behave, communicate, and interact. These departures from the past suggest a variety of topics to investigate and directions to pursue.

The essays in this anthology on food and festivity consider personal as well as social symbols, the dynamics of interaction among family and friends as well as among residents of suburbs and cities, some of the varied meanings of actions and multiple interpretations of events, and—of particular importance—the linkage of food and festivity in a wide range of situations in contemporary American society. Although the subject of food and festivity might be exhausted for years to come (thanks to the present volume) there are other research opportunities. This volume inspires greater attention to the microcosmic, that is, observation and interpretation of individual behavior manifested in specific events. In addition, because aesthetic concerns underlie many of the essays, there are also implications for better understanding food choice.

More research might be done in the future, therefore, on what is a good cook and a gracious host or hostess. Significant aspects of artistry include not only the appearance, taste, and smell of the final product but also the way in which the raw ingredients are prepared, the attention to details of kitchen maintenance, and the rhythm of preparation as well as the nature and ambience of the serving of the food. What distinguishes "special" meals? To some married couples, the first major meal served in the home of the newlyweds, whether gastronomically successful or not, remains memorable years later. While we tend to emphasize the pleasant aspects of experiences with food, what are the worst meals in people's memory? These probably consist of overcooked, tasteless items repulsive in texture and appearance, indicating how important sensual appeal is to eating (and hence significant for understanding and overcoming many aversions); or they were socially disastrous, demonstrating that we tend to associate the taking of food together with feelings of good will; or they conveyed or were assigned negative messages affecting our sense of self-esteem, revealing that we are likely to view the quantity, quality, and apportionment of food as a symbol of values, attitudes, and relationships. What concessions do members of a household make to one another's tastes, preferences, and aversions; how do they manage to compromise, if they do; to what extent do they respect differences, even celebrating these, as well as develop common habits and customs? How and why do the food habits of particular individuals continue or change in relation to changing work, family, and other circumstances? In any given situation, how is individual food choice affected by the nature of the event, the identity and interests of participants, recent and past experiences with food and meanings assigned to them, conceptions of self and of others, the sensory qualities of the food and aesthetic dimension of the setting, and so on?

A second direction for future research is to consider once again the complex question of foodways in America. As early as 1848 a visitor proposed that the national motto should be "gobble, gulp, and go."[12] A dozen years ago *Esquire* carried a full-page "ad" at the back of one issue. A satire of the Evelyn Wood speed reading method, it describes Evelyn Food's program to "cut your eating time in half & triple your consumption in just five days!" Beneath a photo of Ms. Food, seated before an empty plate with knife and fork in upraised hands, is the statement, "It sounds incredible. But Evelyn Food graduates can eat a seven-course meal in four minutes! 4187 calories at that speed with total recall of every bite of every morsel." Some of the skills taught at the Evelyn Food Eating Dynamics Institute are "how to eat without chewing and swallowing," "how to eat up and down as well as from right to left across the plate," and "how to spit out bones and seeds while actually still eating." An additional course will teach post-graduates "How to take advantage of neglected body pockets!" Thus, "you can retain undigested food for weeks, and you can draw on it when you want it."[13]

In 1974, *National Lampoon* featured an article on "The Cooking of Provincial New Jersey." Patterned after *Gourmet Magazine* and richly illustrated with photos of such "traditional fare" as Coke, Twinkies, Hostess Cupcakes, frozen fishsticks and frozen vegetables, boxes of Minute Rice, and pots of boiling water, the article welcomes the reader to "the cooking of provincial New Jersey: Twenty-one cuisines, one great taste." New Jersey cooks learn their art traditionally, "the same way their girl friends did. . . . Each time they use a box of Roast 'n Boast or whip up a batch of French's Potato Pancake Mix, they depend solely on their inherent skills and excellent reading ability." The propensity toward processed foods and prepared mixes grows out of an attitude "reflecting the kind of tradition we hope will never die in provincial New Jersey cooking. . . ."[14]

Much has been made of regional and ethnic traditions, of the abundance of food in America and the technological wonders of flash freezing and microwave cooking, and of the prevalence of convenience- and fast-food as well as sugar and fat in the American diet. Excesses are easy to deplore and satirize. Is there such a thing as "American cuisine" or national eating habits? Does the enormous variety of identities, experiences, and behaviors of people in the United States prevent an attempt to investigate or write about food customs and symbolism in this country?

Some researchers have retreated from the complexity of contemporary eating behavior in America, preferring to investigate customs historically among allegedly isolated rural and ethnic groups. The authors in this volume confront the eclectic variety of foods and confusing array of circumstances head on. Implicit is a method for studying eating behavior in America. This entails realizing that Americans eat what they do, prepared as it is, and served and consumed on certain occasions in particular ways for a multiplicity of reasons. Considerations in the background may include regional or ethnic identity in some instances, as well as technological developments, general values and attitudes, and childrearing practices. Contemporary Americans' eating behavior is also affected by the mass media and by advertising. It is a function, too, of trends, the popularity of certain ideas, and changing lifestyles and concerns generally in society. But for all that, people experience food directly and in interaction with selected others. Compelling influences, then, would seem to be found in the qualities that make eating unique and that inhere in specific situations of food preparation, service, and consumption. In the final analysis, regardless of what is available and what we are told to eat or what is good for us, we make choices. What we eat, when, and for what reason is as much an outcome of individual predilection and situational factors as it is a product of history, culture, and technology.

A third set of opportunities for the future includes application of insights and hypotheses. This volume on food and festive performance includes attention to city-wide celebrations. Increasingly prominent in folkloristics is the matter of public folklife programming some of which includes attention to food customs and symbolism. But there are other applications.

One entails improving programs sponsored by the federal government, taking into account, for example, the varieties of eating behavior, conceptions of food, and food preparation in the United States in order to avoid what the authors of one article call "the government's one-dish dinner."[15] A second involves improvements in institutional food preparation and service. College students used to joke that at the dorm cafeteria they could have "trichinosis for breakfast, salmonella for lunch, and ptomaine for dinner." Recent years have witnessed attempts to improve the quality of foodstuffs and to include greater variety in menu selection. However, food still is overcooked and unseasoned or unimaginatively prepared. It is dished up by people who do not know what is in it. It is consumed in unappealing surroundings. Its selection and preparation are overseen by a manager worried about profit and loss and/or a dietitian preoccupied with the four food groups.

A notable exception is one of the dietitians in a state mental hospital in Osawatomie, Kansas. Writing in *American Journal of Nursing* in 1972, Mary Lou Chappell recommends ways in which staff can understand and help patients through food. This care begins with offering the newly arrived patient a meal, providing something familiar and security-producing. "If the food items served are familiar, the temperatures right, the personnel attitude supportive and helpful, and the surroundings pleasant, this could be the first chance to give evidence that we are interested in a person and want to help." Just as subtly, "If we give a geriatric patient ground food without finding out if this is necessary we can tell him he is old and has lived too long," she warns. She also observes that when there is anxiety generally among patients, the consumption of "security foods" such as milk, bread, and hot cereal rises as much as 35 percent. "Food service as well as the food itself communicates with patients," she concludes. "We indicate to the patient a respect for him when we endeavor to put the food on the plate in an attractive manner.... We cannot ignore the responsibility to understand and use wisely communication via food."[16] Far too few who control food in a dormitory, hospital, or other institution, however, have been sensitized to the varieties of cuisine in America as well as to the importance of symbolism, sensuality of food, aesthetics of the setting in which food is consumed, the tendency toward festivity, and the use of food as a medium of communication.

To conclude, the subject of food customs and symbolism is one of the most overlooked and least understood topics in research. Astonishingly few courses are taught on the traditional and symbolic aspects of food preparation, service, and consumption—not only in professional fields such as nutrition, social welfare, and nursing but also in the humanities and social sciences. What is more compelling, however, than the need for food? In what other realm of life do we expend so much of our energy or engage in so many interrelated activities? What else in our daily lives speaks so eloquently of symbolism, aesthetic sensibilities, communication, social propriety, community, performance, and celebration as do our foodways?

Notes

1. Bronislaw Malinowski, "Preface," in Audrey I. Richards, *Hunger and Work in a Savage Tribe* (London: Routledge, 1932): xii.

2. Ibid., xv.

3. Ibid., x.

4. Richards, 1.

5. Ibid., 23.

6. Ibid., 212; see also 20–30.

7. Ibid., 213.

8. I am indebted to Susan Montepio, a Ph.D. candidate in Folklore and Applied Anthropology, for this information. She is one of three research assistants on a pilot project under my direction concerning organizational culture and management practices at UCLA. The other research assistants are Ms. Susan Scheiberg (Folklore and Communications) and Mr. Peter Tommerup (Folklore and Organization Studies). For more information, see Michael Owen Jones, *Exploring Folk Art: Twenty Years of Thought on Craft, Work, and Aesthetics* (Ann Arbor: UMI Research Press, 1987): 197–202.

9. These and other research questions, assumptions, and hypotheses are discussed in Michael Owen Jones, "Perspectives in the Study of Eating Behaviour," in *Folklore Studies in the Twentieth Century: Proceedings of the Centenary Conference of the Folklore Society,* ed. Venetia J. Newall (Rowman and Littlefield: Totowa, N.J., 1980): 260–65; and Richard M. Mirsky, "Perspectives in the Study of Food Habits," in *Foodways and Eating Habits: Directions for Research* (California Folklore Society: Los Angeles, 1981), ed. Michael Own Jones, Bruce S. Giuliano, and Roberta Krell, 125–33.

10. A point made by Linda Keller Brown and Kay Mussell (eds.) in their book *Ethnic and Regional Foodways in the United States: The Performance of Group Identity* (Knoxville: The University of Tennessee Press, 1984): 5, although it is not always clear how authors utilized "internal" markers of group identity.

11. For the notion of "interactional, communicative, and experiential network," see Beth Blumenreich and Bari Lynn Polonsky, "Re-evaluating the Concept of Group: ICEN as an Alternative," in *Conceptual Problems in Contemporary Folklore,* ed. Gerald Cashion (Bloomington, Ind.: Folklore Forum Bibliographic and Special Series, No. 12): 12–17.

12. A. M. Maxwell, *A Run Through the United States,* cited in Arthur Meier Schlesinger, "A Dietary Interpretation of American History," *Massachusetts Historical Society Proceedings* 68 (1944–1947): 209.

13. *Esquire* 86 (August, 1976): 136.

14. Gerald Sussman, "The Cooking of Provincial New Jersey," *National Lampoon* 1 (June, 1974): 57–63.

15. Judy Perki and Stephanie F. McCann, "Food for Ethnic Americans: Is the Government Trying to Turn the Melting Pot into a One-Dish Dinner?" in *Ethnic and Regional Foodways in the United States: The Performance of Group Identity* (Knoxville: The University of Tennessee Press 1984), ed. Linda Keller Brown and Kay Mussell, 238–58.

16. Mary Lou Chappell, "The Language of Food," *American Journal of Nursing* 72 (July, 1972): 1294–95.

Appendix

Welcome to Soup Night!
Recipes and Philosophy

Lin T. Humphrey

The Legend of Soup Night

You might begin your own Soup Night tradition by re-enacting the folk
story of "Stone Soup":

It seems that some simple peasants who lived in a small village were caught
up in some silly war, in which they had little stake or interest, since a
peasant's life remained much the same, no matter who was in power. When
they heard that some soldiers were coming to their village, they quickly
spread the word to hide all the foodstuffs. By the time the soldiers got there,
all the cupboards and cellars and larders were bare.

The soldiers, of course, were hungry and both surprised and angry to
find nothing to eat in the whole village. One of the soldiers, sensing what
had happened, made the villagers an offer they couldn't refuse: "Bring me
a pot and some water and a stone, I will make stone soup for everyone."
Amazed at the prospect, the villagers did as they were told, and watched
as the soldier built a fire, hung the pot over it, and added one large round
stone. As the water began to boil, he tasted the soup. Turning to the crowd,
he announced that it was not bad, but if he only had some salt and pepper
and perhaps a little garlic, it would be much better. Quickly someone
fetched the spices which he added to the pot. After a second taste, he
declared it would be perfect if only he had a few potatoes. And then, after
dumping in the potatoes, which appeared miraculously from nowhere, he
asked for a few carrots. And then some celery. And then turnips, and dry
beans, and some nice meaty bones, and tomatoes. And on and on and on.
Lo and behold! In a few hours, both the villagers and the soldiers sat down

to the most wonderful stone soup in the world! And to this day, the villagers talk about the wonderful soup the soldier made out of nothing but a stone and some water.

Want to try it? You provide the pot, the water, and the stone, and let your guests bring the rest. Here is the most flexible soup recipe in the world, one that an old soldier gave me.

STONE SOUP

1	large kettle	5–7	qts. water
1	smooth, clean 1–2 lb. stone		

Bring water to a rolling boil. Collect ingredients from your guests: salt, garlic, pepper, soup bones, ham hocks, potatoes cut in chunks, chopped carrots, chopped celery, shredded cabbage, chopped onions, chopped or canned tomatoes, beans, kale, barley, spinach, corn, tomato sauce, mushrooms, even zucchini.

Cover and simmer 2–3 hours. Add a cup of wine, beer, and/or coffee. (These are my own magic secret ingredients that I put in all my soups). Have some innocent, neutral bystander taste before you add more salt or pepper. I always have my husband or one of the newly arrived guests taste the soup; my own taste buds get all clogged up with smells and become completely unreliable.

Remove the stone and the bones.

Ladle soup into bowls; sprinkle with Parmesan cheese.

This is good with any stone-ground (of course) whole wheat bread, but if you are feeling creative or guilty because your guests brought all the ingredients, make Sunflower Whole Wheat Bread.

SUNFLOWER WHOLE WHEAT BREAD

1	pkg. active dry yeast	6	c. (approx.) stone-ground whole wheat flour (I usually cheat and use half all-purpose flour and half whole wheat—the bread rises higher and is lighter)
⅓	c. warm water		
2	c. milk at room temperature		
3	T. melted butter or margarine		
1	T. salt		
½	c. honey	1	c. shelled sunflower seeds.

1. Dissolve yeast in water in large bowl.
2. Add the milk, 2 T. of the butter, the salt and honey.
3. Gradually stir in 5 c. flour to make a soft dough and stir in the sunflower seeds.
4. Spread about half the remaining flour on a board, dump dough, knead for 7–10 minutes until dough is smooth and elastic.
5. Add more flour if necessary.
6. Place in greased bowl, turning to grease the top.
7. Cover with towel and let rise in a warm place until double (about 1–1½ hours).
8. Punch down and shape into two loaves.
9. Place each in a 9 × 5 × 3 or similar sized loaf pan that has been greased on the bottom only.
10. Cover and let rise until almost doubled, about 45 minutes.
11. Brush crusts with remaining T. butter.
12. Bake in 375° oven for about 45 minutes or until golden brown and pulled away from sides of the pan.
13. Remove from pans and cool on racks.
14. Serve warm with lots of butter.

And now your are off and running—or Souping!

The Meat of the Matter

This section contains some really hearty soups, those that stick to your ribs. Since these are often more expensive to make than some of the others that follow, I either save them for a special occasion, or ask everyone to chip in on the beef, fish, or clams, or whatever. Remember, the essence of Soup Night is sharing the soup and the responsibility for a good evening.

For a cold fall or winter's evening, or especially if it's rainy, nothing is better than steaming bowls of chili garnished with shredded cheddar, chopped green onions, sliced black olives, and corn chips. Chili is cheap, filling, and absolutely yummy, for all of those with robust bellies.

SOUPER CHILI

2–3	lb. ground beef (or ground turkey)	1	t. salt
2–3	large onions, minced	½	t. pepper
3	lb. stewed canned tomatoes	½	t. paprika
4–6	T. chili powder	1	T. cumin
2–3	cloves of garlic, minced	1	c. wine/beer and/or coffee
2–3	lb. cans chili beans (purists cook dry beans)	2	T. oregano
			Red pepper for the brave

1. Brown ground beef in bottom of large soup pot that has been sprinkled with a little salt.
2. Add onion and garlic and cook until yellow.
3. Stir in all spices (sometimes we nonpurists use a packet or two of Lawry's or Schilling's chili mix).
4. Add tomatoes and tomato sauce.
5. Add beans.
6. Simmer at least 1 hr. covered.
7. Add wine/beer/coffee.
8. Heat thoroughly over a low-to-medium fire (be careful not to let the bottom burn and stick to the pot!).
9. Ladle into bowls.
10. Provide bowls of cheese, onions, olives, and corn chips for individual garnish.
11. Serve with red wine or good cold beer; feeds 10–15 people.

Chili is especially good with sourdough cornbread. If you don't have a jar of starter hidden away in your refrigerator, try plain cornbread following the recipe on the cornmeal box, or use a mix, or buy a nice loaf of corn-rye bread.

SOURDOUGH CORNBREAD

1	c. starter	1½	c. evaporated milk
1	T. sugar (Yankees like more sugar in their cornbread than this.)	2	beaten eggs
		¼	c. warm melted, butter
		½	t. salt
1½	c. yellow cornmeal	¾	t. soda

1. Mix the starter, cornmeal, eggs, evaporated milk, and sugar.
2. Add melted butter, salt, and soda.
3. Pour into a 10-inch skillet that is well greased and can go into the oven (cast iron is great).
4. Bake in hot 450° oven for 25–30 minutes.
5. Serve and eat while hot. Cut in pie/shaped wedges in skillet.

Everyone knows the virtues of chicken soup; it's good for you, body and soul. And it doesn't have to be expensive. Collect leftover carcasses from your friends, or buy wings and backs cheap at most markets. Cheer up a lonely or depressed friend—ladle out the chicken soup.

CHEERFUL CHICKEN SOUPER

3–5	lbs. chicken	2	bay leaves
2	T. Worchestershire sauce	2	lb. canned tomatoes
5	qts. water	½	t. thyme
2	T. salt	1	c. chopped green pepper
3	chopped onions	1	chopped apple
½	t. pepper	¼	c. chopped parsley
3	c. chopped celery	2	T. lemon juice
½	t. paprika	1	t. curry powder
3	c. chopped carrots	1	c. barley, rice, or thin noodles
½	t. poultry seasoning		
4	chicken bouillon cubes	1	c. white wine/beer/coffee

1. Place chicken pieces in water and simmer two hours, covered.
2. Remove bones and skin, skim off as much chicken fat as possible, and add spices (all of them).
3. Add vegetables and anything else you've forgotten, *except* the rice, barley, etc. and the alcohol or coffee.
4. Simmer 1–2 hours; add coffee/beer/white wine.
5. Add barley, noodles, or rice.
6. Simmer 15–20 minutes.
7. Ladle into bowls.
8. Good with chilled white wine and sympathy.

This recipe makes a lot of chicken soup, but this is a good soup to have left over: you can freeze it and take it to a sick friend.

Chicken soup is good with store-bought or bakery made French bread, but if you want to try something really fun and exotic, try Tomato Bread.

TOMATO BREAD

1	pkg. active dry yeast	1	T. sugar
1	T. vegetable oil	½	t. salt
¼	c. warm water	4½–5	c. whole wheat flour
½	t. powdered basil		(substitute half all-
1½	c. tomato juice		purpose white for
			lighter bread)

1. Grease one 9 × 5 × 2 bread pan or two smaller loaf pans.
2. Dissolve yeast in water for five minutes.
3. Stir in tomato juice, sugar, salt, oil, and basil.
4. Stir in enough flour to make a stiff dough.
5. Turn onto floured board and knead 5–7 minutes until dough is smooth and elastic.
6. Shape into a loaf and place in pan (or loaves into pans).
7. Cover with dish towel and let rise 1–1½ hours until doubled in size.
8. Bake in preheated 350° oven for 50–60 minutes.
9. Cool on rack and serve warm with butter.

People new to Soup Night are often curious about the all-time favorite soup of the group, but we've never voted on it. My husband always gallantly claims that each night's soup is the absolute best. I know, however, that this next soup, if not the absolute favorite, is certainly one of the top three. This might be because so many of the soup groupers are from the east. At any rate, whatever the reason, clam chowder is special. I usually serve it for celebrations—weddings, birthdays, anniversaries, hellos, and good-byes. And if friends request it, I always let them chip in on buying the clams.

SOUPER CLAM CHOWDER

12	slices of crisp bacon	3	diced green onions
2	large chopped onions	¼	c. chopped parsley
4–5	cans (6½ oz. each) chopped clams	3	c. water
		3–4	bottles clam juice
1	t. thyme	2	t. salt
6	c. diced potatoes	6	c. milk
2	bay leaves	¾	t. pepper
4	diced carrots (optional)	1½	c. cream
		1	T. butter
2	c. diced celery	1	c. white wine or beer
			Mashed potato flakes if necessary

1. Fry bacon, drain, and crumble.
2. Sauté onion in 2 T. bacon drippings in large soup pot.
3. Add celery, carrots, green onions, potatoes, salt, pepper, thyme, and bay leaves, and stir about 5 minutes.
4. Add water, clam juice, 1 c. beer or white wine.
5. Simmer covered about 30 minutes.
6. Add clams, milk, cream, and butter.
7. Heat until steaming—don't boil (if mixture isn't thick enough, add instant mashed potatoes).
8. Sprinkle with crumbled bacon and parsley.
9. Ladle into bowls and serve with good, dry white wine. Serves 12–15 people

This chowder is great with big chunks of sourdough or sheepherder's bread. If you need something to go with it, do something simple, like biscuits. Follow the directions on a box of biscuit mix (double for a larger group), or try these triple wheat treats.

Triple Wheat Biscuits

2½	c. sifted all-purpose flour	1	c. wheat germ
1½	t. salt	6	t. baking powder
½	c. shortening		
½	c. whole wheat flour, stirred		

1. Stir in mixing bowl flour (both kinds), wheat germ, baking powder, and salt.
2. Cut in shortening until mixture resembles coarse meal.
3. Add milk and stir with fork until well moistened.
4. Turn out on lightly floured surface and knead about 20 strokes, until smooth.
5. Roll dough to ½ inch thickness.
6. Cut with floured 2½ inch cutter.
7. Place on ungreased cookie sheet.
8. Bake in 450° oven for about 10 minutes or until lightly browned. Makes about 20 biscuits.

Biscuits are much simpler than yeast breads, and these complement the chowder. Your guests will compliment you.

Vegetable Soups for Nonorthodox Vegetarians

I suppose everyone these days has at least one vegetarian friend. The following soups can be adjusted for either the carnivore or the orthodox vegetarian by simply adding more meat or removing the soup bones. However, I must confess that I like them just the way they are. The core of these soups is vegetable—from one or two to many. In all cases you can add or delete according to what you have on hand or what is in season. I think the more fresh vegetables you can use, the better, but canned and frozen probably work just as well.

The first soup is very similar to the stone soup recipe but without the rocks. It's probably the healthiest soup in the entire book.

KITCHEN SINK VEGETABLE SOUPER
(contains everything but the kitchen sink)

2–3	lbs. meaty soup bones		1	t. sugar
1	c. frozen or fresh broccoli, zucchini, crookneck, or turnips		2–3	chopped potatoes
			1	t. pepper
4	qts. water		3	lbs. canned stewed tomatoes
1	T. salt		1	t. basil
1	t. garlic powder		1	c. frozen or canned lima beans
1	head of shredded cabbage		2	bay leaves
2	T. chopped parsley		1	c. frozen or canned green beans
2	large chopped onions		1	c. frozen or canned corn
1	6-oz. can tomato paste		1	c. fresh or canned mushrooms
6	sliced carrots		1	c. beer/wine/coffee
1½	c. chopped celery		1	bunch fresh or 1 pkg. frozen spinach (if you can think of anything else, feel free to add it)
½	t. ground cloves			
½	c. chopped green pepper			

1. Place bones, salt, garlic, and water in soup pot and simmer covered for one hour.
2. Skim surface.
3. Add cabbage, onion, carrot, celery, green pepper, tomatoes, and all the spices.
4. Simmer covered about 45 minutes.
5. Add everything else except the spinach and the beer/wine/coffee.
6. Remove soup bones; remove meat from bones; return meat to soup; give bones to dog.
7. Add spinach and beer/wine/coffee; stir and simmer about 15 minutes.
8. Ladle into bowls.
9. Sprinkle with Parmesan cheese.
10. Serve with hearty red wine.

This soup is good with bread sticks or an herb bread like the following:

HUMPHREY'S HEALTHY HERB BREAD

2	pkgs. active dry yeast	½	t. marjoram
1	T. dried chopped onion	½	c. wheat germ
		1½	t. salt
½	c. warm water (110°)	¼	t. sage
1	T. chopped chives	¾	c. cornmeal
2	T. sugar	¼	c. vegetable oil
½	t. dried dillweed	2	c. all-purpose flour
1	13-oz. can condensed milk (1⅔ c.)	2	c. whole wheat flour
½	t. thyme		

1. Dissolve yeast in warm water.
2. Combine milk, sugar, salt, vegetable oil, parsley, onion, chives, dill, thyme, marjoram, and sugar in large bowl.
2. Stir in the yeast and water.
3. Beat in the cornmeal.
4. Add 1 c. whole wheat flour and 1 c. all-purpose flour.
5. Beat in wheat germ.
6. Stir in rest of flour to make a stiff dough.
7. Turn onto lightly floured board and knead 3–5 minutes until smooth.
8. Place in greased bowl, turning once to grease top.
9. Cover with dish towel and let rise in warm place 1 hour.
10. Punch down and divide in half.
11. Shape each half into a loaf and place in well-greased loaf pan or in well-greased 16 oz. coffee can.
12. Cover and let rise until double, about 45 minutes.
13. Bake in 350° oven about 45 minutes; cover the tops if they get too dark.
14. Remove from pans, cool on racks, serve warm with butter.

After you make both the vegetable soup and the herb bread, your kitchen will be bare. Neither of them is complicated; they just use a lot of ingredients. Probably all you have left are a few potatoes, so the next soup is based on potatoes. Potato-cheese soup is my personal favorite in this collection, but do get someone to help you peel all those potatoes the day before.

POTATO-CHEESE SOUPER

10	lbs. potatoes, peeled and chopped	3	onions, peeled and chopped
3	qts. water	1	T. Worcestershire sauce
3	c. stewed tomatoes (optional)	2	c. celery, chopped
⅔	c. butter	2	qts. milk
½	c. chopped parsley	2	t. salt
⅔	c. flour	2	t. dry mustard
1	t. dill weed	1	lb. Cheddar or Muenster cheese
1	t. pepper		
1	c. beer or white wine		

1. Put potatoes, onions, celery, and 1 t. salt into pot with 3 qts. water.
2. Bring to boil, simmer covered 1 hour.
3. Add 1 c. beer or wine.
4. Melt butter in large sauce pan.
5. Blend flour, remaining salt, pepper, mustard, and Worcestershire sauce into butter. (This is called a *roux* if anyone asks.)
6. Add milk gradually to the roux and stir until thickened.
7. Add this mixture to the soup pot and add tomatoes.
8. Heat thoroughly for 30 minutes but don't boil.
9. Stir in cheese.
10. Ladle into bowls and serve with chilled white wine or cold beer.

Because of the tomatoes, this soup may appear a little pink. If this offends you, leave out the tomatoes. It is good either way. Since potato soup is definitely starchy, you could skip the bread. On the other hand, a nice brown rye would be perfect. You can buy excellent pumpernickels and ryes, or you can try this one, but start it the day before you need it.

WRY RYE BREAD

1	c. buttermilk	3	T. caraway seeds
¼	c. warm water	2	c. whole wheat flour
¾	c. beer	3	c. all-purpose flour
1½	c. rye flour	1	T. grated orange peel
½	c. molasses		
½	c. firmly packed brown sugar		
1½	t. salt		
1	T. softened butter		

1. Scald buttermilk with orange peel and pour into large bowl.
2. Stir in beer, molasses, salt, and caraway seed and cool to lukewarm.
3. Mix yeast with warm water to dissolve.
4. Add yeast and rye flour to buttermilk mixture, stirring to blend.
5. Cover and set at room temperature for 12 hours. (Now is a good time to peel potatoes with a friend.)
6. Dump on floured board and knead until smooth (10–15 minutes). Add more flour if necessary.
7. Place in greased bowl, turning to grease top.
8. Cover and let rise until doubled, about 45 minutes.
9. Punch down and divide in half.
10. Shape in 2 loaves and place in greased 5 × 9 inch loaf pans.
11. Cover and let rise until doubled, about 45 minutes.
12. Bake in 350° oven for about 40 minutes.
13. Cool in pan 10 minutes; dump on wire racks. Serve warm.

This next recipe is a transition soup, one that takes us from vegetables to the next section of this collection, Beans. The main ingredient in this soup is a vegetable, split peas, although some people may consider them more closely akin to beans. Let's not split hairs—here is my favorite recipe for split pea soup, straight from Holland, with a dash of Polish sausage. Although you can use either green or yellow split peas, mixing a pound of each makes a nice combination.

Dutch Treat Pea Souper

2	lbs. green and/or yellow peas	12	c. water
4	t. salt	2	t. savory leaves, crumbled
2	kielbasa (Polish sausage) about 1 lb. apiece, scored	2	large leeks (or onions), chopped
4	potatoes, peeled and diced	1	t. pepper
4	c. chopped celery with leaves	1	c. beer/wine/coffee

1. Wash, rinse peas, and place in soup pot with water.
2. Bring to boiling, add leeks and salt.
3. Cover and simmer for 45 minutes.
4. Add sausage and simmer for 1½ hours.
5. Add potatoes, celery, savory, and pepper; simmer an hour until thick and rich.
6. Add 1 c. of wine, beer, or coffee and simmer 15 minutes.
7. Remove kielbasas and cut them into small chunks; return to pot.
8. Ladle into bowls for 15–20. (Cut recipe in half for a smaller crowd.)

Suggest that your guests bring dark rye or pumpernickel bread and hearty red wine or good dark beer. If the season is right, make some bock beer bread. Bock beer is usually available only in the early spring; if it's the wrong time of year, use any dark beer and make your bread anyway.

Bock Beer Bread

1	c. bock or dark beer	3–3½	c. all-purpose flour
1	t. salt	3	T. soft butter or margarine
1	pkg. active dry yeast	3	T. brown sugar
1	well-beaten egg	½	c. wheat germ

1. Warm the beer (110°–115°) and pour into large bowl.
2. Sprinkle yeast on top and let stand 3–5 minutes.
3. Add half the flour, the sugar, salt, and beaten egg.
4. Beat until smooth.
5. Mix butter with the remaining flour and add wheat germ.

6. Add this mixture to the dough a little at a time—spread it around and together with your fingers until well blended.
7. Add flour until mixture cleans the bowl.
8. Dump onto a lightly floured board and knead 8–10 minutes.
9. Place in greased bowl, turning to grease top and cover.
10. Let rise until doubled, about 45–60 minutes.
11. Punch down, shape into a loaf, and place in a greased 9 × 5 × 3 loaf pan.
12. Cover and let rise until doubled, about 45 minutes.
13. Bake in 375° oven for 35–40 minutes.
14. Remove from pan and cool on rack. Serve warm with butter.

This is a delicious bread and fun to make since you get to mess around in it with your fingers.

Human Bean Soups

The very essence of humble homemade soup is the lowly bean. Cheap, plentiful, as basic as bread and butter, as versatile as poetic license, bean soup is the center of this collection, and the best way to feed a bunch of people in style. Furthermore, bean soup is practically indestructible. Add anything to it; it will enhance the flavor. Double it, triple it, halve it—you still get good basic bean soup. In this section are four favorites from Soup Night, using four different kinds of beans. Mix and match; create your own exclusive beanery.

The place to begin is the basic bottom: plain ol' navy bean soup. The recipe is simple; the taste is fantastic. A pound of beans in soup ought to feed at least 8–10 people.

SOUPER SIMPLE WHITE BEAN SOUP

1	lb. white beans—marrow, navy, pea, or great northern	1½	t. salt
		1–2	c. instant mashed potatoes
1	c. diced celery	½	t. pepper
2–3	cloves minced garlic	2	chopped onions
1	meaty ham bone	1	c. beer

1. Wash beans, cover with water, bring to boil, and simmer 2 minutes.
2. Remove from heat, cover and let stand 1 hour.
3. Bring to boil again, adding ham bone, and simmer covered 2 hours.

4. Add other ingredients and simmer 1 hour longer.
5. Remove soup bone; remove meat from bone; return meat to soup; give bone to dog.
6. Simmer covered about 30 minutes. (If you want to jazz this soup up a bit, now is the time to add other ingredients such as winter squash—seeded and cubed, chopped green peppers, mushrooms, chopped tomatoes, etc.)
7. Ladle into bowls. Pass salt and pepper.

Since this is such a simple, righteous, honest soup and is so easy to make, why not get carried away and make some good contrasting bread. Since the soup is basically white, get some color in your bread. Buy dark breads or make carrot wheat bread, which is a little sweet and complements the bean soup well. Besides, it's good for you.

CARROT AND WHEAT BREAD

1	pkg. active dry yeast	⅓	c. warm water
1	c. raisins	5	T. melted butter or margarine
2	c. milk at room temperature	2	t. salt
6½	c. whole wheat flour (if you are not a purist and want your bread to rise better and be lighter, substitute half all-purpose bleached or unbleached flour)	½	c. honey
		1	c. shredded carrot

1. Dissolve the yeast as usual in the warm water in large bowl.
2. Add milk, 3 T. of the melted butter, salt, and honey.
3. Gradually stir in 5 c. of flour to make a stiff dough.
4. Add carrot and raisins.
5. Spread ¾ of remaining flour on board and dump out dough.
6. Knead for 10–15 minutes, using remaining flour to prevent stickiness.
7. Place dough in greased bowl, turning once to grease top; cover with a towel and let rise until doubled (1½–2 hours).
8. Punch down and divide in half.
9. Knead each half about 30 seconds and shape into smooth round loaves.

10. Place on greased cookie sheet; cover and let rise until almost doubled (about 1 hour).
11. Brush tops with the remaining 2 T. butter, and bake in 350° oven about 30 minutes or until well browned.
12. Cool on rack and serve warm with butter.

After you've mastered the art of simple white bean soup, move on to explore the dark mysteries of black bean soup. Black kidney beans really are black, much darker than ordinary red kidney beans. This soup is nearly as simple as the simple white-bean soup—it just requires more bones and a few more ingredients.

BEAUTIFUL BLACK BEAN SOUPER

1	lb. black beans	2	parsnips, chopped
2½	qts. water	2	T. flour
2	bay leaves	½	t. pepper
5	strips bacon in pieces		Rind and bone from ham *or*
2	cloves garlic, minced or mashed		2 smoked ham hocks, split
2	stalks celery, chopped	2	t. salt
2	onions, chopped	½	c. sherry
2	carrots, chopped	3	lbs. beef bones
2	green peppers, chopped	4	c. cooked white rice
3	sprigs parsley, chopped	2	hard-cooked eggs, finely chopped
		1	c. beer/wine/coffee
			Optional: lemon slices, olive oil, white wine vinegar

1. Wash beans, cover with cold water, and soak overnight.
2. Drain; add 2½ qts. water; cover and simmer 90 minutes.
3. Cook bacon in large skillet; add celery, onion, green pepper, and garlic, and sauté until soft.
4. Blend in flour and stir one minute.
5. Add skillet mixture, bones, parsley, bay leaves, carrots, parsnips, pepper, and salt to beans in soup pot and stir well.
6. Cover and simmer 3 hours, stirring now and then.
7. Remove bones from pot, meat from bones; return meat to pot; give bones to dog.
8. Add about 1 c. beer, wine, or coffee.
9. Simmer 30 more minutes.
10. Add chopped egg and sherry.

11. Place ½ cup rice in each bowl and ladle in the soup.
12. Pass lemon slices, olive oil, and vinegar at table.

With this thick black soup, serve a simple bread. After all, the soup took all day to make. Try bread sticks or warm, buttered tortillas, or maybe Arabic pita bread. If by now you've become an addict and simply have to have homemade bread with your soup, try something simple like a casserole bread, such as this one made with Parmesan cheese.

PARMESAN CASSEROLE BREAD

1	pkg. dry yeast	1½	c. all-purpose flour
½	t. salt	1	beaten egg
¼	c. warm water	1	T. sugar
⅓	c. butter or margarine	½	c. Parmesan cheese
		2	T. chopped parsley

1. Soften yeast in warm water as usual.
2. Cool milk to lukewarm.
3. Sift together flour, sugar, and salt in large bowl.
4. Blend in butter with pastry fork or 2 knives until mixture resembles coarse meal.
5. Add beaten egg, softened yeast, and milk to mixture.
6. Beat well and stir in cheese and parsley.
7. Turn into a greased round 8 × 1½ cake pan.
8. Cover with damp cloth and let rise until double, about 40 minutes.
9. Dot with butter and bake in 370° oven 20–25 minutes.
10. Cut into pie-shaped wedges and serve with butter.

Both the color and the taste go extremely well with the black bean soup.

Now for something more exotic, a bean and minestrone soup combining both Italian and Portuguese ideas about what constitutes good bean soup. It's an easy soup for varying the ingredients. Remember the Cardinal Rule of soup cookery: use plenty of whatever you have on hand. This pot should easily serve 8–10 people.

MINESTRONE-BEAN SOUPER

1	lb. small white beans	¼	c. chopped parsley
10	c. beef stock (or 10 beef bouillon cubes, dissolved)	2	chopped carrots
		3	cloves minced garlic
		4	c. shredded cabbage
1	lb. bulk sausage or ground beef	1	lb.-12-oz. can stewed tomatoes
1	large onion, chopped	1	c. beer/wine/coffee
		1	15-oz. can garbanzo beans
1	t. basil		
1	c. chopped celery	1	12-oz. pkg. frozen spinach, thawed
1	t. oregano		
1	4-oz. can mushroom pieces	3	oz. vermicelli, broken short

1. Wash and sort beans.
2. Bring to boil in 10 c. beef broth; simmer 2 minutes.
3. Remove from heat, cover, and let sit 1 hour.
4. Brown sausage or ground beef in skillet. (Salt the bottom of the skillet and use no shortening.)
5. Add onions, celery, and mushrooms, and sauté until soft.
6. Add to beans in pot and simmer covered 2 hours.
7. Add carrots, tomatoes, cabbage, garlic, basil, oregano, parsley, and beer/wine/coffee.
8. Cook 45 minutes.
9. Add garbanzos, spinach, and vermicelli.
10. Cook 20–30 minutes.
11. Ladle into bowls and sprinkle with Parmesan cheese.

This is an extremely filling soup. It combines something from all of the first three categories of this collection—meat, vegetables, and beans. Truly, this soup deserves good bread, brought by your grateful guests, such as good French or sourdough. Here's a very simple do-it-yourself recipe for beer buns that even your children could make for you. This recipe makes 10 or 12 medium sized buns—double it for a Soup Night crowd.

SOUPER BEER BUNS

2	c. buttermilk biscuit mix	⅔	c. beer
		2	T. sugar

1. Stir together the mix and the sugar.
2. Stir in beer until moistened.
3. Spoon into greased muffin pan.
4. Let stand 15 minutes.
5. Then bake in 400° oven 15–18 minutes or until tops are golden brown.
6. Serve warm with butter.

This bean section is not complete until we have tried the mighty lentil. Lentils are those tiny little beans that blend well with everything. They make excellent salads, great fillings for pita bread sandwiches, and, of course, very good soup. As with most beans, you can add almost everything to lentil soup and change the taste, though not the character, of the soup. Lentils are very adaptable. The following recipe is fairly basic: try adding noodles, sausage, potatoes, leeks, carrots, lemon, or even lettuce. I especially like spinach or chard added the last 10 minutes, sliced garlic sausage, and even sliced wieners. This soup feeds a lot of people; a little lentil goes a long way.

BASIC LENTIL SOUPER

1	lb. lentils	1	t. basil
2	diced onions	2	bay leaves
4	qts. water	1	t. salt
1	finely chopped green pepper	3	T. vinegar or sherry
5	beef bouillon cubes	2	12-oz. cans or bottles of beer
2	bunches of chard *or* 2 pkg. frozen spinach	1	t. thyme
2	c. diced celery	1	t. pepper
2	c. diced carrots	6	garlic sausages or wieners

1. Combine lentils, water, and beef bouillon cubes in soup pot and boil for 2 minutes.
2. Remove from heat, cover, and let stand 1 hour.
3. Add beer, celery, carrots, onion, green pepper, and all spices; simmer covered 1½ hours or until the lentils are tender.
4. Add sausage/wieners and spinach.
5. Stir in sherry or vinegar.
6. Ladle into bowls.
7. Pass alfalfa sprouts to sprinkle on each bowl.

Such simple healthy soup deserves good healthy bread. Buy some at a health-food store or use this recipe for oatmeal bread.

THURSDAY NIGHT OATMEAL BREAD

2	pkg. dry yeast	½	c. light molasses
1	T. salt	4	T. raw rolled oats
½	c. warm water (110°)	⅓	c. shortening
6–6½	c. all-purpose flour	1	c. rolled oats (quick cook)
1½	c. boiling water		
2	beaten eggs	1	egg white
		1	T. water

1. Soften yeast in ½ cup warm water.
2. Combine 1½ cups of boiling water, 1 cup quick cooking oats, molasses, shortening, and salt.
3. Cool to lukewarm.
4. Stir in 2 c. sifted flour and beat well.
5. Add 2 beaten eggs and the dissolved yeast.
6. Add enough remaining flour to make soft dough.
7. Turn out onto lightly floured surface; let rest 10 minutes.
8. Knead until smooth (7–10 minutes).
9. Place in lightly greased bowl, turn once to grease top; let rise covered until doubled (1½ hours).
10. Punch down and divide in half.
11. Coat 2 well-greased 8½ × 4½ × 2½ inch pans with 2 T. raw rolled oats each (4 T. oats).
12. Shape dough into 2 loaves and place in pans.
13. Cover and let double (45–60 minutes).
14. Brush loaves with mixture of egg white and water; sprinkle with rolled oats (optional).
15. Bake in 375° oven for 40 minutes; cover with foil if tops get too brown.
16. Cool on racks; serve warm with butter.

Grand Finale Soups

This collection of soup recipes is just like a pot of soup: I want to keep adding things to it. Every recipe suggests another. I've saved two rather exotic soups for the end. Soup season usually ends when hot weather begins. Both of the following are good signatures for a successful series of soup nights or as openers for a new season in the fall. The first, a super version of bouillabaisse, is fairly expensive. You might pass the hat before making it to ensure you can afford the ingredients. Some of them might also be a little difficult to obtain, but you can always substitute other kinds of fish, etc. This soup is an ambitious project, not to be undertaken lightly or by the faint of heart. Serves 10–20.

SOUPER SUCCESSFUL BOUILLABAISSE

4	lbs. firm fleshed fish in chunks (red snapper, bass, cod, haddock, salmon, whitefish, perch)
1	lb. shelled and deveined shrimp
1	small lobster tail
½	lb. mushrooms
1	c. red wine
1	c. tomato juice
1	pkg. vegetable broth mix
1	t. thyme

6	mussels or oysters or clams (in shell)
1	6-oz. pkg. Alaskan King crab, thawed
2	c. clam juice
1	1-lb. 12-oz. can stewed tomatoes
½	t. saffron
1	strip orange peel
1	t. salt
½	t. fennel seed
1	minced clove garlic
2	T. chopped parsley
⅓	c. chopped green pepper
4	chopped carrots
2	c. tomato sauce
1	crumbled bay leaf

1. In a large soup pot, heat oil and sauté onion, garlic, green pepper, carrots, and mushrooms.
2. Add tomatoes, clam juice, wine, beer, tomato sauce, tomato juice, and all spices and condiments except parsley.
3. Boil mixture 15 minutes and add fish; simmer 10 minutes.
4. Add shrimp and simmer until shrimp turns pink.
5. If shrimp are pre-cooked, add at the same time as the lobster, crab, clams, oysters, and mussels.
6. Cover and simmer until shells open.
7. Ladle into bowls and sprinkle with parsley.

Soup this elaborate deserves only the best in bread. The ultimate, of course, is the sourdough sold on the wharf in San Francisco. If you can't

afford to fly to San Francisco after buying the ingredients for the soup,
here is a simple shortcut sourdough that will make a nice substitute.

SHEEPHERDER'S SOURDOUGH

1 pkg. active dry yeast	1 egg slightly beaten
1 t. salt	2 c. whole wheat flour
½ c. warm water (110°)	1 t. extract malted
1 t. soda	barley
1 c. sourdough starter	1 c. granola-type cereal
1 T. honey	

1. Dissolve yeast in water in large electric mixer bowl.
2. Add starter, honey, salt, soda, malted barley, egg, and cereal.
3. Beat at low speed and add 1 c. flour; beat 2 minutes.
4. Beat in remaining flour with heavy spoon until very elastic.
5. Place dough in a well-greased 5 × 9 inch loaf pan.
6. Cover lightly and let rise in a warm place until almost doubled (1 to 1½ hours).
7. Bake in 375° oven until well browned, about 35 minutes.
8. Cool in pan 5 minutes, then turn out on rack to cool.
9. Serve warm with butter. (If you're expecting a crowd, better make two loaves.)

This last soup differs from all the others because it is chilled and not
served steaming hot. If summer catches you still making soup, quickly
switch from the stove to the refrigerator and make gazpacho. If you can
get the same friend who helped you peel potatoes for the potato soup to
come help you chop vegetables, it will be a lot easier.

END-OF-THE-SEASON GAZPACHO

1	lb. green and Italian red onions, chopped fine	3	cloves minced garlic
6	T. red wine	1½	c. chopped celery, chopped parsley, chives, cilantro
2	T. paprika		
12	tomatoes, peeled and chopped (or a large 2 lb. can chopped tomatoes)	2	5¾ oz. cans sliced black olives
		1½	c. chopped cucumber, peeled
2	t. Worchestershire sauce	1–2	qts. Snappy Tom
12	drops hot sauce		Salt and pepper to taste
1	c. condensed beef broth		
1	c. dry white wine or beer		

1. Mix all chopped vegetables in large crock or bowl.
2. Add garlic, vinegar, paprika, Worchestershire sauce, hot sauce, beef broth, wine or beer, Snappy Tom.
3. Chill 24 hours.
4. Add pepper and salt to taste.
5. Ladle into chilled bowls and sprinkle with parsley, chives, cilantro, or croutons.

Since you can make this soup a day ahead, you might as well round out the season with one last batch of homemade bread. If you still have any beer left after adding it all year to various soups, use a 10-oz. can and make this delicious beer-cheese bread.

THE LAST GREAT BEER-CHEESE BREAD

1	12-oz. can beer (or 1½ c. milk)	2	T. sugar
8	oz. processed (not natural) American cheese	1	T. salt
		5	c. flour
½	c. warm water	2	T. butter or margarine
		2	pkg. active dry yeast

1. Combine beer, water, sugar, salt, butter, and cheese in a large pan.
2. Heat until warm and cheese is mostly melted.
3. Cool to lukewarm.
4. Dissolve yeast in ½ c. warm water.
5. Combine 2 c. flour and dissolved yeast in large bowl.
6. Add warm cheese mixture.
7. Beat 3 minutes at medium speed.
8. Gradually stir in remaining flour with wooden spoon to make a fairly stiff dough.
9. Turn onto floured surface and knead lightly until smooth and elastic (about 5 minutes).
10. Place in greased bowl, turning to grease top; cover and let rise until doubled (45–60 minutes).
11. Punch down and divide into two halves.
12. Now the tricky part: shape each into a 11 × 12 inch rectangle with rolling pin.
13. Cut each rectangle into three long strips, leaving them joined at one end.
14. Braid each loaf and place in a well-greased loaf pan.
15. Cover with towel and let rise until doubled (45–60 minutes).
16. Bake in 350° oven for 40–45 minutes.
17. Turn out of pans immediately and cool on racks.
18. Serve warm with butter.

After the Soup Is Over...

And so ends Soup Night. You are left with dirty dishes, leftover soup, and perhaps a few leftover guests, the good friends who linger for one more cup of coffee and to help with the final cleanup. Use the leftover soup for "seed," freeze it, and the next time you make a similar soup, add it to the pot. Or use it for a quick warm meal for two or three people.

If you have a lot of soup left over, send a jar home with deserving guests. This makes a great lunch the next day, especially for people who normally don't make homemade soup at all. Or deliver it to good friends who were unable to come to dinner.

The essence of Soup Night is participation and sharing. If I made a pot of delicious soup and no one came, there wouldn't be a Soup Night. Involve your friends in the whole process. Collect their old ham bones and turkey carcasses; invite them to help you peel and chop. A good Soup Night is a group endeavor. Give it a try. All you really need are friends and a soup pot to put them in.

Selected Bibliography

Michael Owen Jones and Theodore C. Humphrey

Abrahams, Roger. 1984. "Equal Opportunity Eating: A Structural Excursus on Things of the Mouth," *Ethnic and Regional Foodways in the United States: The Performance of Group Identity,* ed. Linda Keller Brown and Kay Mussell, pp. 19–36. Knoxville: The University of Tennessee Press.

———. 1987. "An American Vocabulary of Celebrations." In *Time Out of Time: Essays on the Festival,* ed. Alessandro Falassi, pp. 173–83. Albuquerque: University of New Mexico Press.

Adams, Jane Lilly. 1981. Changes in Southern Food and Table Customs, 1860–1930. M.A. thesis, Home Economics, George Peabody College for Teachers.

Adler, Thomas A. 1979. "Sunday Breakfast Was Always Special With Us": A Report on Foodways in South Central Georgia. Folklore Forum Preprint Series, 7 (No. 1).

———. 1980. "Making Pancakes on Sunday: The Male Cook in Family Tradition." *Western Folklore* 40:45–54.

The American Heritage Cookbook and Illustrated History of American Eating and Drinking. 1964. New York: American Heritage Publishing Company.

Anderson, Janet. 1986. *A Taste of Kentucky.* Lexington: University Press of Kentucky.

Anderson, Jay A. 1971. "The Study of Contemporary Foodways in American Folklife Research," *Keystone Folklore Quarterly* 16:155–63.

———. 1973. "Scholarship on Contemporary American Folk Foodways," *Ethnologia Europaea: Revue Internationale d'Ethnologie Européenne* 5:56–62.

Arnott, Margaret L., ed. 1975. *Gastronomy: The Anthropology of Food and Food Habits.* The Hague: Mouton.

Babcock, Charlotte. 1948. "Food and Its Emotional Significance," *American Dietetic Association Journal* 24 (No. 5): 390–93.

———. 1962. "Attitudes and the Use of Food," *American Dietetic Association Journal* 38 (No. 6): 546–51.

Back, Kurt W. 1977. "Food, Sex and Theory." In *Nutrition and Anthropology in Action,* ed. Thomas K. Fitzgerald, pp. 24–34. Assen, The Netherlands: Van Gorcum & Comp. B.V.

Bailey, Adrian. 1975. *The Blessings of Bread.* New York: Paddington Press.

Baker, Edward A., and D. J. Foskett. 1958. *Bibliography of Food. . . . 1936–56.* New York: Academic Press.

Bales, Robert F. 1962. "Attitudes Toward Drinking in the Irish Culture." In *Society, Culture, and Drinking Patterns,* ed. David J. Pittman and Charles R. Snyder, pp 157–87. New York: Wiley.

Barber, Edith M. 1948. "The Development of the American Food Pattern," *Journal of the American Dietetic Association* 24 (July): 586–91.

Beeley, Brian W. 1970. "The Turkish Village Coffeehouse as a Social Institution," *Geographical Review* 60:475–94.

Befu, Harumi. 1974. "An Ethnography of Dinner Entertainment in Japan," *Artic Anthropology* 11 (Supplement): 196–203.

Bell, Adele. 1966. "Sorghum Molasses Making Time," *Good Old Days* 2 (No. 10): 30–31.

Bennett, John W., Herbert Smith, and Herbert Passin. 1942. "Food and Culture in Southern Illinois—A Preliminary Report," *American Sociological Review* 17:645–60.

Booth, Sally Smith. 1971. *Hung, Strung, and Potted*. New York: C.N. Potter.

Bossard, James H. 1943. "Family Table Talk—An Area for Sociological Study," *American Sociological Review* 18:295–301.

Botkin, B. A. 1947. "Old New England Dishes." In *A Treasury of New England Folklore*, pp. 359–76. New York: Crown.

————. 1949. "Pleasures of the Palate." In *A Treasury of Southern Folklore*, pp. 550–81. New York: Crown.

————. 1951. *A Treasury of Western Folklore*, pp. 553–62. New York: Crown.

Boyd, Julian P. 1929. "Hog and Hominy: A Gastronomic Interpretation of Southern History," *The Archive* (Trinity College, Durham, N.C.) 37 (January): 5–9.

Brett, Gerald. 1968. *Dinner is Served: A Study in Manners*. Hamden: Shoe String.

Brillat-Savarin, Jean Anthelme. 1926. *The Physiology of Taste: Or Meditations on Transcendental Gastronomy*. New York: Boni and Liveright (orig. publ. 1825). See "On Gastronomy," "On Gourmandise," and "On the Pleasures of the Table," pp. 33–38, 109–18, and 131–40, respectively.

Bringéus, Nils-Arvid. 1970. *Mat och Miljo: En bok om svenska kostvanor*. Lund: Gleerups. Translated by Alexander Fenton (1970) as "Man, Food and Milieu," *Folk Life* (Cardiff) 8:45–56.

Bronner, Simon J. 1981. "The Paradox of Pride and Loathing, and Other Problems," *Western Folklore* 40:115–24.

Brown, Linda Keller and Kay Mussell, ed. 1979. "Focus on American Food and Foodways," *Journal of American Culture* 2 (Fall): 407–570.

————, ed. 1984a. *Ethnic and Regional Foodways in the United States: The Performance of Group Identity*. Knoxville: The University of Tennessee Press.

————. 1984b. "Introduction." In *Ethnic and Regional Foodways in the United States: The Performance of Group Identity*, ed. Linda Keller Brown and Kay Mussell, pp. 3–15. Knoxville: The University of Tennessee Press.

Brown, M. H. De La Peña. 1981. "*Una Tamalada*: The Special Event," *Western Folklore* 40:64–71.

Camp, Charles. 1974. "Federal Foodways Research, 1935–1943," *The Digest: A Newsletter for the Interdisciplinary Study of Food* 2 (No. 2): 4–17.

————. 1978. America Eats: Toward a Social Definition of Foodways. Ph.D. dissertation, Folklore and Folklife, University of Pennsylvania.

————. 1979. "Foodways." In *Handbook of American Popular Culture*, ed. M. Thomas Inge, Vol. 1, pp. 141–61. Westport: Greenwood.

————. 1979. "Food in American Culture: A Bibliographical Essay," *Journal of American Culture* 2:559–70.

————. 1982. "Foodways in Everyday Life," *American Quarterly* 34:278–89.

Chittenden, Varick. 1980. New York State Sanitary Code, Part 14, Subpart 14–1 vs. The Covered Dish Supper. Unpublished paper presented at the American Folklore Society Meeting, Pittsburgh.

Cohen, Yehudi A. 1961. "Food and Its Vicissitudes: A Cross-Cultural Study of Sharing and Nonsharing." In *Social Structure and Personality: A Case Book,* ed. Yehudi A. Cohen, pp. 312–50. New York: Holt, Rinehart, and Winston.

Cook, D. H., and A. J. Wyndham. 1953. "Patterns of Eating Behavior," *Human Relations,* 6:141–60.

Cosman, Madeleine P. 1976. *Fabulous Feasts: Medieval Cookery and Ceremony.* New York: Braziller.

Craigie, Carter Walker. 1976. A Moveable Feast: The Picnic as a Folklife Custom in Chester County, Pennsylvania, 1870–1925. Ph.D. dissertation, University of Pennsylvania.

Cummings, Richard Osborn. 1940. *The American and His Food: A History of Food Habits in the United States.* Chicago. (Reprinted New York: Arno Press, 1970.)

Cussler, Margaret and Mary L. De Give. 1952. *Twixt the Cup and the Lip.* New York: Twayne.

Deetz, James and Jay Anderson. 1972. "The Ethnogastronomy of Thanksgiving," *Saturday Review* 55 (Nov. 25): 29–39.

DeGarine, Igor. 1971. "Food is Not Just Something to Eat," *Ceres* 4:46–51.

————. 1976. "Food, Tradition, and Prestige," *Food, Man and Society,* Dwain Walchner, et al. New York: Plenum Press.

Digby, Joan and John Digby, ed. 1987. *Food for Thought: An Anthology of Writings Inspired by Food.* New York: William Morrow and Company.

Douglas, Mary. 1970. *Purity and Danger: An Analysis of Concepts of Pollution and Taboo.* Baltimore: Penguin.

————. 1972. "Deciphering a Meal," *Daedalus* 101 (Winter): 54–72.

————. 1973. *Natural Symbols.* New York: Vintage.

————. 1974. "Food as an Art Form," *Studio International* 188:83–88.

————. ed. 1984. *Food in the Social Order: Studies of Food and Festivities in Three American Communities.* New York: Russell Sage Foundation.

Douglas, Mary and Michael Nicod. 1974. "Taking the Biscuit: The Structure of British Meals," *New Society,* 30:744–47.

Farb, Peter and George Armelagos. 1983. *Consuming Passions: The Anthropology of Eating.* New York: Washington Square Press.

Feeley-Harnik, Gillian. 1981. *The Lord's Table: Eucharist and Passover in Early Christianity.* Englewood Cliffs: Prentice-Hall.

Fisher, Annie May. 1931. Food and Table Customs of the South, 1607–1865. M.A. thesis in Home Economics, George Peabody College for Teachers.

Fisher, M. F. K. 1937. *Serve It Forth.* New York: Harper.

————. 1941. *Consider the Oyster.* New York: Duell, Sloan and Pearce.

————. 1942. *How to Cook a Wolf.* New York: Duell, Sloan and Pearce.

————. 1943. *The Gastronomical Me.* New York: Duell, Sloan and Pearce.

————. 1949. *An Alphabet for Gourmets.* New York: Viking.

————. 1976. *The Art of Eating.* New York: Random House. [A reprint of Fisher, 1937, 1941, 1942, 1943, 1949]

Geffen, Alice M. and Carole Berglie. 1986. *Food Festival: The Ultimate Guidebook to America's Best Regional Food Celebrations.* New York: Pantheon Books.

Georges, Robert A. 1984. "You Often Eat What Others Think You Are: Food as an Index of Others' Conceptions of Who One Is," *Journal of Folklore Research* 43:249–56.

Gizelis, Gregory. 1971. "Foodways Acculturation in the Greek Community of Philadelphia," *Pennsylvania Folklife* 20 (No. 2): 9–15.

Glenn, Viola. 1936. "The Eating Habits of Harlem," *Opportunity* (March): 82–85.

Goode, Judith G., Karen Curtis, and Janet Theophano. 1984. "Meal Formats, Meal Cycles, and Menu Negotiation in the Maintenance of an Italian-American Community." In *Food in the*

Social Order: Studies of Food and Festivities in Three American Communities, ed. Mary O. Douglas, pp. 143–218.

Graham, Andrea. 1981. "'Let's Eat!': Commitment and Communion in Cooperative Households," *Western Folklore* 40:55–63.

Gutowski, John. 1978. "The Protofestival: Local Guide to American Behavior," *Journal of the Folklore Institute* 15 (No. 2): 113–32.

———. 1977. American Folklore and the Modern American Community Festival: A Case Study of Turtle Days in Churubusco, Indiana. Ph.D. dissertation, Indiana University.

Harris, Marvin. 1974. *Cows, Pigs, Wars and Witches: The Riddles of Culture.* New York: Random House.

———. 1977. *Cannibals and Kings: The Origins of Cultures.* New York: Random House.

Honigman, John J. 1961. *Foodways in a Muskey Community: An Anthropological Report on the Attawapiskat Indians.* Ottawa: Northern Co-ordination Research Center.

Hufford, David. 1971. "Organic Food People: Nutrition, Health, and World View," *Keystone Folklore Quarterly* 16:179–84.

Humphrey, Linda T. 1979. "Small Group Festive Gatherings," *Journal of the Folklore Institute* 16:190–201.

Ireland, Lynne. 1981. "The Compiled Cookbook as Foodways Autobiography," *Western Folklore* 40:107–14.

Jacobs, Jay. 1975. *Gastronomy.* New York: Newsweek Books.

Jenner, Alice. 1973. *Food: Fact and Folklore.* Toronto: McClelland and Stewart.

Jerome, N. W. 1969. "American Culture and Food Habits." In *Dimensions of Nutrition: Proceedings of the Colorado Dietetic Association Conference,* pp. 223–34. Boulder: Colorado Associated Universities Press.

Joffe, Natalie F. 1943. "Food Habits of Selected Subcultures in the United States," *Problems of Changing Food Habits.* National Research Council Bulletin, No. 108, pp. 97–103.

Jones, Ewan. 1975. *American Food: The Gastronomic Story.* New York: E. P. Dutton and Company.

Jones, Michael Owen. 1980. "Perspectives in the Study of Eating Behaviour." In *Folklore Studies in the Twentieth Century: Proceedings of the Centenary Conference of the Folklore Society,* ed. Venetia J. Newall, pp. 260–65. Totowa, N.J.: Rowman and Littlefield.

Jones, Michael Owen, Bruce S. Giuliano and Roberta Krell. 1981. "Prologue," "The Sensory Domain," "The Social Dimension," "Resources and Methods," and "Epilogue." In *Foodways and Eating Habits: Directions for Research,* pp. vii-xii, 1–3, 41–44, 91–93, and 134–137, respectively. Los Angeles: California Folklore Society 40 (No. 1) of *Western Folklore;* reprinted 1983.

Joos, Sandra K. 1984. "Economic, Social, and Cultural Factors in the Analysis of Disease: Dietary Change and Diabetes Mellitus among the Florida Seminole Indians." In *Ethnic and Regional Foodways in the United States,* ed. Linda Keller Brown and Kay Mussell, pp. 217–37.

Kanter, Rosabeth Moss. 1972. *Commitment and Community: Communes and Utopias in Sociological Perspective.* Cambridge, Mass.: Harvard University Press.

Karp, Ivan. 1980. "Beer Drinking and Social Experience in an African Society." In *Explorations in African Systems of Thought,* ed. Ivan Karp and Charles S. Bird. Bloomington: Indiana University Press.

Katz, S. H. et al. 1974. "Traditional Maize Processing Techniques in the New World," *Science* 184:765–73.

Kearney, Michael. 1970. "The Social Meaning of Food Sharing in Mexico," *Kroeber Anthropological Society Papers* 43:32–41.

Khare, Ravindra S. 1976. *Hindu Hearth and Home.* New Delhi: Vikas Publishing House.

Knutson, A. L. 1965. "The Meaning of Food." In *The Individual, Society and Health Behavior,* ed. A. L. Knutson, pp. 132–43. New York: Russell Sage Foundation.

Kottak, Conrad P. 1978. "Ritual at McDonald's," *Natural History Magazine* 87 (No. 1): 75–82; also in *The World of Ronald McDonald,* ed. Marshall Fishwick, pp. 398–402. Bowling Green, Ohio: Popular Culture Press.

Kupper, Jessica, ed. 1977. *The Anthropologists' Cookbook.* New York: Universe Books.

Langlois, Janet. 1972. "Moon Cake in Chinatown, New York City: Continuity and Change," *New York Folklore Quarterly* 28:83–117.

Lehrer, Adrienne. 1969. "Semantic Cuisine," *Journal of Linguistics* 5:39–55.

———. 1972. "Cook Vocabularies and the Culinary Triangle of Levi-Strauss," *Anthropological Linguistics* 14:155–71.

Leverton, R. M. and A. G. Marsh. 1939. "Comparison of Food Intakes for Weekdays and for Saturday and Sunday," *Journal of Home Economics* 31:111–16.

Levi-Strauss, Claude. 1966. "The Culinary Triangle," *The Partisan Review* 33:586–95.

———. 1969. *The Raw and the Cooked.* New York: Harper & Row.

———. 1973. *From Honey to Ashes.* New York: Harper & Row.

———. 1977. "The Roast and the Boiled." In *The Anthropologists' Cookbook,* ed. Jessica Kupper, pp. 221–30. New York: Universe Books.

———. 1978. *The Origin of Table Manners.* New York: Harper & Row.

Levin, Channie Milowsky. 1934. "A Study of Jewish Food Habits," *American Dietetic Association Journal* 9:389–96.

Levin, Kurt. 1943. "Forces Behind Food Habits and Methods of Change." In *The Problem of Changing Food Habits.* National Research Council Bulletin, No. 108.

Levy, Sidney J. 1981. "Personal Narratives: A Key to Interpreting Consumer Behavior," *Western Folklore* 40:94–106.

Lincoln, Waldo. 1929. Bibliography of American Cookery Books, 1742–1860. *Proceedings of the American Antiquarian Society* 39, part 1 (April 17): 85–225. Reprinted: Worcester, Mass.: The Society.

Linsenmeyer, Helen Walker. 1976. *From Fingers to Finger Bowls: A Sprightly History of California Cooking.* San Diego: The Union-Tribune Publishing Co.

Lloyd, Timothy Charles. 1981. "The Cincinnati Chili Culinary Complex," *Western Folklore* 40:28–40.

Lockwood, William and Yvonne Lockwood. 1986. "Ethnic Roots and American Regional Foods." In *A Conference on Current Research in Culinary History: Sources, Topics, and Methods: Proceedings,* pp. 130–37. Higham, Mass.: Culinary Historians of Boston.

Loeb, Martin. 1951. "The Social Functions of Food Habits," *Journal of the American Academy of Applied Nutrition* 4:227–29.

McKim, Marriott. 1968. "Caste Ranking and Food Transactions." In *Structure and Change in Indian Society,* ed. Milton Singer and Bernard Cohen, pp. 133–71. Chicago: Aldine (Viking Fund Publications in Anthropology, No. 47).

McKnight, David. 1973. "Sexual Symbolism of Food Among the Wik-Mungkan," *Man* 8 (New Series): 194–209.

McMahon, Sarah. 1986. "Sources and Documents: The Study of Diet and Foodways in Colonial America." In *A Conference on Current Research in Culinary History: Sources, Topics, and Methods: Proceedings,* pp. 130–37. Higham, Mass.: Culinary Historians of Boston.

Mandelbaum, David G. 1965. "Alcohol and Culture," *Current Anthropology* 6:281–93.

Marett, Robert Randolph. 1934. "Food Rites." In *Essays Presented to C. G. Seligman,* ed. E. E. Evans-Pritchard, et al., pp. 197–208. London: Paul, Trench, Trubner.

Marshall, Howard Wight. 1979. "Meat Preservation on the Farm in Missouri's 'Little Dixie'," *Journal of the American Folklore Society* 92:366 (October-December): 400–17.

Marshall, Mac, ed. 1979. *Beliefs, Behaviors, and Alcoholic Beverages.* Ann Arbor: University of Michigan Press.

Mauss, Marcel. 1967. *The Gift: Forms and Functions of Exchange in Archaic Societies.* New York: Norton (orig. pub. 1925).

Menzies, Isabel E. 1970. "Psychosocial Aspects of Eating," *Journal of Psychosomatic Research* 14:223–27.

Michaels, Craig. 1971. *Sunday Breakfast: A Cookbook for Men.* Concord, CA: Nitty Gritty Publications.

Mintz, Sidney W. 1985. *Sweetness and Power: The Place of Sugar in Modern History.* New York: Penguin.

––––––. 1986. "American Eating Habits and Food Choices: A Preliminary Essay," *The Journal of Gastronomy* 2 (No. 3): 15–22.

Mirsky, Richard M. 1981. "Perspectives in the Study of Food Habits," *Western Folklore* 40:125–33.

Moe, John. 1977. "Folk Festivals and Community Consciousness: Categories of the Festival Genre," *Folklore Forum* 10 (No. 2): 33–40.

Montell, Lynwood. 1972. "Hog Killing in the Kentucky Hill Country: The Initial Phases," *Kentucky Folklore Record* 18:61–67.

Montgomery, Edward and John W. Bennett. 1979. "Anthropological Studies of Food and Nutrition: 1940s and 1970s." In *The Uses of Anthropology,* ed. Walter Goldschmidt, Session 5, Washington, D.C.: American Anthropology Association.

Moore, Harriet Bruce. 1957. "The Meaning of Food," *American Journal of Clinical Nutrition* 5:77–82.

Munro, Sarah Baker. 1985. "Basque Celebrations in Eastern Oregon and Boise." In *Idaho Folklife: Homesteads to Headstones,* ed. Louie W. Attebery, pp. 91–100, Salt Lake City: University of Utah Press.

Newman, Jacqueline M. 1986. *Melting Pot: An Annotated Bibliography and Guide to Food and Nutrition Information for Ethnic Groups in America.* New York: Garland Publishing.

Niethammer, Carolyn. 1974. *American Indian Food and Lore.* New York: MacMillan.

Norman, Barbara. 1972. *Tales of the Table: A History of Western Cuisine.* Englewood Cliffs: Prentice-Hall.

Palmer, Earl. 1966. "Apple Butter Time," *Scenic South* 23 (No. 10): 14–15.

Palmer, Edward. 1878. "Indian Food Customs," *American Naturalist* 12 (No. 6): 402–3.

Paranatella, T. B. 1921. "Sumptuary Laws and Social Etiquette of the Kandyans," *Journal of the Ceylon Branch of the Royal Asiatic Society* 21 (No. 6): 48–50.

Passin, Herbert, and John W. Bennett. 1943. "Social Process and Dietary Change," *The Problem of Changing Food Habits.* National Research Council Bulletin, No. 108, pp. 113–23.

Pearson, Leonard, Lillian R. Pearson, and Karola Saekel. 1974. *The Psychologist's Sensational Cookbook.* New York: P. H. Wyden.

Potter, David M. 1954. *People of Plenty: Economic Abundance and the American Character.* Chicago and London: The University of Chicago Press.

Pound, Louise. 1959. "Some Old Nebraska Folk Customs." In *Nebraska Folklore,* pp. 184–208. Lincoln: University of Nebraska Press.

Powdermaker, Hortense. 1932. "Feasts in New Ireland: The Social Function of Eating," *American Anthropologist* 34:236–47.

Prosterman, Leslie. 1981. "Food and Alliance at the County Fair," *Western Folklore* 40:81–90.

––––––. 1982. The Aspect of the Fair: Aesthetics and Festival in Illinois County Fairs. Ph.D. dissertation, University of Pennsylvania.

Pullar, Philippa. 1970. *Consuming Passions: A History of English Food and Appetite.* London: Hamish Hamilton.

Pumpian-Mindline, E. 1954. "The Meaning of Food," *Journal of the American Dietetic Association* 30:576–80.

Pyke, Magnus. 1968. *Food and Society.*. London.

———. 1970. *Synthetic Food.* London: John Murray.

———. 1972. *Technological Eating: Or Where Does the Fish-Finger Point?* London: John Murray.

———. 1975. "The Influence of American Foods and Food Technology in Europe." In *Superculture: American Popular Culture and Europe,* ed. C. W. E. Bigsby, pp. 83–95. Bowling Green: Popular Culture Press.

Reinecke, George F. 1965. "The New Orleans 12th Night Cake," *Louisiana Folklore Miscellany* 2 (No. 2): 45–54.

Remington, R. E. 1936. "The Social Origins of Dietary Habits," *Scientific Monthly* 43:193–204.

Renner, H. D. 1944. *The Origin of Food Habits.* London: Faber and Faber.

Richards, Audrey I. 1932. *Hunger and Work in a Savage Tribe: A Functional Study of Nutrition Among the Southern Bantu.* London: G. Routledge and Sons.

———. 1939. *Land, Labour and Diet in Northern Rhodesia.* London: Oxford University Press.

Root, Waverly and Richard De Rochemont. 1976. *Eating in America: A History.* New York: Morrow.

Rozin, Elisabeth. 1973. *The Flavor-Principle Cookbook.* New York: Hawthorn.

Rozin, Paul. 1976. "Psychological and Cultural Determinants of Food Choice." In *Appetite and Food Intake,* ed. Trevor Silverstone, pp. 286–312. Berlin: Dahlem Konferenzen.

Sackett, Marjorie. 1963. "Kansas Pioneer Recipes," *Western Folklore* 22:103–6.

———. 1972. "Folk Recipes as a Measure of Intercultural Penetration," *Journal of American Folklore* 85:77–81.

Samuelson, Susan Camille. 1983. Festive Malaise and Festive Participation: A Case Study of Christmas Celebrations in America. Ph.D. dissertation, University of Pennsylvania.

Santich, Barbara. 1985. "Word of Mouth: Language and Gastronomy," *The Journal of Gastronomy* 1 (No. 3): 35–42.

Santino, Jack. 1983. "Halloween in America: Contemporary Customs and Performances," *Western Folklore* 42:1–20.

Sass, Lorna J. 1975. *To the King's Taste: Richard II's Book of Feasts and Recipes Adapted for Modern Cooking.* New York: Metropolitan Museum of Art.

———. 1976. *To the Queen's Taste.* New York: Metropolitan Museum of Art.

Schafer, Robert and Elizabeth A. Yetley. 1975. "Social Psychology of Food Faddism," *Journal of the American Dietetic Association* 66:129–33.

Shenton, James Patrick, et al. 1971. *American Cooking: The Melting Pot.* New York: Time-Life Books.

Shifflett, Petty A. 1976. "Folklore and Food Habits," *Journal of the American Dietetic Association* 68 (No. 4): 347–50.

Shuman, Amy. 1981. "The Rhetoric of Portions," *Western Folklore* 40:72–80.

Simoons, Frederick J. 1961. *Eat Not This Flesh: Food Avoidances in the Old World.* Madison: University of Wisconsin Press.

Slocum, R. 1944. "Friendship Through Food: What's Cooking in Your Neighbor's Pot?" *Common Ground* 4 (No. 3): 79–81.

Smallzried, Kathleen Ann. 1956. *The Everlasting Pleasure: Influences on America's Kitchens, Cooks, and Cookery from 1565 to the Year 2000.* New York: Appleton-Century Crofts.

Smith, C. Earle, Jr., ed. 1973. *Man and His Foods.* University: Unviversity of Alabama Press.

Sokolov, Raymond. 1974a. "Some Like It Hot," *Natural History* 83 (No. 4): 64–68.

———. 1974b. "The Ritual of Maize," *Natural History* 83 (No. 7): 64–65.

———. 1975a. "The Melting Pot," *Natural History* 84 (No. 1): 98–100.

_____. 1975b. "A Plant of Ill Repute," *Natural History* 84 (No. 2): 70–71.

_____. 1980. "An Original Old-Fashioned Yankee Clambake," *Natural History* 89 (No. 6): 96–102.

_____. 1981a. *Fading Feasts.* New York: Farrar Straus & Giroux.

_____. 1981b. "Planter's Lunch," *Natural History* 90 (No. 8): 88–92.

_____. 1985. "The Way We Eat Now," *Natural History* 93 (No. 10): 108–11.

_____. 1986a. "The Real Thing," *Natural History* 94 (No. 1): 102–5.

_____. 1986b. "Chowder Chauvinism," *Natural History* 94 (No. 5): 98–101.

_____. 1988. "A Simmering Sabbath Day Stew," *Natural History* 97 (No. 2): 88–91.

Soler, Jean. 1979. "The Semiotics of Food in the Bible," In *Food and Drink in History,* ed. Robert Forster and Orest Ranum, pp. 126–38. Baltimore: Johns Hopkins University Press.

Sorre, Max. 1962. "The Geography of Diet." In *Readings in Cultural Geography,* ed. Philip L. Wagner and Marvine W. Mikesell, pp. 445–56. Chicago: University of Chicago Press.

Stratton, Joanna L. 1981. *Pioneer Women: Voices From the Kansas Frontier.* New York: Simon and Schuster.

Tannahill, Reay. 1970. *The Fine Art of Food.* Cranbury: Barnes.

_____. 1973. *Food in History.* New York: Stein and Day.

Towsend, Mary A. 1973. "Hog Killing on a Queenfield Farm, Marquin, Virginia," *North Carolina Folklore* 21:32–34.

Trillin, Calvin. 1974. *American Fried: Adventures of a Happy Eater.* Garden City: Doubleday.

Trulson, Martha F. 1959. "The American Diet—Past and Present," *The American Journal of Clinical Nutrition* 7:91–97.

Visser, Margaret. 1987. *Much Depends on Dinner: The Extraordinary History and Mythology, Allure and Obsessions, Perils and Taboos of an Ordinary Meal.* New York: Grove Press. (First published Canada: McClelland and Stewart, 1986.)

Weintraub, Linda. 1979. "The American Still Life: A Document of the American Diet 1800–Present," *Journal of American Culture* 2:463–79.

Welsch, Roger. 1966. "Pioneer Cooking." In *A Treasury of Nebraska Pioneer Folklore,* pp. 307–28. Lincoln: University of Nebraska Press.

_____. 1971. "'We Are What We Eat': Omaha Food as Symbol," *Keystone Folklore Quarterly* 16:165–70.

Widdowson, John D. A. 1975. "The Things They Say about Food: A Survey of Traditional English Foodways," *Folk Life* (Cardiff) 13:5–12.

Williams, Roger J. 1978. "Nutritional Individuality," *Human Nature* 1 (No. 6): 46–53.

Wilson, Christine S. 1973. "Food Habits: A Selected Annotated Bibliography," *Journal of Nutrition Education* 5 (No. 1, Supplement 1): 39–72.

Wolff, Peter H. 1972. "Ethnic Differences in Alcohol Sensititivty," *Science* 175:449–50.

Wurtman, Richard J. 1978. "Food for Thought," *The Sciences* 18 (No. 4): 6–9.

Yoder, Don. 1961. "Sauerkraut in the Pennsylvania Folk-Culture," *Pennsylvania Folklife* 12 (No. 2): 56–69.

_____. 1961a. "Schnitz in the Pennsylvania Folk-Culture," *Pennsylvania Folklife* 12 (No. 3): 44–53.

_____. 1971a. "The First International Symposium on Ethnological Food Research." *Kentucky Folklore Quarterly* 16:185–88.

_____. 1971b. "Historical Sources for American Traditional Cookery: Examples from the Pennsylvania German Culture," *Pennsylvania Folklife* 20 (No. 3): 16–29.

_____. 1972. "Folk Cookery." In *Folklore and Folklife: An Introduction,* ed. Richard M. Dorson, pp. 325–50. Chicago: University of Chicago Press.

Yudkin, J., and J. C. McKenzie. 1965. *Changing Food Habits.* London: McGibbon and Kee.

Contributors

THOMAS ADLER is a folklorist interested in bluegrass and foodways who earned his Ph.D in folklore in 1979. He has authored numerous articles on traditional foodways and has presented papers to scholarly societies and public audiences on food traditions, bluegrass music, and computers. He is now studying the traditionalizing culture of the microcomputer-using world.

CAROL EDISON is coordinator for the Folk Arts Program of the Utah Arts Council. She received her M.A. in English from the University of Utah. She is the author/compiler of *Cowboy Poetry from Utah: An Anthology* (1985) and a contributor to *Idaho Folklife Reader: From Homesteads to Headstones* (1985).

BARBARA FERTIG is completing her dissertation on the Feast of the Holy Ghost as celebrated in Stonington, Connecticut for George Washington University. She has worked as a folklife researcher, curator, and grant writer, and has published articles on a variety of topics including weaving, tobacco, and Turkish rugs.

JAMES S. GRIFFITH earned his Ph.D. in Cultural Anthropology and Art History in 1974 from the University of Arizona where he has been Director of the Southwest Folklore Center since 1979. He remains deeply involved in the annual production of Tucson Meet Yourself, which he helped found in 1974. He publishes on the traditional music, religious arts, and legends of southern Arizona and northwest Mexico.

LIN T. HUMPHREY earned her M.A. in English at the University of Arkansas, Fayetteville in 1963, has been an NEH Fellow, and currently teaches composition and folklore at Citrus College. She has published articles on small group festive gatherings and the ethnic riddle joke.

THEODORE C. HUMPHREY earned his Ph.D. in English literature at the University of Arkansas, Fayetteville in 1972 where he was an NDEA Fellow. He has taught English and folklore at California State Polytechnic University, Pomona since 1968, has been an NEH Fellow, and studies family folklore, narrative, folk belief, and foodways.

MICHAEL OWEN JONES is Professor of Folklore and History at U.C.L.A. as well as Director of the Center for the Study of Comparative Folklore and Mythology. He has authored or edited nine books on various subjects including faith healing, folk art, fieldwork, foodways, culture and symbolic behavior in organizations, and applied folklore. He is a Woodrow Wilson Fellow, a Fellow of the American Folklore Society, and a member of the California Council for the Humanities.

ANNE R. KAPLAN is an editor at the Minnesota Historical Society. She received her Ph.D. in folklore and folklife from the University of Pennsylvania and is coauthor of *The Minnesota Ethnic Food Book* (1986).

NANCY KLAVANS trained and worked as a professional chef with Madeleine Kamner for five years. She is currently in a graduate program in folklore at the University of Pennsylvania. She served as Editor of *The Digest* and continues as contributing editor. She is an active member of the Culinary Historians and Les Dames D'Escoffier.

KATHY NEUSTADT is completing her Ph.D. from the University of Pennsylvania with a dissertation on the Allen's Neck Clambake. While continuing to study New England folklife in particular and foodways and festivity in general, she also does research in gender studies. On the third Thursday of every August for the indefinite future, she can be found at the Allen's Neck Clambake, enjoying the work, the company, and the food.

ANTHONY T. RAUCHE is an assistant professor of music theory and ethnomusicology at the Hartt School of Music of the University of Hartford in Hartford, Connecticut where he works on American Indian music, ethnic American music, popular music, music in northern New Mexico, and music in the life of the Italian community in Hartford. A pianist, Mr. Rauche has specialized in performing works by Schoenberg, Messiaen, Stockhausen, Cage, as well as composers from New England and the Midwest. He has recorded for Spectrum Records and the Musical Heritage Society. He is completing his doctoral dissertation in ethnomusicology at the University of Illinois, Urbana-Champaign.

Sue Samuelson earned her Ph.D. in folklore and folklife from the University of Pennsylvania. She has taught courses on food and culture at Rutgers University and Pennsylvania State University-Harrisburg. Her research specialties include the role of food in American holidays and in family settings and the history of the study of food.

Sharon R. Sherman earned her Ph.D. in folklore from Indiana University and currently directs the folklife program at the University of Oregon where she teaches folklore, film, and popular culture. Her principal research interests include the use of film to document folkloric events, family folklore, and material culture. Her films and videos include *Tales of the Supernatural, Kathleen Ware: Quiltmaker,* and *Passover: A Celebration.*

Amy E. Skillman received her masters in folklore and mythology from U.C.L.A. in 1979. Her work in the Los Angeles area included folklife projects with the Craft and Folk Art Museum, the National Park Service and the American Folklife Center. She served for two years as the Coordinator of Cultural Heritage Programs at the Missouri Cultural Heritage Center, University of Missouri-Columbia. She is currently Director of State Folklife Programs at the Pennsylvania Heritage Affairs Commission.

Eleanor Wachs is Director of Exhibits, The Commonwealth Museum at Columbia Point, Boston, Massachusetts, and she has taught folklore at Brown University and the University of Massachusetts-Boston. She has conducted fieldwork in Massachusetts for the Smithsonian Institution's Festival of American Folklore 1988 and was a member of the fieldwork team for the Lowell Folklife Project, American Folklife Center, Library of Congress and the Lowell Historic Preservation Commission.

Index